D1738719

ALBANIAN STALINISM:

IDEO–POLITICAL ASPECTS

by

Arshi Pipa

EAST EUROPEAN MONOGRAPHS, BOULDER
DISTRIBUTED BY COLUMBIA UNIVERSITY PRESS, NEW YORK

1990

EAST EUROPEAN MONOGRAPHS, NO. CCLXXXVII

Copyright © 1990 by Arshi Pipa
ISBN 0-88033-184-4
Library of Congress Card Catalog Number 90-80366

Printed in the United States of America

FOREWORD

Collected in this volume are political writings from 1958 to 1989, which are, however, far from covering the whole span of that period. The first four articles were written during the first four years of my residence in the United States. At that time I still entertained hopes of returning to my native country once it was freed from communist rule, which I thought was bound to end soon after Albania broke with the Soviet Union to join China.

Yet the odd alliance with China lasted as long as Albania's alliances with Yugoslavia and the Soviet Union put together. And my interest in Albanian politics waned after I became a U. S. citizen. This was in Berkeley, California, where I was then teaching. The Berkeley Free Speech Movement awoke me to the reality of the American way of life. In Minneapolis, where I moved in 1966, I became involved in American politics, whereas my writings followed the bent of my profession as a teacher of Italian literature at the University of Minnesota. There I also began writing on Albanian literature and folklore.

The Kosova riots of 1981 immersed me once again in Albanian politics. The remaining articles in this volume were all written in the eighties.

They have one main theme, Albanian Stalinism, considered in some major 'ideo–political' aspects. Since the reader won't find 'ideo–political' listed in a common English dictionary, I explain it here briefly, referring him also to the last article in this book, where the Leninist–Stalinist term is treated at some length. What it means is politics dominated, one can even say determined, by ideology—not by economy, as the reader might think, led astray by the deceptive description of Stalinism as Marxism–Leninism. I note, by the way, that Albanian Marxism–Leninism is an ossified Stalinism which works as a monistic religion, pervading and imbuing nearly all areas of human

activity and life. It has been little studied so far. My approach, which is phenomenological rather than theoretical, opens a trail for study in depth.

All of these writings, here assembled in chronological order, have been previously published, except for the last article and the poem in the appendix. Two earlier writings are translations from Albanian. The essay on Archbishop Prendushi appears in an abridged form, whereas the other, which traces the eastward trend of Albanian Stalnism, has been somewhat expanded. All pieces have been reviewed for the sake of orthographic uniformity and stylistic refinement. In the revision process factual errors were corrected and superfluous wording was pruned.

I thank the periodicals in which the articles were published, *Telos, East European Quarterly, Labour Focus on Eastern Europe, Dielli [The Sun], Shqiptari i lirë [The Free Albanian], Flamuri [The Flag] Zâni i katholikvet shquiptarë në mërgim [La voce dei cattolici albanesi]*, for permission to reprint the articles. Particular thanks go to Dr. Jeffrey Fruen, who edited and typed the manuscript, while also working with me on the translation of the poem.

A.P.

I.   ON ALBANIAN INDEPENDENCE*

In commemorating the anniversary of our Independence Day, it has become customary to begin by eulogizing the man who was the protagonist of this most memorable event of our history. We shall not make an exception to the rule, and we shall mention with reverence the name of the national hero Ismail Kemal. He rendered the country a capital service at a turning point in her history. Had it not been for his political ability, as well as his courage, Albania would not have won her independence in the fateful year 1912. And one may doubt that Albania would ever have won her independence, had that unique occasion been allowed to slip away. There is in the historical process of some nations a critical moment which may be decisive for a nation's survival or death.

But, having paid tribute to the venerable wise man of Valona, we must go further, bearing in mind that what he accomplished, together with other patriots of the time, was only the last act in a vast drama which had been maturing for centuries among the Albanian people. This drama began with the League of Lesh, when Scanderbeg laid the foundations of the Albanian nation, emerging from the medieval darkness. Then there was another darkness, the period, centuries long, of Asiatic darkness. Yet Albania lived, albeit in slumber, and from time to time gave flashes of awakening. Those sparks converged finally in that national movement which is the League of Prizren. From that time on, the drama of Albania's creation rushes towards a solution.

---

* A speech for the 47th anniversary of the proclamation of Albania's independence, Carnegie Endowment International Center in New York, November 28, 1959. Published in *Shqiptari i lirë* [*The Free Albanian*], November 1959.

And yet, what kind of a solution was it! The great powers that legalized Albania's birth, after mutilating her to satisfy our neighbors' greed, presented her with a king, a foreigner. This king left Albania and her throne as soon as the First World War broke out to join the army of his Kaiser. Albania was occupied by foreign armies. The period of Albania's real independence began only in 1920. In that year, delegates from all parts of Albania met at a congress in Lushnje. The Congress of Lushnje restored to the country its lost sovereignty, vesting it in a Council of Regents; provided for a legislature; and set up a national government. The new Albanian state legitimized itself by winning the battle of Valona, liberating from Italian occupation the town where Albania's independence had been proclaimed. On the opposite border, it drove back the Yugoslav army which had invaded our territory. Albania was finally integrated within her internationally recognized frontiers, and commenced her normal independent life.

* * * * *

A year ago today, I was in Detroit, where I participated in a celebration of our holiday arranged by the Albanian–Americans of that city. The speaker praised Ismail Kemal, indulged in recalling facts which illustrated the great contribution to the cause of independence made by Albanian ethnics in the United States, and said something about Scanderbeg. Somebody after him recited a poem about Scanderbeg. The ceremony was closed with a religious prayer. But not one word was said about the period of independence itself, not one word concerning the present situation in Albania. A kind of taboo seemed to prevent any mention of communism. One had the impression that the history of Albania was complete with the achievement of independence. But how this independence evolved afterwards, and how it was lost, and especially what its significance is today, these did not seem to interest the assembly.

The generation of Albanian emigrés who flocked to the United States before and after the First World War is today almost extinguished. A new generation has replaced it, an American generation. These descendants of the old generation have only vague reminiscences of their mother country; evidently, they cannot feel about it as we feel, we fresh exiles who are carrying about in our bones the marks of our country's latest events. But to ignore these events purposefully, to bury in silence what is crying out to the heavens, to

approve with silence a state of affairs which their consciences cannot but disapprove, this is wrong. For the sake of these people, so that their consciences might be awakened and freed of all kinds of fears, misapprehensions, and prejudices, I must briefly recall here the salient points of Albania's political development, with particular regard to the present situation. I hope thus to help them begin to realize at least one thing: that the independence at which they rejoice in their celebrations today is, in fact, nonexistent.

The period of factual independence of our country covered less than two decades (1920–1939). It started with a stage of Occidental-patterned democracy, which proved to have been introduced prematurely in a country just emerging from long oriental domination. This democracy developed into an autocracy. For all the serious shortcomings of our period of independence, one may agree with the general opinion, expressed especially by foreigners, that Albania had already achieved notable progress at the time when she was invaded by fascist Italy.

Let me here make the point that to Albanians fascism means chiefly denationalization. In this respect, of the two kinds of fascism that we had to endure, Italian fascism was by far the more dangerous. The Nazi army wanted our territory mainly for strategic aims. Fascist Italy wanted to colonize Albania with Italian citizens, so that in a few years the country would become an Italian province, where the Albanian language would be spoken as it is today in the Albanian colonies of Calabria and Sicily. It is thus understandable that the Albanian people should bear a grudge against those Albanians who showed too much zeal in serving Italian fascism.

From fascism Albania passed straightway to communism, from one dictatorship to another. I cannot dwell here on the evils of dictatorship; I must limit my discussion of communism to its pertinence to nationality. The question may be formulated thus: Is communism less destructive to the Albanian national entity than was fascism?

Albanian communism grew to unbelievable proportions out of almost nothing because it artfully championed the national feeling of resistance to the foreign invader. For a long time communism concealed its nature under the catchword of "Movement of National Liberation," with "antifascism" meant to be a synonym. Now every Albanian knows that Albanian communism was fathered by Yugoslav communism. The growing dependence of Albania on Yugoslavia reached such an extent that, had it not been for the spectacular

split of Yugoslavia from the Russian–dominated camp, Albania would have been today the seventh republic of the Yugoslav Federation.. And in saying this, please note, I am simply relating the official version of the Albanian government.

The same man was then, as he is now, the number one of communist Albania: Enver Hoxha. I recall people shouting in 1945 "Enver–Tito!" Some years later the shouts were "Enver-Stalin!" I lived long enough in communist Albania to experience a third "Enver–Khruschev

Take the official organ of the Tirana regime. Read the editorial carefully, pay attention to events of national life; then pass to the international section, and compare the place given the Soviet Union to that given to all the other countries of the world, noting also the sources of the news. Then read the paper once more, this time underscoring with red ink such phrases as "The Albanian people," "The People's Republic of Albania," and the like, while underscoring with black ink all that bears the label of "Soviet Union." Now work out their proportions, record your results, and see in all honesty whether your impression of the whole is that you have read an Albanian paper published in an independent country or rather in some part of the Soviet Union.

While in Yugoslavia, I happened to hear a witticism about Montenegro. The proud Montenegrin, if asked about the number of inhabitants of his republic—which is less than half a million—would answer: We were two hundred million together with the Soviet Union. The joke is a grim reality in Russianized Albania. A relentless propaganda is trying to convince Albanians that their country is "an inseparable part of the socialist camp headed by the great Soviet Union." One must thank God that Albania is geographically separated from Russia. Otherwise, the fanaticism of Albania's rulers would have long since incorporated her into the Soviet Union, where the Albanian people would have no greater national distinction than, say, the Tadjik people.

It is true that people still speak Albanian in Albania, but only because it is too early for them to speak Russian. It is also true that the Albanian communist government defends Albania's frontiers against Greek chauvinism. But what is meritorious in this? Albanian communism defends its own regime, while only incidentally defending Albanian territory. Were a pro–Moscow regime to establish itself in Greece, the attitude of the Albanian leaders would change overnight.

To those who might doubt this, I would point out the recent experience with Yugoslavia. The Tirana government discovered the existence of a Kosova question only after Tito became a renegade. And during all this time of bitter conflict with Yugoslavia, did the government ever claim the Albanian territories under Yugoslav rule? The government never did, because it is not at all interested in the integration of Albania within her truly national borders, which remains the basic tenet of Albanian patriotism. What the government is interested in doing is simply to annoy Tito, create difficulties for him, thus making easier the collapse of a regime distasteful to Moscow.

* * * * *

It has been exactly twenty years since Albania lost her independence, and ever since she has been passing from one dependence to another. Dependence is no less such when wearing the mask of independence. Albania had a formal independence even during the fascist occupation. It is on this formal independence that Greece bases her assertion of being in a state of war with Albania.[1] True independence cannot but be national. And those who think that communism can fraternize with nationalism have a poor idea of the former's essence. Those Albanian–Americans who may entertain such illusions should give attention to some simple facts.

Do they think the five–ecked star superimposed on our flag is a sign of nationality? A thing is made manifest by its signs. And don't they know that in communist Albania "Independence Day" has been coupled with "liberation day" to blur the significance of the former: To be convinced, let them look at the Independence Day newspapers, where the picture of Haxhi Qamil is found beside those of Scanderbeg and Ismail Kemal.[2]

The Albanian–Americans are happy with the formal aspect of Albanian independence. Is not Albania represented in the United Nations, they say? Yes, it is, along with the Ukraine and Byelorussia. Albania is ruled today by Albanians, they insist. Her rulers are of Albanian origin, that is true. But are they to be called Albanians only because of that? Independence may be lost not only through foreign invasions, but also through treasonous devotion to foreign powers. The chief mark of national sovereignty is the will to preserve and increase, within the frame of a truly independent state, those elements which make for the individuality of a nation. Communist Albania is the negation of that concept.

The Albanians recall with deepest gratitude what their brothers in the United States have done in the past for the cause of Albania. Suffice it to mention here their role at the Peace Conference of Versailles, when the partition of our territory planned by our neighbors had already received the blessings of the great European powers. These plans, however, were frustrated by the energetic opposition of the President of the United States, who had been briefed by Albanian–American delegates.

This was forty years ago. What is their stance today?

By mute complacency or active support, the new generation of Albanian–Americans uphold a regime that undermines Albania's independence while also being openly hostile to the United States. Seldom has human aberration gone so far.

I cannot believe that they are ignorant of the presence in Albania today of political prisons and slave labor camps. Do they approve of this fact, these citizens of a free, democratic country? An estimated 7–10 percent of Albania's population has been arrested, tortured, jailed, deported, interned during the fifteen years of Communist rule. Of this total, some 10,000 have been shot, hanged, killed by torture, or brought to death by diseases contracted in horrible jails or by inhuman labor conditions in camps. Only a very small part of these people (not more than 1 percent) were "collaborators with occupation powers" or "enemies of the people," as communist propaganda has branded them. The bulk of them were nationally–minded people, from all regions and strata and conditions, who opposed communism openly or clandestinely, by word or by gun, in individual rebellions or mass insurrections, for various reasons: religious, moral, intellectual, as well as political, social, economic. Among them were distinguished patriots belonging to this very Albanian extraction; and among them also were people whose only crime was their admiration for the United States.

To those who praise the Tirana regime for its achievements, I should point out that those achievements—grossly exaggerated in accordance with communist practice—are accomplished at the expense of our very independence, let alone freedom and human worth. Albania has been turned into a springboard for Russian imperialism with the Sazani island a Russian submarine base, and plans to make Albania an atomic base.

For the sake of the future of their relatives and friends, if not for the sake of the Albanian people as a whole, I appeal to these

Albanian–Americans to change their attitude, bearing in mind that what applies to communism in general applies also to that part of it which is today Albania.

And let me finish by reminding them that to us Albanian exiles who have left our country only because compelled to, with a longing to see it again when both independence and freedom will be restored, Independence Day is not an occasion for celebration and entertainment, but one for mournful thoughts.

II. A MEMORIAL FOR ARCHBISHOP PRENDUSHI*

Behind the walls of the Durrës Prison stands a low building which serves as a restaurant and a classroom for policemen. In November 1947, a number of political prisoners were brought before a military tribunal convened there. At the time juridical proceedings were quite perfunctory. Once arrested, the accused was taken to prison to await trial. Since the verdicts were decided by the Ministry of the Interior, the courtroom proceedings were a mere formality.

The prisoners, tried individually or in groups, were sentenced in groups. A military tribunal was composed of a chief judge, two members, the prosecutor, and a sergeant–recorder. There was no defense attorney. The prosecutor would read the charges for each prisoner, who would then be told to respond. This done, the court would retire and come back after a while. The chief judge would pronounce the sentence.

On the day of my sentencing, I joined about sixty fellow prisoners in the above–mentioned building. The prosecutor, Petrit Hakani, made a brief statement, then began reading his list. When he mentioned the name of Vinçenc Prendushi, a white–haired, elderly man rose slowly from his bench. He was charged with being an enemy of the people, a collaborator with the occupation, and a fascist. His rank as Archbishop of the Catholic Church was pointed out, together with phrases such as "reactionary cleric" and "agent of the Vatican." The prosecutor requested twenty years imprisonment at hard labor. When the defendant was allowed to address the court, he said in a broken voice: "I wished no one ill. I have tried to do good." And he sat down.

---

* Abridged translation of "Kujtime mbi Vinçenc Prendushin," published in *Flamuri*, 1959, Nos. 105–108.

1. Sharing Prison with Prendushi

I met Archbishop Prendushi after we were sentenced—we both got twenty years. We were locked up with twenty other prisoners in the isolated room number 8 of the Durrës Prison, reserved for the "most dangerous" prisoners—it had once been an ammunition storeroom. The walls were very thick, the ceiling high, and there was only one tiny front window. Although the fifty–square–meter room was overcrowded, the prisoners squeezed closer together to give more space to the Archbishop. I happened to be placed next to him.

In a short time we became friends. Our conversation about political matters was whispered so that the others could not hear (torture had taught us to be cautious). But the Archbishop was not interested in politics, and we would more often talk about literature, folklore, and personal experiences. The Archbishop occasionally gave counsel to ease the suffering hearts of his fellow prisoners. Whenever he spoke, his vocabulary was simple, so that even the peasants could understand. The entire room would listen in respectful silence.

Sometimes he would quietly gaze for hours out the small window. Probably he prayed. His generosity (he would share with others the little food a devoted old lady would sometimes bring him), as well as his understanding of the needs and failings of people, won the friendship and trust of all those around him.

Eventually he gave me permission to call him by his Franciscan name "Father Vinçenc," that name sounding more appropriate in prison, where all differences in rank between people disappear.

2. A Pure Life

The life of Msgr. Prendushi was given to the service of God and the fatherland. His name is especially dear to the people of Shkodër. As a young Franciscan friar, Fr. Vinçenc showed great tact and understanding in first calming and then mediating disputes between the intolerant religious factions that emerged with the creation of the Albanian nation in 1912. The Albanian nation is indebted to the Order of St. Francis for its great service in religious, cultural, social, and national matters.

Shkodër elders of all three religions were stirred by the patriotic speeches of young Fr. Vinçenc at national holiday celebrations or historical festivities. They also admired him as a poet and a folklorist. With his publication of a collection of north–Albanian folk songs, Fr.

Vinçenc gave a more scientific direction to the collection of Albanian folklore. His first lyric poems were published by the Shkodër literary periodicals. The collection of his poems, *Gjethë e Lule* [Leaves and Flowers], gained widespread recognition. He also translated and adapted into Albanian a number of European masterpieces.

His talent as a spiritual leader was recognized by his confrères, who elected him their provincial. The Holy See later named him Bishop of Sapë (1930). By the time the Italian armies occupied Albania in April 1939, Prendushi held the post of Archbishop of Durrës. His was the highest ecclesiastical rank next to that of the Primate of the Catholic Church in Albania.

As a religious dignitary and one of Albania's representative literary figures, Archbishop Prendushi could not long be at peace with the communist regime that overtook his nation and attacked his faith. He told me that the communist leader Enver Hoxha had invited him to a "consultation" about the problems of the Catholic Church in Albania. The sole purpose of the meeting was to impose on him the communist viewpoint on religion and the Vatican. Following the Archbishop's arrest, Hoxha attacked him viciously in several public speeches.

3. The Prelate Tortured

Shortly after his "consultation" with Hoxha, the sixty–five–year–old Archbishop was arrested. He was taken to the Durrës Security Section and mercilessly tortured. He told me how the police beat him with wooden sticks. They bound his hands and feet and suspended him, "like a ram on a crook," from a hook in the ceiling of the Security bathroom, leaving him there until he fainted.

Durrës prisoners regularly performed hard labor chores. One day the guards assigned the Archbishop to a party which had to carry logs. Because the prison compound is situated on a hill, the delivery trucks would unload logs at the base of it. 'Volunteers' would then carry the logs uphill and stack them near the prison walls. The guard who selected the 'volunteers' for this task ordered the Archbishop to join the party by yelling, "You, priest!" Everyone was shocked, since the Archbishop was not only old, but also suffered from an acute hernia which caused each step to be extremely painful. The Archbishop joined the other workers without voicing any complaint.

Fellow prisoners later told me what occurred. The policemen placed logs on the Archbishop's shoulders which he could not carry.

He would struggle, stumble, and fall. This happened three times, yet he never uttered a word of complaint. All the while the Prison Director and the Commissar, watching the scene, laughed and made sarcastic remarks. Fellow prisoners tried in every possible way to lighten his burden, leaving the smallest logs for him to carry. Even without the added weight of the logs, the walk uphill was painful to him. Whenever he fell, the guards gave him a few moments to recover and then urged him to work harder with shouts of, "Hey, priest, did you ever do any hard work?" The director of the prison and the police constantly referred to the Archbishop as "priest," using the word as an insult.

During that time the Archbishop's main concern was for one of his priests, the Reverend Anton Zogaj, pastor of the Durrës parish. Zogaj had been sentenced to be executed and was locked up in solitary confinement. It was dangerous to communicate with those condemned to death. However, thanks to prison friends, the Archbishop was able to learn of the pastor's last will. Father Zogaj wanted the buttons of his cassock saved and removed from prison. The Archbishop was very pleased when the request was carried out.

Once I asked the Archbishop if he had left any manuscripts at home. He told me that he had translated and adapted Weber's *Dreizenlinden*. I asked why he had selected that particular work rather than some more notable piece of German literature. His answer was that the Austrian mountain people share many common customs with our Albanian mountain people.

4. The Ailing Archbishop

Archbishop Prendushi and I were roommates until the summer of 1948. Then I was sent to the Vloçisht labor camp in Southern Albania. On my return in November, I found the Archbishop ailing. He suffered from a heart disease and could seldom leave the prison room even for the daily scheduled walk in the courtyard. When his condition worsened, he was taken to the hospital. I followed soon after. The prison hospital barracks, annexed to the main hospital of Durrës, was a one–storey building constructed by prisoners and situated on a narrow street not far from the boulevard Dalip Tabaku. Our hospital ward was small and old, with two tiny windows which looked out to the sea.

The doctors' diagnosis was that the Archbishop had acute asthma as well as heart trouble. This was a particularly dangerous condition

for a man of his age. The asthma bothered him especially at night. The attacks increased in severity until he could not muster enough energy to speak. Dr. Propopulli, who was in charge of our ward, a man with a heart of gold who compassionately felt the suffering of prisoner patients, did everything in his power to help cure the Archbishop. At the risk of his own position, he visited the Archbishop several times a day, in addition to making his normal rounds. The doctor often brought special medicines which were not usually found in the hospital.

In June 1948, the Albanian government broke off relations with Yugoslavia. Rumors were heard of a forthcoming amnesty which would especially benefit the political prisoners. Although the Archbishop's condition was steadily deteriorating, the hope that he might spend his last days quietly at home rallied him. I doubted the communists would release him, yet I hoped that the government would shorten his sentence. Throughout this time, I tried to keep alive his hope for freedom.

5. A Moving Scene

Father Jul Bonati, the parish priest of Vlorë, was brought to the hospital annex to await committal to the Durrës mental institution. I had met Fr. Bonati years before, when I was a student in Florence. At the time he was trying to publish his translation of Father Gjergj Fishta's *Lahuta e Malcís* [The Lute of the Mountain]. I told Fr. Bonati that the bedridden man gasping for breath was Archbishop Prendushi. Although Fr. Bonati could hardly stand upright because of his own infirmities, he hurried to the Archbishop's bedside and tried to kiss his hand, which the Archbishop withdrew. Bonati then asked for his blessing. With great effort the Archbishop placed his hand on the father's head and then collapsed.

The Archbishop did not die then, but passed away several days later. In those final days he suffered greatly. The nights were filled with apprehension and trepidation. The light was on until midnight. In the darkness of the room after midnight, his suffering increased. The lack of light seemed to cause lack of breath for him. During those dark hours, his rattling breath was like the howl of a wounded creature. It was heart–rending to hear a man fighting for every gasp of air; no one could close his eyes during those attacks. We massaged his feet to ease his pain. We also kept a fire going all night long, because the light and heat of the fire seemed to comfort him.

6. Seeking the Light

Often we could not secure enough wood to keep the fire burning. When the last embers were dying and the darkness weighed heavily upon the room, we took turns at the Archbishop's bedside, assuring him that it would soon be dawn. Our words would ease his pain.

One such night, the Archbishop told me: "Now I can understand Goethe's phrase, '*Mehr Licht*'." The light which the poet sought in his hour of death certainly was not the light which we perceive with our sense of sight, something the Archbishop was well aware of. For when the thoughts of man pass from the material realm to the spiritual, the medium of the transition is usually light. From Neoplatonism through St. Augustine and then the Franciscan school of Oxford, the image of light illuminated the concepts of philosophy, while bridging poetry and mysticism. And Ugo Foscolo wrote, "For the eyes of a dying man seek the sunlight." The Albanian blessing, "May your eyes be the light of the world," expresses a similar idea.

Archbishop Vinçenc Prendushi died in February 1949. On that night of his death the fire burned brightly in our room. When I last closed his sunken eyes which had so long sought the light, I saw in his drawn face the quiet peace of a soul at rest after so much suffering. The soul that shrinks in physical pain shines bright when pain relinquishes the body. One may or may not believe in the immortality of the soul. But I find it difficult to accept that everything comes to an end when we see how men die for their ideals.

III. FIFTEEN YEARS OF COMMUNIST ALBANIA*

Khrushchev's visit to Albania in May 1959 brought our country into the limelight of politics. It was from Albania that the Soviet boss threatened the Western world with turning the smallest Russian satellite into a missile base. The threat was meant especially for two NATO countries, Italy and Greece, which had agreed to build missile bases in their territories. These two countries are Albania's neighbors. Greece borders with Albania along a slanting northeast line from the Ionian Sea to the Pindus range, while Italy stands opposite her, separated by the Adriatic Sea, which at the Otranto Straits narrows down to less than fifty miles. On the north and east, Yugoslavia's massive bulk weighs heavily upon Albania's weak shoulders.

The strategic position of Albania accounts for the interest shown in her. Ever since Yugoslavia's split with the Russian–dominated bloc, it is only through Albania that the Soviet Empire has been able to reach the Mediterranean Sea. The trouble is that access to Albania is not easy. Unlike the other satellites, which have a common border with Russia, Albania is geographically isolated, sandwiched between Yugoslavia and Greece. How is it then that she belongs to the Eastern bloc?

The last Balkan country to achieve independence (1912), Albania emerged from World War I a mutilated state which had to cope with many shortcomings inherited from four centuries of Turkish domination. Her difficulties were adroitly exploited by her neighbor, fascist Italy. In his dreams of restoring the Roman Empire, Mussolini conceived of Albania as a natural springboard for expansion into the Balkans. As early as 1939 the Italian army invaded Albania and kept

---

* Published in *Shqiptari i lirë*, February 1960, March 1960, April 1960, May 1960.

her subjugated until the breakdown of the fascist state. The country was then occupied by Nazi troops.

The Albanian people rose up against both dominations in an unrelenting struggle that eventually grew into an organized national armed resistance. While almost all political parties and groups were unanimous in opposing the Italian oppressor who wanted to turn Albania into a colony, some leaders of the nationalist parties showed reluctance in fighting the German invaders, who had achieved the integration of Albania within her ethnic borders. Their pro-German stance played into the hands of the Communist Party, which managed, in the name of 'national liberation,' to outplay its opponents, the true nationalist parties. The tide was with it, so communism won.

The policy of the Albanian Communist Party during the liberation period was in fact dictated by the Yugoslav Communist Party through its emissaries. They were instrumental in giving birth to 'the younger sister' (1946), and then tutored her. The Albanian Communist Party became a mere appendage of the Yugoslav Communist Party. By the end of 1947, Albania was practically a Yugoslav-ruled country. Plans for the formal merger of Albania as the seventh republic of the Yugoslav Federation were already being worked out. The new Yugoslav republic would have included in its administration the Albanian regions of Kosova and Metohija ('Kosmet'), which Albania has always claimed as integral parts of the nation.

Belgrade's defiance of Moscow was like lightning from a clear sky. The prevailing pro-Yugoslav faction in the Albanian Central Committee lost ground at once. The Albanian Premier, Enver Hoxha—who at the time had already been superseded by his rival, the omnipotent Minister of the Interior and Belgrade's chief agent, Koçi Xoxe—made good use of the opportunity. He accused Xoxe of treason to both Party and nation. Xoxe was arrested, tried, and executed. Dependence on Yugoslavia was over.

As Yugoslavia reacted furiously, Albania turned to Stalin for protection. But Stalin, while gladly accepting her conversion, was slow to take the orphan under his wing. The situation in the Balkans was then uncertain, and the Soviet Union could not commit herself to an alliance with a little country surrounded by enemies who had more than once planned its partition.

As the years went by, Albanian communism consolidated itself. Its policy was one of complete conformism to all that bore the label of the Soviet Union: in none of the other satellites was the copy so

similar to the original. In 1956 the Soviet bloc decided to include
Albania in the Warsaw Pact. The Albanian Red leaders saw their
victory sealed, and took a long breath.

1. Albanian Communism a Southern Phenomenon

Albania is divided by the river Shkumbin into two halves characterized by two dialects, Gheg in the north and Tosk in the south. The
language differences reflect psychological idiosyncracies. The Northerner, sober in his manners and slow in his judgments and acts, is
conservative, strongly attached to his soil, and devoted to traditional
customs and mores, including religion. The Southerner is more open-
minded, quick to react, has a remarkable gift for assimilation, and
likes the adventurous, the new, the exotic—the bulk of Albanian em-
igrants before World War II were of southern origin.

Albanian communism is chiefly a southern phenomenon.

On the eve of 'liberation,' communism controlled vast areas in
the South, while the North continued to remain closed, hostile to it.
The North had to be 'conquered.'

The conquest was bloody, as the Ghegs' resistance proved stub-
born. It exploded in revolts which forced the partisan troops to keep
'the reactionary North' under a military state of siege. One of these
revolts, that of the Postriba peasants (September 1946), barely missed
capturing the chief northern town of Shkodër. Repression was fero-
cious. There is hardly a family in the North that did not suffer, in one
way or another, from vindictive measures such as shooting, hanging,
torture, jailing, internment, confiscation, heavy taxation, public humiliation, and other offenses. Communist leaders of Northern origin
are numerically irrelevant.

Although the chief communist forces stem from the South, they
constitute even there a minority of the population. Communists in
the South clashed in a bitter civil feud with nationalists, who were
prepondant there. These were later suppressed with the same cruelty
as their Northern brothers.

By promising the peasants of the fertile plains of Central–South
Albania the land of their feudal owners, communism won them to
its cause. It won the warlike shepherds of mountainous Southern
Albania by skillfully appealing to their instinct for conquest under a
cover of wounded national pride. With these two forces combined,
communism crushed the resistance of the Southern nationalists.

Contents

The communists at that time were numerically negligible (no more than 700 at the first Party Conference in 1943, according to official data). Only a few of them were industrial workers. A working class was almost nonexistent in Albania, which was—and still is—an agrarian country. The towns are rather small, and no important industry was to be found when communism took over, the only agglomeration being found in the oil fields of Central–South Albania. Communism was imported into Albania mainly by students who had had a taste of it during their university studies in Western countries. Many of them became schoolteachers. Their students spread the rudiments of the doctrine to workers and employees, as well as to some low–ranking officers. Such elements constituted the core of the Albanian Communist Party.

Since seizing power, the Party has tried to improve the education of its members through compulsory attendance at Marxist–Leninist night school courses, but the level continues to be low. Unlike other communist parties which, along with rank–and–file members, included well–educated people with communist training and political experience, the Albanian CP had very few such people. The Party 'intelligentsia' is a phenomenon only of the last few years, and carries no weight in the political field. The key posts in the Party and in the government are always held by the old guard, semi–educated almost all of them. Even admitting that they have learned something in the meantime, it is hard to conceive of such leadership administering a state.

2. Survey of Communist Achievements and Failures

It is fifteen years since communism established itself in Albania. Let us review its effects in the various fields of national life, beginning with the political.

Albania is today virtually a Russian–ruled country, with no more autonomy than any of the national federal republics of the Soviet Union. The Russians are the undisputed masters of the country. The attitude of the Albanian leaders toward their bosses is one of servile obedience.

Albania's communist rulers have made it an outpost of Russian imperialism in a zone of Europe which is potentially a powder keg. They have already handed over to the Soviets the Sazani Island in the Straits of Otranto, which has become a Russian submarine base. And they might allow them to establish missile bases on the mainland.

In the event of war, Albania is likely to be a target of NATO forces, involving widespread destruction and inviting another invasion by her neighbors, with whom at present she is in bitter enmity. And who will be paying for their follies but the Albanian people?

Albanian leaders boast about their chief political achievement, their alliance with Russia, overlooking the fact of having brought Albania into complete geographical isolation. The country would otherwise be much more interested in friendship and good relations with her neighbors, the Balkan states and Italy.

Albania is today a militarist state with a relatively strong army—and a stronger police, by means of which communism rules the country. The Albanian army is well trained and equipped, and the Albanian leaders like to make a parade of their military strength on festival days. But is that genuine strength?

Among the countries of the communist bloc, Albania is the one with the lowest standard of living, almost the same as that in the prewar years. The Albanian army may have tanks and airplanes; the Albanian citizen does not have sufficient food and clothes.

A considerable part of the Albanian budget is swallowed up by armaments and other military expenses. These represent huge expenditures for a little country like Albania, and keep her from gaining health and prosperity. Other financial burdens are the overgrowth of the diplomatic apparatus (Albania now has diplomatic relations with many countries of Asia and Africa) and the vast propaganda machine. Even more serious is the damage caused to the national economy by the foreign trade policy. By exporting her products solely to countries of the Eastern bloc, communism has doomed Albania's economy to deficit. Those countries, mainly agrarian like Albania herself, are little interested in Albania's agricultural products. It would be much more profitable for Albania to export her products to Western countries, where they are in demand. Previously, the bulk of Albanian exports, such as oil, chrome, wool, leather, timber, and tobacco, went to Italy, which stands at the door of Albania, transport to her being easy and cheap. Now Albanian goods are shipped to Russia, Poland, or Czechoslovakia, circumnavigating Europe, and are paid for at lower prices. The communist leaders extol the 'disinterested' economic aid Russia is giving to Albania. But Albania would need no such aid were the doors open for normal trade exchanges with the West.

A basic cause for Albania's economic backwardness lies in her rulers' inadequacy to the tasks at hand. Reviewing the previous ca-

reers of the Treasury Ministers of the communist period, one finds
that they were a land–surveyor of roads, a student in economics, a
bank employee, and a teacher of gymnastics. Their incompetence
calls for foreign economic 'advisers,' who in fact dictate. These were
Yugoslavs formerly; now they are Russians. These foreigners tend to
look at the economic problems of Albania through their own ethnic
lenses, and often advise 'the younger sister' to do things detrimental
to her national economy. Thus Yugoslav experts advised Albania to
raise industrial crops, such as cotton and sunflowers, instead of wheat
and corn. Only when the break occurred did the Albanian leaders recognize that their Yugoslav brothers had deprived the Albanian people
of their bread.

Albania's economy is built on an artificial basis, one which is
at odds with its natural basis, agriculture. According to Marxism,
economic factors determine politics. What one sees in fact is the contrary: political concerns determine the economic structure. Strange
as it may seem, Albanian communism based its economic policy on a
syllogism: Communism is the ideology of the working class. No such
class exists in Albania. Then let us create it.

Thus, in order to have a working class, communism proceeded to
build more and more factories and plants, regardless of the fact that
many of them are quite unprofitable. Albania could, for instance,
import sugar for less than half of its actual cost in producing it. The
same can be said of textile plants, cotton mills, etc.

Industry is good if devised to meet the needs of the population.
And some profitable industry, in the form of oil refineries, olive oil
factories, lumber mills, and especially power plants, is in order. The
communists have done fairly well in this sector. What one objects
to is their irrational drive to create new industries for the mere sake
of industrializing the country. An agrarian country, Albania should
develop only those branches of industry which are related to her own
raw materials, and in such a way that the cost of producing an item
does not exceed the cost of importing it.

The peasantry constitutes the bulk of Albania's population. Before the advent of communism, some 80 percent of the population
lived by tilling the soil. To ingratiate themselves with the peasantry,
the communists hurried to enact the Agrarian Reform Law. This
reform, however, had little effect upon the social composition of the
Albanian peasantry. Only on the fertile plains of South–Central Albania were there some big estates to expropriate; in the other parts

of the country, especially in the mountainous zones, the land has for
centuries been owned in small parcels by free peasants and shepherds.
Most of the small estate expropriations claimed (about 4,500 according to official figures) consisted in fact of averaging corrections.
As the peasants had little to gain from the Agrarian Reform Law,
they could not be won over to communism. On the contrary, since
the various restrictive government ordinances cut heavily into their
incomes, the cooperative movement being forced upon them, they
grew hostile toward the regime.

The reluctance of the peasantry to carry out the communist
agrarian policy has had repercussions in the country's agrarian situation. Little advance has been made in agriculture; in some branches,
as in cattle raising, there has even been recession. The advance is
found chiefly in the state–owned agricultural section. Stripped from
the expropriated estates of the rich 'beys,' the best parcels have been
transformed into state farms.

Through the drainage of marshes and irrigation of arid territories,
the area of the nation's cultivated land (about 10 percent of the whole)
has been considerably expanded. These achievements are marred by
the fact that most of the work has been done by forced labor. The
drainage of the Maliq marsh, from which Albania's sugar now comes,
has been carried out mainly by political prisoners. "Our sugar smells
of blood," they say in Albania.

Remarkable progress is to be found in mining. Albania's soil
is rich in minerals, and mining has been given particular attention.
Chrome mining has undergone development: Albania is a major pro-
ducer of chrome. The extraction of oil, another important branch of
the Albanian economy, has also advanced. In the oil fields of South–
Central Albania, formerly exploited by Italian capital, new wells are
now operating, and a refinery plant has been set up.

Little has been achieved, on the other hand, in the field of public construction. In all these fifteen years, only one major building
project has been carried out—the hydroelectric plant on the Mati
river, which furnishes a conspicuous part of the country with power.
A few public roads have been added to the existing network, along
with a fragment of railroad connecting the capital with the town of
Elbasan.

Factories and plants have absorbed almost all the construction
work in Albania. Only a small number of houses have been built.
A visitor who comes to Albania after long years of absence finds

little change in the aspect of her cities (Tirana, the capital, being an exception). Better work has been done in the field of Public Health. New hospitals and sanatoriums have been built. The death rate has decreased. Still, diseases run high; tuberculosis, in particular, is widespread. Its chief cause, according to competent sources, is a protracted underfeeding. Communist health policy often finds itself operating in a vicious circle: it has to heal wounds that it inflicts itself through a low standard of living.

The work of communism in Albania is still more tangible in the field of Public Education. Communists are eager to found new schools. Elementary education for all people is a main target; they want all Albanians to read their newspapers and their propaganda brochures. They have waged a relentless war on illiteracy. Discounting their usual exaggerations, one must recognize that the rate of illiteracy has declined considerably, and in a few more years may almost disappear. Apart from elementary schooling, what they aim at is technical education. They have multiplied Normal Schools (corresponding to American Teachers' Colleges) and established vocational schools. On the other hand, they have abolished the classical gymnasium. The State University in Tirana rates among their highest achievements. They strongly sponsor science and the arts. But as their practice is conditioned by strict conformity to the Party line, the results are poor. Literature, in particular, has fallen low. Having silenced by execution or imprisonment some of the best Albanian writers, communism has reduced literature to a panegyric of the leaders and to a second-hand copy of Soviet socialist realism.

3. The People under Communism

We shall begin with the working class. What has communism brought to this group which it considers its backbone, its pride?

The monthly salary of the Albanian worker ranges between 2,400 and 4,000 leks, the latter figure being arrived at by a minority of skilled workers. The bulk of the working class receives a monthly 2,700 to 3,000 leks. Now 3,000 leks corresponds to ca. $20.00. Bread costs 10 leks a pound; sugar, 60 leks; olive oil, 100 leks; butter, 200 leks, coffee, 450 leks. A quart of milk costs 25 leks; one egg, 6-7 leks; one orange, 10-12 leks. A good pair of shoes costs 1,500-2,000 leks, and a decent suit, 10,000-15,000. In other words, the daily pay of the worker (about 100 leks) will buy one of the following: one gallon of milk, one and a half pounds of meat, half a pound of butter, 10–15 eggs, or 8–10 oranges. How, then, does a worker keep himself alive? He lives mainly on bread (not bread and butter), adding an occasional bowl of soup, or a piece of cheese, or some vegetables. It is quite usual to see a worker lunching on a piece of bread plus an onion or a tomato. He washes this down with a glass of water, lights one cigarette (a pack of cigarettes costs 15–25 leks), and goes back to work. True, in most factories a worker can have a meal at a reduced price; its food value, however, is poor.

And how about clothing? At evening one may see people decently dressed walking along the streets in Albanian cities. But let us follow one of them on his way home. He takes off his suit, examines it, then brushes it carefully. A manual worker has only that one suit; a manager may have another. People who own three suits and four shirts in Albania are part of the *nomenklatura*. Such being the condition of the Albanian worker, is it possible for him to like communism? Yet he cannot even express his dislike, any such expression being considered a crime. But, one might argue, could not the union defend his interests? Impossible: unions in communist Albania are government agencies for ruling the working class. Strikes are forbidden. Striking, communists argue, makes sense when workers are exploited by capitalists. But to strike against a state that represents their interests is absurd. With such sophisms, behind which stands the iron fist, communist union leaders try to dull the workers' consciousness. At least once a week they submit them to lengthy and compulsory ideological lectures, and if a daring fellow risks a critical observation, the lecturer promptly reminds him of the 'class enemy' rejoicing at his criticism and turning it to his own profit. A boss may at times admit a mistake, excusing himself by invoking Lenin's truism, "Only those who work make mistakes." And if the complaint about working conditions gains steam, he will fall back on the never-failing argument of sacrifice: the working class, as the leading class in the revolution, has to prove itself by accepting the sacrifices involved as a consequence of capitalist encirclement.

Exploitation and humiliation characterize the situation of the Albanian working class under communism. Its attitude toward the peasantry is even worse.

The initial Agrarian Reform Law was hailed by the peasants of Central–South Albania, most of whom were tenants on large estates owned by a handful of powerful Moslem 'beys' who had oppressed and exploited them for centuries. These peasants gave active support to communism because of the land they received. The bulk of the peasantry, who owned their own small parcels of land, remained indifferent. Their indifference shifted to hostility as communism impaired their living conditions by exacting heavy taxes. And when the Party tried to impose on them its policy of collectivization, encroaching brutally on their customs and religions feelings, they reacted with anger.

The Albanian peasant resists collectivization for a double reason. By entering the cooperative, he will lose his independence to become a salaried worker under the orders of the state. Moreover, his salary will be low. On both counts he will be a loser.

The prisons and the forced labor camps are full of peasants who have disobeyed communist laws or offended the authority of the rulers. One has hidden a part of the wheat due the state; another has grumbled about the regime in the presence of the tax collector. A third has publicly sneered at Stalin's picture (and for that crime has been sentenced to five years of prison and forced labor). Many others are behind bars for beliefs or actions that run counter to the communist code of ethics. One man has refused to send his daughter to join the railroad team, expressing doubts about the morals of communist youth. Another has dared shelter an 'enemy of the people' in his house. Still another has not only refused to be an informer but has divulged this secret. A fourth has been convicted of 'propaganda' against the cooperative movement, thus revealing himself as a 'kulak.'

'Kulak' in Russian means 'fist.' In communist jargon it means a rich peasant opposed to the Party's policy of collectivization. This policy was started, in Albania as in the Soviet Union, under the slogan: "War to the death against the kulak!" In the opinion of a brainwashed Party member, a kulak is a base fellow, hypocritical, treacherous, one who by means of well-calculated hints and insinuations keeps a peasant from joining the cooperative. The kulak is drawn on placards as a big-bellied brute with evil, squinting eyes, his yellow teeth like those of a crocodile and his claw-like nails dripping blood.

This is the bugbear with which communism terrorizes the peasants. To be branded a kulak is to lose both freedom and property. The kulak is responsible for all that goes wrong in the agrarian sector. Has a peasant shown any reluctance to 'volunteer' for a collective team? Don't look too far: the kulak's finger is there. Has a cooperative's horse caught cold and died? A kulak has poisoned him. The wheat has rotted in the state storehouse because the kulak has managed to evade the 'vigilance' of the supervisor. And who but a kulak could burn the cooperative's haystacks or break the windowpanes of the newly-built village school at night?

The first agricultural cooperatives were created in the expropriated estates of the Myzeqe plain shortly after the communist takeover. The communists, however, judged it premature to impose cooperativism on the whole of Albania before being safely established in the country themselves. Having just finished distributing the land to the peasants, it would have been nonsensical to proceed immediately to forced collectivization. So they took a roundabout way. They began putting all sorts of remoras in the ways of the individual peasant's economies. They forced him to sow according to a state plan; they exacted from him such heavy taxes (while almost exempting the collectives from them) that he could only live by toiling twice as much as before. The goal was to force him into accepting collectivization.

The peasantry reacted. There were cases of open rebellion, like that of the peasants of Postriba in September 1946. Serious troubles arose in the districts of Shijak and Tepelenë during the period 1947–48. Some peasants shot Party executives who confiscated their crops.

A pitiless repression followed. Peasants were shot and herded into jail by the hundreds. Many of them took to the mountains. Others burned the wheat due the state, killed the surplus cattle they were not allowed to raise, or felled fruit trees upon which a tax had been laid. By the end of 1948, there was such a scarcity of wheat in the country that people fed on legumes and berries.

Facing bankruptcy, communism loosened the screws. An attempt to tighten them up through collectivization was repeated at the end of 1950, soon to be dropped again. Only after Albania's entering the Warsaw Pact did the Albanian rulers proceed to the decisive collectivization of the land. Officially, this was to be completed on a voluntary basis. In practice, pressure was brought to bear upon the reluctant peasantry. Often the authorities would pick up a peasant suspected as a sympathizer of previous regimes and jail him on some trumped-up charge, his example being a lesson to others.

The following was related to the author by a native of the Daragjat village near Shkodër who escaped to Yugoslavia because he "preferred death to collectivization."

In September 1957 the Party delegated its leaders to carry out the collectivization campaign. To the Shkodër district, known for its opposition, came Premier Shehu himself.

A former military academy student, Shehu joined the International Brigades in the Spanish Civil War and won his general's epaulets fighting the fascist–Nazi occupiers of Albania. Known in his country for being both valiant and cruel, he is reported to have knifed with his own hand Italian soldiers captured in battle. On another occasion, in a fit of rage against Albanian nationalist, he is said to have torn the Albanian flag to pieces.

Upon his arrival in the above–mentioned village, Shehu first had a short talk with its parish priest, the old man trembling all over with fear. Then he gathered the peasants and had another short talk with them. He told them he knew of their patriotism and their devotion to the Party. But he also knew that there were two or three kulaks among them. These dirty enemies of the people, these agents of capitalism, were trying to keep the honest, loyal, patriotic peasants from joining the cooperative. The overwhelming majority, he was sure, would agree with him to enter the cooperative. Was there anyone against it? Such a person could speak his mind freely; the Party was pledged to respect criticism, when, of course, it was honest and constructive. When no one spoke, Shehu went on to say this left no doubt that the village approved his proposal. The parish priest, he added, also favored it, being a true servant of the people and not that reactionary type of priest who is its worst enemy. And since all those present agreed to join the cooperative, the village executive could proceed to register them.

Now a few words about the intellectuals. They have from the outset shown communism a cold face, provoking the communists to fury. The many show–trials in Albania resound with the names of doctors and lawyers, professors and writers, technicians and engineers, who have not bent knee before the despotic regime. Most of them have been shot or hanged, and a great many have disappeared and are disappearing into the Communist dungeons and slave labor camps. Their story is a separate chapter of Albanian communism, the most shameful and hideous. Albania could perhaps pardon communism many crimes, but not that of having deprived her of her sons' energy of mind and spirit, a nation's most valuable capital. And when one further considers that Albania is not a nation with an abundance of intellectuals, one can more sensibly evaluate her loss. Indeed, the present situation has been brought about just because of deficient statesmanship and incompetent administration.

The communist leaders tried to lure intellectuals into their ranks. Their gains being meager, they resorted to violence. By killing and jailing a considerable number of them, they forced the rest into submission or quiescence. In the meantime, they proceeded with feverish speed to build up their own intelligentsia. Here, so far, they have met with failure. Except for a number of fanatics, the majority of the new intellectuals pay only lip service to communist ideology; their eyes are turned toward the West. The legacy of the former generation of intellectuals, all of them imbued with Western civilization, is still too much alive for the new generation to become devotees of an ideology which is alien to the frame of mind and traditions of the Albanian people.

4. The Party

The Albanian—be he peasant, worker, or intellectual—dislikes communism. The Party membership does not exceed 5 percent of the total population, a significant figure considering that membership in the Albanian communist "Party of Labour" is not so strictly regulated as in other communist countries.

The rank–and–file Party member is not happy either. He has a number of duties and responsibilities and much of his time is spent in conferences and meetings. As for income, he is no better off than anyone else, and he realizes that the Party has become the fief of a few dignitaries who hold its key positions and share its benefits. They live in comfortable houses, are driven in costly cars, and feed and dress themselves in special shops, where they get the most expensive items at ridiculous prices. At gala receptions, their wives appear in elegant gowns. And they usually take their vacations abroad. The leaders are still called 'comrades,' and as proof of their comradeship they occasionally shake hands in public with some worker or peasant. But actually they are as remote from the people as any ruling clique. The concentration of power in their hands has totally alienated them not only from the people, but also from the Party rank and file.

In February 1951, a bomb exploded in the Soviet Legation in Tirana, where a joint conference of Soviet diplomats and Albanian leaders had been called. The government accused 'reactionary elements' opposed to the regime. Some thirty non–communists were dragged out of their beds and shot without trial. Among them was a professor of biology, a woman. Later on, it was discovered that the man who had set the bomb was a subordinate officer, a Party member.

In the summer of 1956, widespread discontent burst out among the rank and file. Delegates to the Party Conference in the Tirana district rose up against the leadership with violent criticism of its high-handed policy. They repeated again and again that, while the working class was being exploited to the point of starvation, the leadership wallowed in wealth.

The rebellion was promptly crushed, the rebels silenced. There were trials, followed by executions. Terror struck at the roots of the Party, widening still more the cleavage between the bureaucratic-militarist class and the rest of the nation.

The kind of dictatorship that exists today in Albania has nothing in common with the official 'dictatorship of the proletariat.' It is, in fact, the dictatorship of a handful of rulers, backed by a class of officers who guard them and, accordingly, share in the benefits created by the toil of the peasants and workers. Ideology means little or nothing to the military class constituting the real backbone of the communist regime. The former peasants and shepherds, at present colonels and generals, have not assimilated Marxism–Leninism, except for a few formulas and slogans which they display along with their epaulets and decorations. They would not give up these decorations for any price and would fight to the death to preserve the privileges they have acquired. This group has kept the communists in power during its critical moments. Their sons are being assiduously trained for leadership in the Party schools of Albania and the Soviet Union. But time will pass before they can assume their fathers' role. To this day the reins of power are firmly in the hands of the old guard.

It is military power that maintains communism in Albania, not ideology and doctrine, not Soviet support. Time and again, the leaders have complained about the ideological shortcomings of Party members. They are particularly worried about the vestiges of religious education, which systematic atheistic indoctrination has not been able to eradicate. It is also true that religion has lost ground in Albania, even if there have been cases of Catholic Party members being married by a priest, or of Moslem Party members breaking Party discipline for the sake of religious customs and traditions.

5. Conclusions

An alien, imported ideology, forced upon the people with utmost brutality, communism remains to this day as alien as ever. Unlike most of the other communist–ruled countries where communism has absorbed something of the national character, Albania allows no such special characteristics. Albanian communism is merely a copy of Bolshevism, without the slightest originality of its own.

Various authors who have written about Albania are almost unanimous in acknowledging the Albanian's fierce instinct of freedom, his high esteem of what is brave and heroic, his proverbial abiding by his pledged word, his awesome 'vendetta' tempered by chivalrous forgivensss, his stern code of family life in which the 'pater familias' has full authority, and his house is considered a sanctuary for the guest.

Communism imposed upon this people an ideology which makes a herd of slaves out of free individuals, brings about a psychology of cruelty and torture unknown to the Albanian, enforces a code of ethics which turns children into spies on their own parents. Such an ideology has traits antithetical to those which characterize the Albanian mind. Therefore, it cannot thrive. But it can produce confusion and aberration.

Fifteen years of communist dictatorship have produced a sad and negative record in Albania, which can be summed up as follows:

It has inflicted irreparable damage on the intellectual life of Albania by destroying a great part of her intelligentsia and by subjecting activities of the mind to Party dictates;

It has impoverished Albania's economy by imposing an economic and trade policy unsuited to her geo–political conditions;

It has grafted onto the nation's ethics Bolshevik practices and patterns;

It has dealt a severe blow to the national unity of the country by causing a rift between the North and the South;

It has jeopardized the very existence of Albania as a state by a selfish, short–sighted, unilateral policy in international relations.

In view of these results, one cannot deny that there have been a few gains, such as enlargement of the cultivated area of land, more intensive exploitation of the soil, some aspects of industrialization, and progress in the fields of public health and public education. Yet compared to the negative records as described, the losses far outweigh the gains.

Communism boasts of them, exaggerating as usual. Any democratic regime could have achieved the same and much more in a period of fifteen years.

It remains to explain how this regime has reached its fifteenth year.

During her existence as an independent state, Albania was continually threatened with being swallowed up by her neighbors. A first partition between Italy, Greece, Montenegro, and Bulgaria was planned as early as 1912, the very year when Albania won her independence. In 1915, a secret treaty was signed in London on Albania's partition between Italy, Greece, Montenegro, and Serbia. In 1939, the Italian army occupied Albania. At the Paris Conference of 1946, Greece proposed to Yugoslavia a bilateral partition of Albania. Yugoslavia rejected the offer, her objective being the total annexation of the country. In 1949, plans were made for a military occupation of Albania by Greece. To this day, Greece considers herself in a state of war with Albania, claiming almost all the southern part of the country.

Struggling for its own existence, Albanian communism has also struggled for Albania's independence. It has rebuked the fantastic claims of Greek chauvinism and, since the break with Yugoslavia, has stigmatized its former ally for the repression and denationalization policy practiced against the Albanian minority in Yugoslavia. In this way communism, by a bitter irony of history, has come to be a champion of Albanian nationalism.

This last feature of Albanian communism explains, in the last analysis, its survival through the agitated period of its rule. Although Albanians hate communism, they would rather live under it than lose their independence. They know that while communism is a transitory state in the history of their country, the life of the nation goes on.

The day when Albania is no longer surrounded by enemies planning her destruction, communism in Albania will be living its last hours. The overthrow of the regime may come from the people by means of a general uprising. More likely it will come from a military coup. It may also occur from some more educated Party members when they realize that the existing situation is untenable and debasing.

IV. ALBANIA'S FOREIGN POLICY VIEWED THROUGH HER ALLIANCES*

Half a century has elapsed from November 28, 1912 when Albania achieved independence. During this period the Albanian state has gone through a number of political vicissitudes in which sovereignty has been defended, lost, regained, given up, patronized, and reasserted, depending on alliances with invariably totalitarian states. This article first sketches the forms of the Albanian state in chronological order, and then focuses on the degree of sovereignty as affected by the alliances with those states. The article concludes with a geo–political interpretation of the alliances.

A. Forms of the Albanian State

1. The First State (1912–1920)

Albania is the last Balkan country to achieve independence. The London Conference (July 29, 1913) recognized the new Albanian state, whose boundaries are fixed by the Florence Protocol (December 17, 1913). Born a rump state through amputations of large parts assigned to Albania's neighbors and forthwith invaded by foreign armies during the Balkan Wars and World War I, the state lacks true sovereignty. A foreign prince, Wilhelm zu Wied, chosen by the great powers, arrives in Durrës in November 1913, only to leave the country as soon as World War I breaks out. During his short–lived reign, whole Albanian regions remain outside the government's reach. In Central Albania peasants rebel, while in the South a pro–Greek government with Gjirokastër as capital is formed.

---

* Elaborated version of "Zhvillimi politik i shtetit shqiptar" [The Political Development of the Albanian State], published in *Shqiptari i lirë*, November–December 1962.

During World War I, the occupying powers—Austria–Hungary, Italy, and France—set up local administrations in their zones of occupation. At the end of the war, Albania is occupied by the victorious Allied powers. A government in Italian–occupied Durrës is formed, whose delegates represent Albania at the Versailles Conference.

2. The Democratic State (1920–24)

A sovereign Albanian state as the expression of the will of the people through elected representatives begins functioning after the Lushnje Congress (January 21, 1920). Sovereignty is vested in a Council of Regents, with a government issued from representatives of the people divided into two chambers. In the Parliament, the Popular Party and the Progressive Party adopt European parliamentary procedures. Democracy is superficial—the Progressive Party is in fact a feudal coalition. In June 1924, the liberal wing of the Popular Party, constituted into an Opposition Party, seizes power through an armed revolution. Bishop Fan Noli heads the revolutionary government. It is soon after toppled by a counterrevolution led by Ahmet Zogu (December 1924). As Premier of the new government, Zogu first settles accounts with his adversaries, then gets himself elected as President of the Republic. The republican cocoon gives birth to monarchy.

3. The Autocratic State (1924–39)

During the Zogu period, the agitated internal situation stablizes. The leader's carrot–and–stick policy subdues *bajraktars*[1] while ingratiating feudal cliques. Various attempts to dethrone "the tyrant" fizzle. Foreign policy is Italian–oriented. Mussolini guarantees the country's integrity from neighbors' threats while pouring cash into the empty Albanian treasury. In exchange, Albania grants Italian companies concessions to build roads and bridges, exploit the subsoil, and run the National Bank of Albania, founded with Italian capital. Albanian foreign policy is a facsimile of its Italian model. The form of the state is a "constitutional monarchy," with a government at the monarch's command and a parliament without political parties which rubber–stamps governmental decrees. Poverty reigns supreme in both cities and the countryside while the royal family immerses itself in luxury and pomp.

4. The Fascist Occupation State (1939–1943)

The fascist aggression against Albania (April 7, 1939) seals eighteen years of Italian dependency.[2] The Emperor of Ethiopia receives the additional title of King of Albania. The Albanian state is a miniature copy of the Italian fascist state, with a Corporative Council and a pro-Italian government at the behest of the Italian Viceroy. Later a certain autonomy is granted to the government by the inclusion of nationalist elements. Yet the government remains antipopular. When Italy invades Greece to "liberate" Çamëria (October 1940), the Albanian government joins Italy in declaring war on Greece. And when Yugoslavia disintegrates as a consequence of the German aggression, Kosova and other Albanian-inhabited regions are incorporated into Greater Albania (April 1941). In November 1941, the Albanian Communist Party is founded. Resistance to the occupation forces grows with the formation of two nationalist parties, the National front and the Royalist Party.

5. The Nazi Occupation State (1943–44)

In August 1943 Nazi troops occupy Albania. A Constituent Assembly declares the end of the Italian occupation and elects a regency and a pro-German government, which is even weaker than the former quisling governments. When the National Liberation Movement led by communists liberates whole districts in South Albania, a Provisional National Liberation Government is formed in Berat (October 22, 1944), based on people's councils in accordance with the Soviet (and Yugoslav) pattern.

6. The Communist State (1944–1962)

On November 27, 1944, the Partisans liberate Tirana. The new state, named the People's Republic of Albania, is a tool of the Albanian CP in imposing its dictatorship on classes, groups, and persons hostile to communism. The internal policy has two objectives: to industrialize the country by creating a working class almost *a nihilo*, and to build socialism in the countryside by forcing peasants into agricultural cooperatives.

While the Party's internal policy is a linear process with occasional slowdowns, foreign policy presents opposite features, characterized as it is by eccentric flights resulting in ideological breaks. Having begun its career as Yugoslavia's satellite, Albania first swerves into the Soviet orbit and then, attracted by Maoist China, follows her at a certain distance, no longer a satellite, now a fellow traveller. Passing from one state's ideological grounds to another's without settling down in any one of them, Albania resembles the Wandering Jew in search of a home.

B. State Sovereignty and Alliances

Conceived as the visibility of independence, sovereignty presents itself on a scale. A state is totally sovereign, partially so, or totally dependent, according to whether sovereignty remains in the full possession of the state, is more or less shared with other states, or is in the full possession of another state. Dependency can be political, or economic, or both. In the case of the Albanian state, the degree of sovereignty varies with its degree of dependency on other states through alliances with them. We now apply this premise to the various forms of the Albanian state as reviewed in the preceding section, leaving out the 1912–1920 period during which Albania is a state without real sovereignty.

1. Democratic Neutrality

During the period 1920–24, Albania is a fully sovereign state, not allied with any foreign state and therefore neutral. Its sovereignty is, however, inconspicuous, the state being engrossed in internal problems, such as building up the state apparatus, repressing rebellions, and defending frontiers. International relations are limited mostly to establishing diplomatic relations. One such case has fateful consequences. The Noli government, after recognizing the Soviet Union, seems inclined to accept communist technical aid. This causes consternation in the rest of the Balkan states, all of them monarchies. Royalist Yugoslavia arms the exiled Zogu, who, at the head of his tribe, reinforced with a contingent of White Russian exiles, defeats the revolutionary government.

2. The Alliance with Italy

Once in power, the Albanian leader reneges on his Yugoslav promises and makes overtures to Italy. The Adriatic power, which considers Albania a zone of Italian influence, is ready to comply. A Pact of Friendship and Security (November 1926) is followed by an Alliance Treaty (November 1927). Yet the Italian penetration is not all–pervasive and sovereignty is preserved. The king controls the administration, and to a great extent, the army, while his gendarmerie, organized by English officers, remains his prerogative. When he chafes at an Italian proposal for a customs union, and then dismisses the Italian military advisers, Italy replies by sending an Italian fleet on the Durrës waters (June 1934). Zogu retreats while continuing to temporize. Having failed to change his regime through pressure and bribes, Mussolini orders the aggression (April 7, 1939).

3. Albania under Axis Powers

The aggression catches national consciousness unawares. The population, used to an autocratic regime, is slow to react. Ideological confusion grows when Kosova and Çamëria join Greater Albania, touted by fascism as Italy's gift to the Albanian nation. The formation of the Albanian CP is a first voice of protest, soon followed by the formation of a Zogist party and of a republican front. Guerrillas of the three parties begin operations. An attempt to coordinate their actions is torpedoed by the Yugoslav CP, which enjoins the Albanian CP to withdraw from a planned coalition in which the nationalist parties flaunt the flag of Greater Albania, including Kosova. With Kosova as the apple of discord flung between nationalists and communists, civil war breaks out, fomented by the latter.

The short interval of German occupation is marked by important developments. The nationalist parties have no intention of fighting the Germans, who support an "independent" Greater Albania (a Kosovar SS division fights on their side). Albanian communists, on the other hand, are on the side of Yugoslav communists, who fight the Germans as both invaders and Nazis. Because Kosova is claimed by Yugoslav communists, the Albanian communists cannot but be silent about it. Their silence is construed by nationalists as national treason. Communists retort by calling them fascists for their pro–German stance. Their national liberation war is in fact an ideological war against fascism–Nazism. As such it coincides with the war against Germans by the Western Allies and the Soviet Union. And since the Allies' immediate objective is defeating the Germans, whoever fights them is an ally. Their military aid and the thrust of their propaganda are for the Albanian communists, not for the Albanian nationalists. Ironically enough, the communists seize power in Albania carried on the tide of democratic victories in Europe.

4. The Yugoslav Tutelage

In November 1944 Albania regains its independence. But this independence is more apparent than real. The Yugoslav CP, which has organized the Albanian CP, continues to tutor it. The Albanian leaders, inexperienced in statesmanship, let their Yugoslav 'brothers' command. A Treaty of Friendship and Mutual Aid (June 1946) is followed by a Treaty of Customs and Monetary Union (November 1946). Albanian sovereignty is reduced to its shadow, the country slips back to a form of dependency worse than that of monarchist Albania. Agreement in principle is reached by the two governments for a republic of Albania (together with Kosova) as Yugoslavia's seventh republic.

Suddenly Stalin denounces the Yugoslav leadership as ideologically deviant. Yugoslavia ripostes by breaking loose from Soviet control. The break prompts Albania in turn to shake off Yugoslav dominance. Under the pressure of Koçi Xoxe, Yugoslavia's strong man in the Albanian CP, Enver Hoxha, the Secretary General, reluctantly approves the annexation. Now, assisted by Mehmet Shehu, a general with a hero's reputation, Hoxha takes Stalin's side, backed by the people. Xoxe is demoted, tried, and finally hanged as a traitor to both the Party and the nation (July 1949).

5. The Soviet Patronage

The regained independence is more like a vacuum. Execrated by Yugoslavia and looked at askance by the Soviet Union for her subservience to that country, Albania is alone in a world of nations hostile to or, at best, distrustful of her because of her bad international record.[3] She is at risk of disappearing from Europe's map. In the past Zogu turned to Mussolini after double–crossing Pašić.[4] Having abjured Tito, Hoxha resorts to Stalin. Albanian diplomacy at this juncture is dead set on winning his patronage by singing his praises while hurling sewers of verbiage against the Yugoslav renegade. The strategy works; Stalin takes Albania under his wing.

6. Alienation from the Soviet Union

Albania's inclusion in the Warsaw Pact (May 1955) gives her some international relief. Stalin has died in the meantime, to the great loss of the Albanian rulers. For Khrushchev, the new man at the helm, does not continue his former master's ostracism of Yugoslavia, which he tries to bring back into the fold. He also finds fault with Hoxha's defiance of Tito and advises the Albanian leader to make peace with his former boss. But reconciliation with Tito implies Xoxe's rehabilitation, thus encouraging the remains of his faction to reorganize and vie for power. Hence Hoxha's quarrel with Khrushchev, which comes to a head when the Soviet leader visits Albania in May 1959. The Albanian leadership feels sold out, a sentiment shared by most of the population, loath to see Yugoslav rule reinstated.

7. The Alliance with China

In their efforts to get free of Soviet patronage, now felt as a yoke, the Albanian leaders are lucky to have a communist state, and a great power at that, listen sympathetically to their complaints. Like Albania, China disapproves of the de–Stalinization process going on in the Soviet Union while also condemning Yugoslav "revisionism." Finding themselves on the same ideological journey, the two countries form an alliance. It seems to defy logic, considering the distance separating them, not to mention their difference in size. It was a *do ut des* logic. When the Soviet Union suspended a shipment of wheat badly needed by the Albanian population, China rushed to the rescue by buying it from Canada. Albania repaid with services, becoming China's mouthpiece in the United Nations.[5] Albania may be as a mouse compared to China, the Mountain. But the mouse has a voice, which the Mountain does not. In competing with the Soviet Union for world hegemony, it is no small feat for China to have Albania aligned with herself rather than with her rival. For now the mouse can be used to pester the rival. Khrushchev reacted as angrily as Stalin did in the past. The Soviet bloc excommunicated Albania.

8. The Albanian Pendulum

We can say that the sovereignty of Albania oscillates like a pendulum under the gravitation of single alliances with totalitarian states. Having reached a terminal point in the direction of dependency, the pendulum swings back to its independence point. National sovereignty remains the axis of Albanian foreign policy in alliances with totalitarian states aiming at her annexation or vassalage. In both cases national pride is offended, and the reaction is rebellion.

King Zog's rebellion against the annexational aims of fascist Italy was an irresolute one, a *rebellion à genoux*. More significant cases are found in the history of communist Albania. The nationalist Party faction frustrated Yugoslavia's attempt at annexation. The revolt against the Soviet Union's patronage was provoked by Khrushchev's heavy–handed treatment of the Albanian leaders. In all three cases survival played a decisive role, the nation's interests being of secondary importance. Indeed, from an economic viewpoint, the revolts were counterproductive. The alliance with China, an exception to the rule in that it does not offend national pride, was mainly determined by economic interests.

9. Developmental Orientation

Starting as a premature European–like democracy, the Albanian state (d)evolves into autocracy by going through a revolution and a counterrevolution. Foreign intervention promotes autocracy to dictatorship. In this new mold, the Albanian state passes from fascism, through Nazism, over to Stalinism. Then, within the contours of Stalinism, it experiences all three types of that ideology in the Old World, which are representative of the three geo–political divisions in a European–Eurasian–Asiatic continuum. Viewed from this angle, the Albanian state is paradigmatic of a political development increasingly alien to European democracy.

The orientation, initially westbound in the republican, monarchist, and colonialist period of the state, brusquely reverses itself to become eastbound. Starting from Adriatic shores and covering the distance Marco Polo did seven centuries ago, it reaches the East Pacific coast, thus tracing an arc of ca. 180 degrees. Once arrived at this point, the possibilities for further advancement are nil. For in whatever direction the move is made, the result will be an approach to the West, either by way of the western hemisphere, or, what seems more likely, in the direction of home.

C. The Eastbound Drive

The section on the forms of the state has shown that the Albanian state has developed in a direction contrary to democracy. The section on the degree of sovereignty of those forms has explained why the state has never achieved full sovereignty, i.e., both political and economic, the degree of sovereignty varying with the antidemocratic bearing of the state with which Albania has been forced into an alliance. What is to be learned from these inferences?

1. Review of the Alliances

The Albanian state is small, compressed by stronger and richer neighbors, which have, moreover, territorial claims over it. The country is also poor, with an economy that scarcely meets the elementary needs of its population. Such being the case, Albania does need aliances with stronger and richer states.

But alliances are of different kinds. An alliance with a stronger neighbor intent on swallowing its ally is a way of national suicide. This was the case of Albania's alliance with Yugoslavia. Convinced that Yugoslav communists are different fron noncommunist Yugoslavs and aptly lured by them into beileving in the mirage of a union of all Albanian lands in the form of a republic enjoying the same rights as the other republics of Federal Yugoslavia, the Albanian leaders handed the keys of Albania to their Yugoslav comrades.

The alliance with Yugoslavia was also proposed to Zog. But the wily tribal chief knew enough not to fall into the Serbian trap. He could not, however, elude the Italian snare.

An alliance with democratic Italy is less dangerous, for Italy, while not innocent herself, has more than once defended Albania's interests. Yet an alliance with a fascist imperialist Italy is more dangerous, as proved by what happened.

The (mis)alliance with the Soviet Union, dictated by the imperative of survival, presented no risk of annexation. Yet the Albanian leaders forgot that when a prince marries a Cinderella, she has to be his princely slave (Boccaccio's story of Griselda), ready to comply with his every wish and whim.

Albania's alliances with Italy, Yugoslavia, and the Soviet Union, and now with China, are all single alliances with invariably totalitarian states. Why does Albania enter into such alliances?

2. Lack of Democratic Tradition

The phenomenon occurs four times in a row; it cannot possibly be accidental; it must have a reason. And this is not terribly hard to identify when we compare Albania to a state with approximately her own area and population and which is situated geographically not too far away. Such is Switzerland—and Albania has more than once been called the Switzerland of the Balkans, a mountainous country with a breathtaking range in the north and a beautiful riviera in the south.

Yet whereas Switzerland is a rich country with a centuries–long democratic tradition and an advanced civilization, Albania is a destitute country with no modern democratic tradition, and with a civilization still in the way of formation. Both countries are republics, but the name means quite different things, Switzerland being a democratic republic with free elections and one bound to respect civil and human rights, but Albania a dictatorship where 99 percent of the voters vote for the platform of a single party, with prisons and forced labor camps for those who dare to disobey her ukases.

3. Birds of a Feather Flock Together

While sovereignty in a democratic country rests with the collectivity of its people(s), in a totalitarian/authoritarian country it is vested in a power élite or even in one sole person. These power élites or dictators tend to form alliances with others of their ilk. Exceptions occur in emergency situations, the alliance in World War II of the two great democratic powers with the Soviet Union being a case in point. The rule explains communist Albania's tendency to form alliances with invariably totalitarian states. The rule applies also to the alliance with Italy, Zog having ruled Albania pretty much as Mussolini ruled Italy. The question whether a democratic state could have prevented Italy's fascist aggression is a moot point. But if a democratic Albanian state could not have prevented fascism from invading the country, it could have prevented communism from seizing power. For had it not been for the country's fascist occupation, infant Albanian communism, which grew rapidly while disguised as a movement of national liberation, could easily have been defeated by Albanian nationalism.

4. The Oriental Burden

Analysis of the development of the Albanian state suggests that this development is a causative chain. Lack of democracy can in turn be explained by the legacy of Ottoman absolutism. What Albania experienced in the late Middle Ages is a feudal form of state, which did not lead, as was the case with other Balkan states, to a unitary form of state. The Ottoman occupation, which nipped in the bud a first attempt made by Scanderbeg at a unitary state, brought in an alien culture which caught on in Albania faster than in any other part of the Balkans (except Bosnia). The Ottoman heritage weighs heavily

on Albanians' shoulders, a burden of which they will not easily be rid.
No wonder then that after a short–lived West–oriented democratic
start, followed by a longer period during which oriental habits got a
western veneer, the needle of the Albanian politics shifted brusquely
to the East.

5. The Logic of the Curved Line

Now Albania's eastward drive, we saw, has reached a terminal
point, from which the needle cannot but swing back. A first move in
that direction will be followed by a second, that by a third, and so
on. The needle won't stay put until it reaches a point that represents
the vectorial sum of Albania's physical, socio–economic, and politico-
cultural factors. This locus cannot but be in the western world, in
the part of it inhabited by European families of nations. Albania will
have to come back to the home from which communist ideology has
banished it.

The question is when the homecoming will occur: when will Albania be disgusted in turn with Maoist China?

6. Albania's International Position

Albania's alliance with China is not like the alliance with the
Soviet Union. China can hardly match the economic–technical aid
the Soviet Union gave to Albania. And what the Soviet Union was
expected to do in case of aggression, i.e., defend Albania, China cannot.

Albania's exit from the Soviet bloc has weakened her international position. For a change in the equilibrium of forces in Europe—
say the end of Yugoslavia's neutrality—might be catastrophic for
Albania. Other scenarios can be imagined. If Albania becomes a
Chinese base for Maoist penetration into Africa, the Mediterranean
countries would raise a hue and cry against Albania, and the question of her partition will be reproposed. Albania's membership in the
United Nations would not obviate an aggression. Considering Albania's ill- repute, very few countries would protest, and certainly not
the two superpowers, which Albania continues to antagonize.

By allying herself with the Soviet Union Albania secured her
political independence. By allying herself with China Albania risks
losing it.

7. A Political Absurdity

In their convulsive efforts to keep communism going on in Albania, her rulers have twice formed and dissolved alliances with communist countries. Will she likewise undo her alliance with China? An alliance with China after the breaking of one with the Soviet Union is an absurdity from a security point of view. And political absurdities cannot last long. By accepting, however reluctantly, an alliance with the Soviet Union, the Albanian people let it be understood that a life of misery and oppression under Albanian bosses is a lesser evil than the loss of the country's independence. By aligning the country with Maoist China, the Albanian rulers have made it clear that holding power is dearer to them than national independence.

They have exhausted their repertoire of acrobatics. In one way or another, they must go.

V. KOSOVO BETWEEN YUGOSLAVIA AND ALBANIA*

Q. What would you say are the affinities and differences between Kosovo and Albania today?

bf A. The Albanians feel very strongly about Kosovo being part of Albania. Not only because of historical elements, but I would say for political reasons, too. There is no Albanian who does not feel that Kosovo should be an integral part of Albania.

Q. Do you think this is also true for the younger generation which has grown up and gone through Yugoslav schools? Do you think they also feel themselves closer to Albania than to Yugoslavia?

A. That I really don't know, because I have not visited Kosovo. But I would say that in general there is a greater attraction towards Albania: the Kosovars feel they are part of Albania and would like to join it. But this is more a kind of nostalgia or emotional approach, and when one comes to the leadership, they certainly view things differently.

Q. The Albanian leadership in Kosovo?

A. Yes. I am quite sure of that. They feel differently because they know that if Kosovo joined Albania they would be just eliminated. There is no doubt about that. They are officially the representatives of revisionism, Titoism, etc. People in key positions, who were instrumental in creating the existing situation, would be eliminated. Therefore it goes without saying that they don't want just to join Albania, I mean an Albania ruled by the kind of leadership which exists there today.

Q. You think there is a difference between the leadership and the population—that the population does not have fears?

---

* Interview by Michele Lee. Published in *Labour Focus on Eastern Europe*, Summer 1982.

A. That's correct. My feeling is that the population, especially those who don't know exactly the situation in Albania, have a nostalgic desire to join Albania. Those who are more educated and know the difference between the two kinds of socialism are of course much more reserved. I would say that these are in general the educated people who can make out the differences, ideological differences in particular. And when it comes to the leadership then there is no doubt that they are against. But the affinities are there: the common history, common language, common customs. And this constitutes the basis for a union.

Q. You say that they have a common history, and this of course is largely true. Nevertheless Kosovo has been outside Albania for about seventy years now, with the exception of the very short period of Italian occupation. As seventy years in the twentieth century is considerably more than seventy years at any other time, do you think this has created some basis for separate development?

A. In my view, this has to be considered in relation to specific problems. For instance, regionalism—the question of Gheg and Tosk, to begin with—and the economic situation. But there can be no doubt that there is an affective element involved. If, for instance, a referendum were to be held today in Kosovo, then I am sure that a great deal of the population would vote for union with Albania just because of these affective ties. Speaking of affinities, we should also include the important folklore elements. However, the differences are also very relevant. To begin with, Kosovars are nearly all Gheg. The distinction between Ghegs and Tosks has some importance in Albanian history, dating back to the time when the dividing line between the Roman and Byzantine empires passed through the country. This, more than the religious difference, explains why there has always been some friction between the Ghegs and Tosks. Just to give you an example, when Albania became a kingdom, the king was a Gheg Northerner, and there was a great deal of resistance to him on the part of the Tosk Southerners. At least three insurrections started in the South: one in Vlorë, another in Fier, a third in Kurvelesh. The people who led these uprisings were all Tosk. Sometimes there were chieftains from Northern Albania who, for tribal reasons, disliked Zog. But the main trouble came from the South.

Now, since the Kosovars and an awful lot of Albanians in Macedonia are Gheg, then a unification—I will come to this problem later— would immediately change the more or less equal balance of Ghegs and Tosks in Albania. Also, in Albania they have learned to live together. And of course there is a question of religion. In Albania today there are three or four religions (if we include the Bektashi), and the Moslems form a majority of more than 70 percent. The Moslem element in Albania is not generally of a fanatical character—religion has never been important to the Albanians, and to the Moslems even less than to the others. The Catholics are somewhat more religious, but even they only in Shkodër, not in the Highlands. Because of their cultural links with Italy and the Vatican, they are more conscious of their religious identity.

But is is also interesting to know that these are also the most patriotic people in Albania. There is a whole line of Albanian patriotism which has its greatest champions in the Albanian Franciscans. The doctrine of their founder is only loosely binding on Franciscan friars, who have at times taken up a gun and fought the enemy. Now, since the Albanians in Yugoslavia are 95 percent Moslem, the union would completely change the balance in this respect, too.

Q. Surely if the Albanian population is 70 percent Moslem today and 95 percent tomorrow; this is only a matter of degree. Do you feel that there is more to this than numbers? Is it to do with the Moslem schools and the practice of Islam, which is free in Kosovo, while that organizing aspect is completely absent in Albania?

A. Yes, the Kosovars are religious. I would not say they are fanatics, but they do feel religious. And I think that religion to them comes mostly as a kind of differentiating element *vis-à-vis* the Slavs in general.

Q. How about the younger generation? More than half of the Kosovar population is under the age of twenty.

A. No doubt this is important. But I would say that since religion has been left free in Yugoslavia, there is still a kind of religious feeling that could be considered mostly traditional and customary. It is still there, whereas in Albania it is now almost eliminated. So, in the event of a union there would be friction on this score.

Q. Kosovo enjoys a large degree of autonomy in Yugoslavia, and its position in the Federation is very similar to that of the other republics and Vojvodina. What do you think of Kosovo's status in Yugoslavia?

A. What exactly does it mean to say that Kosovo is an Autonomous Province? Politically speaking, the Kosovars do have a great degree of autonomy: they have a territorial army, for instance, and their own security forces; and the chief administrative positions are held

by them as well. But the question is how well this political autonomy
works at the economic level. I am not an economist and I do not
know the situation there very well, but from the information I have
been able to gather, it would seem that the situation could best be
described by the word 'semi-colony.' The Federation has given them
a lot of money, a quarter of a million dollars even goes to Kosovo from
the World Bank to redress the economy, and there are the loans with
low interest from the Federation.

Yet things are clearly in bad shape there. Compare the monthly
industrial wage. In Kosovo it is $180, compared with the Yugoslav
average of $230. Then there is the fact that Kosovo is still to a large
extent an agricultural region: 51 percent of the population lives off
the land, compared with 38 percent in Yugoslavia as a whole. Some
heavy industry has been developed, especially mining and the electri-
cal industry, but the money which goes into these industries does not
produce marketable items which bring money and also jobs. Kosovo
has to buy everything from the other states in the Federation. Also,
the unemployment rate there is fantastic. In 1981 there were 178,000
unemployed and only 57,000 in employment. Even these are mostly
administrative employees, so that employment has the nature of bureaucracy, it is unproductive. And you have this enormous number of
students—51,000, but maybe the figure is a little exaggerated. Where
is this nascent intellectual proletariat to go? A number of Kosovars
are now travelling around trying to find jobs in other states of the Federation, or even going to West Germany and other countries abroad.

Q. This is a general problem in which Kosovo has been caught particularly badly because of the nature of its industry. But throughout Yugoslavia certain branches of industry, primary industry, have always
felt underprivileged as a cheap basis for further industrialization. And
throughout Yugoslavia, not just in Kosovo, youth unemployment is
very high. Kosovo, of course, feels all this much more strongly because
it has no secondary industry.

A. So, there has to be absolute improvement in the economic situation
of the Kosovars, because political economy combined with a semicolonial situation calls into question the meaning of political economy
itself. I don't know how this could be improved. One could say *a
priori* that the Yugoslav government must have tried to solve this
problem, because it is in the interest of Yugoslavia as a whole to have
a healthy Kosovo. But I don't know what the reasons are which have
made economic recovery impossible in Kosovo. For example, I have

read that decentralization has not only not advanced the situation there, but actually worsened it, and I would like to know why. I would like to hear an explanation from people competent in this field, for the fact is that the situation in the economy is very bad.

Q. How about the culture?

A. Here we have the other anomaly. The culture in Kosovo is not really Kosovar but Albanian, so that if the situation from the economic point of view is semi–colonial, in culture we have a quasi–colonial situation. This may be connected with the fact that scholarship has not yet developed as far as in Albania. But the point is that Kosovars have only been absorbing what they get from Albania, and even then without discrimination. So you have all these books from Albania which are simply reproduced. Consider the fact that they have adopted the so–called standard literary Albanian. One understands the political reasons for this: having been called 'Shiftars' for a long time, and having in a way been second–class citizens, it was imperative for them to identify with Albania by all possible means. And since Albanians identify not with religious or political frameworks—I would say even less with ideology—but with their language, they immediately adopted the standard language and have been using it ever since. So I don't know what is going to happen now that the cultural convention between Albania and Yugoslavia has been suspended.

Q. The cultural convention?

A. They have had a cultural agreement with Tirana, and it was working pretty well in the sense that they received a great deal of educational material, especially literature, and tried to absorb as much as they could. So, what are they going to do now that the agreement has been suspended? I have heard that they might reconsider the question of the literary language, and this they may very well do if the situation continues. I expect they will try to develop their own literary dialect. Now that the convention has been suspended they won't have textbooks, for instance, so they will have to produce their own textbooks, and that will take time. It is not so easy. From the cultural point of view, also, autonomy has meant very little.

Q. Perhaps at this point it might be relevant to ask how you think a change of status from Province to Republic might alter the situation?

A. We must look at the question of leadership first in the new situation. If Kosovo received the status of a republic, the first effect would be a rise in the morale of the population, a real mood of elation. The friction would subside, and the economic situation might also improve since Kosovo would have more say in the Federation. That would be almost a necessary consequence of republic status, because it may produce more initiative on the part of the Kosovar leadership, an impulse to start making the reforms for which they have not previously had sufficient power and legitimacy.

I expect that in a new situation the leaders would be in a position to have more influence on the population: for example, to begin some reforms in agriculture, to try to correct its primitive situation—I am not saying to collectivize or anything of that sort. Yet there are ways of correcting the situation perhaps from a technical point of view, and this could bring some improvement in the economy of Kosovo. In culture, too, they would certainly become more positive and develop greater cultural autonomy from Albania.

So, they will be writing their own history from a less dependent point of view. There is something else also. If I am not mistaken, the university there has emphasized the humanities; the departments of technology and agriculture are not very strong. They have been specializing in history, literature, foreign languages, but they lack people with special knowledge of the economy who are able to manage industries. The point is to redress the Kosovo economy, and unless they can create leaders and specialists for this purpose, they will always be in an inferior situation. And if they become a republic, I think they could do it. A change in status would also create an element of stability because, feeling themselves real citizens of the country, they would start to work out more constructive projects. Also from a cultural point of view. So I think that the Yugoslav Federation has almost everything to gain from this and almost nothing to lose. This would be a kind of legal recognition of what they have in practice, and as for the secession problem, I don't think it is real.

Q. Did you not say earlier that if one held a referendum tomorrow in Kosovo the Kosovars would vote in great part to join Albania? This is what the Yugoslav government, the Yugoslav leadership, say they are worried about.

A. In the present situation this may very well be the case. But with the granting of republic status comes also the incentive. First of all because they would become more conscious of the political situation, and the great deal of ignorance which exists would gradually vanish as people came to understand the difference between the two systems. Once they understood that, the kind of nostalgic, affective attachment to Albania would also diminish. They would start realizing that although there is an Albania there, there is also an Albania here. So they have the same language, but they have some freedoms which do not exist there. It is by no means certain that under such conditions a referendum would automatically resolve into the option to join Albania.

Q. You know that after last year's events in Kosovo, Stane Dolanc, a member of the Yugoslav Party Presidency, told foreign journalists at a press conference that republic status for Kosovo would mean creating two Albanias, and that it would be wrong to do this. Do you think there would be two Albanias?

A. There will be two Albanias because there will be something called Kosovo which speaks the Albanian language, and develops Albanian culture within the framework of the Yugoslav Federation. But what does this mean in practice? There are a million and a half Albanians in Kosovo, and nearly another three in Albania, so there would be a smaller Albania here and a larger Albania there. But there is no doubt that this would benefit the Federation. I don't think the Yugoslavs have anything to lose because secession seems to me quite improbable.

I don't think the Albanians really have their sights set on union with Kosovo. As we were saying earlier, the political systems are so different that I don't see how they could amalgamate. A conquest of one side by the other would just create immense problems. It is difficult to see that just joining them together would bring any improvement. The Albanians, and I think they are sincere here, say they don't have any territorial claims. This, I believe, is because of the problems that would be involved.

There would immediately be a problem arising from the still largely private character of Kosovo agriculture. So the Albanians would have to impose collectivization, and the Kosovars just wouldn't take it after living in an atmosphere of freedom from that point of view. There would also be the problem of regionalism all over again. Either there would be a greater Gheg participation in the government and Politburo—which would very much weaken and practically dissolve the kind of leadership existing in Albania today—or the leadership coming from Kosovo would be simply eliminated, and hostility created as a result. The Albanian leadership now—I am not speaking of the future—really doesn't want reunion with Kosovo. So, if neither the Albanians from Albania nor the Kosovo leadership want union (this is just looking at the political differences), there is no basis for the fear of secession and union. I hope the Yugoslav leadership will come to this conclusion, since it is for the benefit of the Yugoslav Federation as a whole and not only of Kosovo.

Q. Before we carry on, do you want to say anything more on Kosovo from the Albanian perspective?

A. I think that the Albanian leadership feel more secure having Kosovo there, as a stake in Yugoslavia, in case of an invasion. They feel it be a kind of buffer zone, and they are very much afraid of an invasion from the Soviet Union. When they go so far as to say that if Yugoslavia were attacked they would come to its aid, then this explains a great deal about the situation. They feel physically more protected by having Kosovo there.

Q. Is the Kosovo issue perceived differently by the Ghegs and the Tosks in Albania? I mean, you suggested that in a certain sense it is also a Gheg–Tosk problem. Does the population in the north have stronger ties to Kosovo?

A. For historical reasons, the Northern Albanians would feel more strongly for union with Kosovo than the Southerners. The dialect, as well as religion, also bring them together. The old tribal relations may still be alive, because I don't think they can be extirpated so easily. For instance, when I speak to Dukagjin people from Albania, they have a feeling that the Kosovars are just the same, that they are Dukagjin mountaineers who have gone down to the plains. So they feel that they are their own tribe in a sense, which is not the case, of course, with Southern Albanians.

Q. What is the cultural scene in Kosovo today?

A. Illiteracy is still very high in Kosovo, around 31 percent. This leads to a disproportion between university students and uneducated people. That, of course, is connected with differences between the urban and rural population, which in Albania, as you know, has been corrected. It was never a real problem in Albania because the cities have always had a close relation with the countryside, but anyhow it has been the policy in Albania to close that gap. And therefore this difference exists between Albania and Kosovo.

Q. Do you think that this gap in Kosovo is a result of the private nature of agriculture, or that perhaps it has been also historically determined by the bigger size of towns, say, their more autonomous development?

A. I am not competent to speak about these problems. But it is true that Kosovars have had a pastoral kind of economy—raising animals and particularly sheep—as well as the custom of transhumance,

which also applies to Northern Albanians. The economy is influenced
by physical and geographical factors which make them somewhat different from the rest of the population in Yugoslavia. The point I
am trying to make is that there is a great imbalance: on the one
hand, there is the intelligentsia, some good scholars being produced
there now; and on the other hand, you have just ignorance and illiteracy. And with ignorance comes fanaticism. This situation can
be corrected, will be corrected, particularly through developing technology, through travel between Kosovo and Albania and, hopefully,
vice versa, but also through the development of a Kosovo culture.
The Kosovars do have a certain tradition which, to some extent, distinguishes them from the rest of Albania. And in order to develop
further their national culture, they will have to use these characteristics and return to the literature produced in Kosovo—they will have
to develop their own literary dialect. To me this kind of copying of
the language does not seem very productive.

First of all, it creates a great problem. I have read a communiqué of one of the meetings of the executive studying the situation
of the language, and they were very despondent about how slowly the
standard literary language has been absorbed. This is to be expected
because of the differences in dialect. Now, if instead they would work
out a kind of literary standard based on the Kosovar dialect, then I
think education would be improved and the population would absorb
it better. This brings us to the question of literature, which is important from a cultural and political point of view. I have noticed myself,
and here I can speak with some confidence, that they were doing some
good work in literature before adopting the literary standard, because
of course they could express themselves easily. There was a great deal
of eclecticism or groping—all manner of currents amalgamated without any discrimination—but these were the trails, these were passes
being opened. I am sure that they have produced some good work.
And sure, the people are there, as well as the intelligence and capacity
for creation—Kosovars have a good deal of imagination. And this has
come almost to a stop now. Gheg and Tosk are the same language,
no doubt about that, but they have some differences. It is not easy
to write in another dialect unless you have been trained very well.
So, my reading now is that what they have produced of late is rather
disappointing. There used to be some real literary potential, but that
has gone. It may well recover, but I don't know exactly how.
Q. Is this felt by some in Kosovo?

A. I don't know if they feel it or not, but the problem is there. Because when you write literature, you create from the subconscious. The phraseology is very important, and they have sacrificed this to some extent. So, when I speak about this problem, it is because I think that they should really be a bit on their own, they should try to do something that better reflects their own cultural situation. I would also like to mention that if they have not yet produced great scholars or great writers, this is understandable in terms of their past situation. But I have also seen them progressing and they have some good people, especially in linguistics and folklore, musical folklore in particular. The publications I have been following speak of real progress, the scholarly standards have improved and have been improving. They have produced a really important scholar, Hasan Kaleshi, who also knew the oriental languages, Turkish and Arabic. That is extremely important, I think, for Kosovo, indeed for the whole of Albania—the Albanians, very strangely, have not given sufficient importance to oriental studies. For instance, there is a book that has just come out, by Zef Mirdita, on the problem of Dardania, which is a scholarly book. So it is not that they lack people, but they will have to get more accustomed to ways of scholarship and to have more contact with the outside world. They don't have the problem they have in Albania of not being able to travel abroad, although in Albania as well things have started to change. I hear that they now send students to France and Italy. But the Kosovars are more favored from this point of view: their greater freedom allows them to develop more contacts and better literature. In the arts they have been doing some good work, especially in music and dance. And there is a good actor, Bekim Fehmiu, who has acted in some good films and has recently been working in the United States. So I think they can produce their own culture. I don't mean to say that they should differentiate themselves absolutely from Tirana, definitely not, but it would be in the interests of Albanian culture generally if they are able to develop their own brand of Albanian culture.

Q. What effect do you think a future Albanian unification would have on the Balkans?

A. I would say that it would have a very positive effect on peace in the Balkans. The Albanians have always felt that injustice was done to them when parts of their territories were left in other states. Since they are also a small nation, they feel that by being united they would come to play a major role in the politics of the Balkans. The

feeling that they are one nation is very strong, despite differences in
dialect and other areas. If the existing situation is not corrected, the
Albanian problem will always be a major source of friction and one
more destabilizing element in the Balkans. The question is how this
unification is to be effected.

There are, of course, two ways of approaching the problem: the
incorporation of Kosovo into a 'Greater Albania,' or the federation
of Albania with Yugoslavia. The Albanians have a very strong wish
to be independent, and I would say that ideology here is really secondary. If you talk to an Albanian, be he rightist or leftist, he will
always be for an independent Albania. So federating with Yugoslavia
seems to me quite an improbable solution. The other alternative,
that Kosovo joins Albania, seems for the moment also very difficult
and improbable. For although the two systems of government both
go under the name of socialism, they are actually very different. It
will be some time before union becomes a real possibility.

What I see happening for the moment, however, is a rapprochement between Kosovo and Albania, and this will certainly be easier
if a change in Albania were to take place so that the Yugoslavs would
not be viewed with hostility from the ideological point of view. Such a
rapprochement would certainly be in the interests of both Kosovo and
Albania. As you know, Yugoslavia is already Albania's major trading
partner. This suggests that ideological differences are to some extent
artificial and involve a great deal of rhetoric. For if you trade with
another country, and this country becomes your major trading partner, then of course there is a *de facto* rapprochement taking place.
Particularly as the two systems, though in many ways very different,
are also basically socialist, and this makes it all very much easier than
if it was a question of a capitalist country.

Q. Both Albania and Yugoslavia are also outside the Eastern bloc.

A. This is another important element in common, because in the
Balkans today only Yugoslavia and Albania do not belong to one of
the blocs. The fact that Albania and Yugoslavia both have a strong
sense of a Soviet threat necessarily brings them together. Therefore
their rapprochement would also be very important in bringing other
Balkan nations together and establishing the contacts which could
later lead to a Balkan federation. When I speak of a Balkan federation I do not, of course, mean just Albania and Yugoslavia. But
things have to start somewhere, and a rapprochement between Albania and Yugoslavia holds most promise for a future Balkan federation.

Considering what happened in the past, and looking at the present situation, this is the best solution for all of us to live in peace. The question of leadership to one side, the population of the Balkans would certainly benefit by that. And the sooner it happens, the better it will be.

VI. PARTY IDEOLOGY AND PURGES IN ALBANIA*

An aging Albanian Little Red Riding-Hood finds herself a lonely
widow after having married and then divorced, one after another, the
Yugoslav Wolf, the Soviet Bear, and the Chinese Dragon. Each divorce entailed a thorough housecleaning, to make sure that the new
partner, upon waking in the morning, would not risk stepping into the
slippers of the preceding husband. Partial housecleanings have also
occurred, involving removal of furniture and other belongings which,
upon closer inspection, were identified as magic objects furtively introduced by the Western Ogre, lurking in the distance and waiting
for his turn.

We can thus speak of purges related to four basic heresies: Titoism, Soviet social-imperialism, Maoism, and Eurocommunism. The
first three are explained as revisionistic variants of Marxism-Leninism
in socialist countries mostly under the pressure of American imperialism. The same pressure on bourgeois European countries breeds Eurocommunism. Of the three revisionistic variants, Titoism stands in
open collusion with capitalism, and therefore is the principal ideological enemy. And since Yugoslavia oppresses an Albanian population—
in Kosova, Macedonia, Serbia, and Montenegro—more than two-
thirds as great as that in the mother country, Albanian Marxism-
Leninism merges with Albanian nationalism to declare Yugoslavia
Albania's archfiend.

After World War I, Albania was Yugoslavia's darling, the Communist Party of Albania (CPA) faithfully following the line of the
Communist Party of Yugoslavia (CPY), its midwife and tutor. Had
it not been for the break between the Soviet Union and Yugoslavia
in 1948, Albania would be the seventh republic of Federal Yugoslavia

---

* Published in *Telos* 59, Spring 1984.

today. Yet the bitter enmity between the two countries goes back
to the Balkan Wars, when Albania frustrated Serbia's attempts to
annex part of it by achieving independence (1912), and then to the
Conference of Versailles which assigned royalist Yugoslavia a part
of the defunct Ottoman Empire that was overwhelmingly populated
by Albanians. Communist Yugoslavia accepted this inheritance, and
then proceeded to incorporate the whole of Albania. The attempt
failed because a nationalist faction in the CPA led by Enver Hoxha
and Mehmet Shehu managed to defeat the Titoite faction, thanks to
Stalin's denunciation of the CPY as anti–Soviet.

The ensuing sweeping purge was approved by the nationalistic
population, which was also pleased to see the Party's name changed
into that of the Party of Labour of Albania (PLA). And since Stalin
had practically saved the country's independence, the leadership's
move to have Albania join the Soviet bloc met with relatively little
resistance. After Stalin's death, Khrushchev tried to lure Yugoslavia
back into the bloc. The Hoxha–Shehu duumvirate interpreted his
move in the sense of a possible revival of the Titoite faction, leading to their own liquidation. Another major purge began, involving pro–Soviet as well as pro–Yugoslav party members. The Soviet
Union reacted by excommunicating the rebel and stopping financial
and technical aid.

Then came the alliance with China, at a time when Mao was
accusing the Soviet Union of having ceased to be a socialist country. Albania readily walked in Mao's footsteps and, in exchange for
economic assistance and technical expertise, espoused China's line,
becoming its mouthpiece in the U.N. But once admitted to that organization (1971), China lost interest in Albania, reconciled with revisionist Yugoslavia, and stepped into world politics with the ambition of a future third superpower. Its clash with the Soviet Union
gradually brought China into collusion with the United States. The
ideological switch of the great ally could not fail to raise questions.
Mao's theory of the three worlds, with Europe occupying a middle
position between the two superpowers and the nations of the Third
World, was bound to make Eurocommunism appealing to the less
doctrinaire party members. Albania's alliance with China began to
look weird from a cultural and economic perspective and downright
absurd from a military viewpoint. Soon pro–Western tendencies co-
alesced into a *modus vivendi et operandi* that ignored the austere
prescriptions of the Hoxha–Shehu leadership. A third wave of purges

started in the army and in the sectors of economy and culture.

The break with China, accused like the Soviet Union of social-imperialism, left Albania the only Stalinist fortress on the planet. To justify that situation, Hoxha set out to demolish all kinds of revisonism in a series of books in which his own version of Stalinism is presented as the quintessence of Marxism–Leninism. He was in the process of writing his major literary work, *The Titoites*, when all of a sudden he found himself to be the target of a plot engineered by none else but his closest associate, Shehu. Hoxha was able to defeat his rival, who then allegedly committed suicide. The purge struck Shehu's family and his henchmen. In *The Titoites*, the First Secretary of the Party accuses his Prime Minister of having been an agent of the Yugoslavs as well as of the two superpowers, i.e., as the monstrous combination of the three evil beasts (the Dragon is missing) ready to pounce upon poor Little Red Riding–Hood, faithfully guarded by her Albanian champion.

1. The Yugoslav Tutelage (1941–48)

The Tirana Founding Conference (November 1941) succeeded in temporarily reconciling the ideological differences among three of the more important communist organizations: the Korçë Group, the Shkodër Group and the Youth Group. Hoxha, then a member of the Korçë Group operating in Tirana, was elected secretary of the Provisional Central Committee, composed of Hoxha, Qemal Stafa, Koçi Xoxe, Tuk Jakova, Kristo Themelko, Ramadan Çitaku, and Gjin Marku.[1] Hoxha's election was the outcome of the stipulation that "none of the former principal leaders [chairmen and deputy chairmen] of the groups would be elected to the leadership."[2] The leaders of the Youth Group, Anastas Lulo and Sadik Premte, were disappointed. Premte managed to get hold of the Vlorë Regional Committee in 1943. His rebellion was quelled. Hoxha participated personally in the punitive expedition. A regional leader "was killed as a traitor,"[3] while another "accidentally fell victim of the plot they [the rebels] had concocted."[4] Premte managed to escape and later fled abroad. Lulo was arrested by partisans and executed.[5]

A second purge struck members of the leadership itself. Ymer Dishnica and Mustafa Gjinishi had been delegated by the Party to deal with the Nationalist Front (Balli Kombëtar) at the Mukje Conference (August 1943) in view of the concerted action against the foreign occupiers. They signed the agreement for the formation of the Committee for the Salvation of Albania. The agreement was immediately rejected, under Yugoslav pressure, by the rest of the leadership as alien to the Party line, and Dishnica was expelled from the Politburo as an "opportunist" (Plenum of the Central Committee, May 1944). Opportunistic, i.e., inclined to collaboration with non–communist nationalist parties, was the whole Party line at the time, according to other Politburo members such as Sejfulla Malëshova and Nako Spiru. They tried to rehabilitate Dishnica after the country's liberation. He ended up in prison instead. As an intellectual with a French background, Dishnica was suspect to the Party leadership dominated by Koçi Xoxe, the leader of the Titoite faction, who was Organizational Secretary as well as Minister of the Interior and Chief of the Security apparatus. Hoxha concurred with Xoxe. They were only too glad to get rid of a brilliant politician who could have eclipsed Hoxha and caused problems to Xoxe.

Gjinishi, a first–rate propagandist and organizer, was the person mainly responsible for the success of the Pezë Conference (September 1942) which saw the CPA emerge as a political–military force, able to conduct guerrilla warfare. He was treacherously killed by a fellow Party leader while marching with a partisan division in Northern Albania, probably on orders from the Commander–in–Chief.[6] Hoxha accuses him of being an agent of the British Intelligence Service.[7] Gjinishi, who knew English, had had contacts with the British Army Mission officers then operating in Albania.

Another victim of the above–mentioned partisan division at about the same time was Lazar Fundo, a veteran communist who had worked for the Comintern in Moscow. Repelled by Stalin's atrocities, he had left the Soviet Union and spent some time in Paris. Upon his return to Albania, he was interned in a fascist concentration camp (1939–1943). When fascism collapsed, aware that the Party wanted to eliminate him as a traitor, Fundo joined an armed band in Kosova, led by Seid Kryeziu, an aristocratic social democrat whom Fundo had befriended while in Paris. Captured by the partisans together with his friend, the "Trotskyite" Fundo was shot "as an agent of the British and the feudals."[8] Kryeziu was saved by the Yugoslavs who insisted on his liberation.

The purges of the war period instituted a pattern. After the country's liberation, many communists who had led the anti–fascist resistance were demoted and even purged as suspects because of lack

of enthusiasm for the Yugoslav line. A major purge was that of Sejfulla Malëshova.

An old communist who had spent his exile years in Moscow working for the Comintern, Malëshova returned to Albania in the spring of
1943, joining the partisans. He was immediately coopted as candidate
member of the Politburo, due to his reputation as an Albanian poet as
well as a Marxist theoretician, indeed the only one of whom Albania
could boast at the time. After the liberation, Malëshova contended
with Hoxha for primacy in the Party. But since his influence there
was weak, he leaned for support towards pro–Western non–party elements in the National Liberation Front, the cover organization for
the CPA (he was Secretary General of that organization). According to Hoxha, Malëshova was purged as a "right–wing opportunist,"
"a liberal parliamentary democrat . . . he was in fact opposed to
socialist revolution."[9] What he was really opposed to was a socialist
revolution of the Stalinist kind, whose horrors he had experienced
while in Moscow. His "pro–Western inclinations," with which the
Yugoslavs found fault, lay less in his Italian background than in his
refusal to ban from the schools authors such as the Franciscan father
Gjergj Fishta, whose epic, *The Mountain Lute*, exalts the Albanians
who fought against the Slavs. Malëshova's theses on the country's
economy and culture (he was then Chairman of the Economic Planning Committee and Minister of Culture), at a time when writers
were being jailed for expressing criticism,[10] and engineers hanged as
saboteurs,[11] made Malëshova an easy target for his rivals. The main
reason, however, for his purge was his nationalism, which in those
days was tantamount to anti–Yugoslavism. Hoxha's report to the
Party's Fifth Plenum (February 1946) had Malëshova as its main target. With the concurrence of Xoxe, for whom Malëshova had utter
contempt, Hoxha managed to liquidate a dangerous rival, his main
one at the time, a person who would not bow to a (to him) upstart
communist who knew little more of Marxism than the jargon of tracts
and the language of Stalin's *Short Course* of the history of the Communist Party.

The elimination of Nako Spiru was a much more complicated
affair. A former student of Political Economy at the University of
Turin, Spiru was, in his capacity as President of the Youth Organization, a member of the Politburo. Hoxha describes him as "intelligent,
clear in the line, courageous and a good organizer."[12] but also as "ambitious and inclined to intrigues."[13] Having been Hoxha's right–hand

man during the war years, Spiru turned against him at the end of the war. The shift occurred at the Berat Plenum (November 1944), where Malëshova, Spiru and Xoxe, under the baton of the Yugoslav delegate Stojnić, submitted the Commander–in–Chief to a volley of damning criticism. Hoxha managed to survive, but his grip on the Party was gone. The victor was the proletarian Xoxe, who suddenly emerged as Albania's strong man, pushed or rather kicked ahead by the Yugoslavs (at a reception for the Albanian delegation in Belgrade in December 1946, Tito offered the seat at the head of the table to Xoxe, not to Hoxha). As President of the Special Court for the Trial of War Criminals and Enemies of the People (March–April 1945), Xoxe set the tune for the ensuing policy of repression against opponents and critics, inside and outside the Party.

A longtime communist and member of the Korçë Group, Xoxe was elected member of the Politburo while still in jail. After his release in April 1943, he was put in charge of the Party cadres. He accompanied Vukmanović–Tempo to Greece twice in 1943, and the two became friends. It was Tempo who, having clashed repeatedly with Hoxha, groomed Xoxe for the top seat. Colonel Stojnić set the stage, working behind the scenes, with Xoxe, Spiru and Malëshova, unhappy with Hoxha's monopolization of power. In *The Titoites*, Hoxha ridicules Xoxe, describing him as a half–literate tinsmith, "swarthy, short, with bulging eyes like those of a frog."[14]

Once Malëshova was gone, a bitter rivalry developed between Xoxe and Spiru. This gave Hoxha an opportunity to arbitrate their disputes, thus helping him retain the reins of the government at a time when Party power was slipping from his hands. And since the stronger contender was Xoxe, Hoxha made use of Spiru to check Xoxe's ascendancy. Eventually he won over Spiru to his side. This occurred when the latter began to have qualms about having signed the Economic Convention for the parification of currency, unification of prices, removal of custom barriers and creation of joint economic committees, which laid the ground for Albania's political union with Yugoslavia. Backing away from his former pro–Yugoslav stance, Spiru oriented himself towards the Soviet Union, asking for economic and technical assistance. The arrival of Soviet advisers infuriated the Yugoslavs, who felt betrayed by one whom they considered their man (Spiru had previously written a letter to Tito, asking him to use his authority for the removal of Hoxha). Not yet strong enough to attack Hoxha frontally, Xoxe demanded Spiru's head. He had Hoxha call a meeting of the Politburo restricted to only four members: Hoxha, Xoxe, his faithful Pandi Kristo, and Spiru. In that meeting, Xoxe accused Spiru of being an "agent of imperialism."[15] Spiru requested five days to prepare his reply. His request was rejected by the other three. The next day Spiru visited Hoxha, insisting that his request be granted and asking him to help. Hoxha's answer was negative: "The Bureau has decided it."[16] That same day Spiru committed suicide.

Hoxha had earlier joined forces with Xoxe to liquidate Malëshova, thus reassuring the Yugoslavs who disliked both Malëshova and himself. This time, the Yugoslav pressure growing on him, he sacrificed the very person whom he had been inciting to resist that pressure. And when pressure reached the point of explosion with the Yugoslav's insistent demand for the creation of a unified command of the army, Hoxha sold out Shehu, the only Party leader who then stood firmly for him. In a telling passage in *The Titoites*, he admits his debt to Shehu for coming to his rescue:

> Although I was Commander–in–Chief, I was virtually pushed to one side. . . . Among the first measures which I decided to take was the reorganization of the General Staff. When we discussed this question, Nako Spiru proposed insistently that Mehmet Shehu should be placed at the head of the General Staff because he was "a born soldier, well trained, who had proved himself." . . . Likewise, the fact that he was studying in the Military Academy in the Soviet Union added to my hope that Mehmet Shehu would strongly oppose the mish–mash the Yugoslavs were creating in our army.[17]

Which indeed he did, thus angering "Xoxe and his clan," who began to attack him, pressuring Hoxha to dismiss him from his post. Shehu is quoted as having declared to Hoxha: "Comrade Commander . . . the Yugoslavs want to eliminate you. . . . I opposed them openly."[18]

Spiru committed suicide on November 20, 1947. At the end of December, Shehu was dismissed. In November of that year, Xoxe demanded that Hoxha write a leading article in a magazine founded by Xoxe

> about the vital relations with the Yugoslav friends, about their aid and especially about the contribution of the Comrade Marshal Tito. . . . The Yugoslavs needed my article as a "certificate of good behaviour" for Yugoslavia and Tito.[19]

Hoxha complied with Xoxe's demand:

In very general terms and with the odd "fact" for the first years of the war, I pointed out the links of friendship between our parties and countries. However, even with this, the Yugoslavs and their agents were satisfied: the important thing for them was that the General Secretary of the CPA should write even one good phrase, even in completely general terms, about Tito's Yugoslavia, as a safe conduct pass for the annexation.[20]

Hoxha had previously approved the Economic Convention signed by Spiru, who "did nothing in this direction without consulting me and received my approval." Now Hoxha wrote and signed with his own hand "a safe conduct pass for the annexation."

In the winter of 1947, Albania's annexation by Yugoslavia in the spring of 1948 was as probable as the succession of winter by spring. If it did not occur, this is because Stalin could not restrain his anger at Tito's growing acts of independence. Hoxha had been assiduously watching the darkening clouds that gradually obscured the relations between Yugoslavia and the Soviet Union, patiently waiting for the "thunderbolt" to strike: "We had some signs and signals in this direction."[21] His strategy of temporization eventually bore fruit. Stalin's letter to the CPY (March 28, 1944) saved him. Understandable therefore is his worship of Stalin. On the occasion of Stalin's death, Hoxha signed an "oath" of allegiance to the Soviet dictator.[22] He has indeed honored his oath, made in the name of the Albanian people, as well as his pledge to Stalin during his last visit with him: "We shall certainly carry out your instructions, Comrade Stalin."[23]

Xoxe was shot as a Titoist and a Troskyite in 1949, setting in motion the most wide–ranging purge in the history of the CPA–PLA. His closest collaborators in the Politburo, Pandi Kristo, Nesti Kerenxhi and Xhoxhi Blushi, as well as the regional Security chiefs and their most zealous dependents, were given prison sentences. Kristo, a tinsmith from Korçë like his old friend Xoxe, was apparently spared because shooting him would have been too much of an honor paid to that "shitty rabbit."[24] who once, when confronted by Hoxha, "had collapsed like a heap of cow–dung in a rain storm."[25]

The anti–Titoite purge was not confined to pro–Yugoslav Party members. Pressing on Shehu to be more exacting against anti–party and enemy elements, Hoxha engineered a radical housecleaning. The Party's 2nd National Conference (April 1950) announced the purge of Abedin Shehu, Minister of Industry, and Niazi Islami, Deputy Communications Minister. They were accused of having criticized the Two–Year plan as "unrealistic."[26] Beqir Ndou, President of the National Council and a former member of the Regional National Liberation Council of Kosova and the Dukagjin Plain, was removed from his post. Two army chiefs were expelled for having undermined the Party's role in the direction of the army. They were Gjin Marku, a member of the 1941 Provisional CC, and Nexhip Vinçani, Chief of the General Staff. On the basis of official sources, it has been calculated that from 1948 to 1951, more than 25 percent of the Party membership was expelled,[27] including more than half of the Central Committee members and about a third of the deputies of the People's Assembly.[28]

2. The Soviet Patronage (1949–1961)

The slogan "Enver–Tito" was soon replaced by its counterpart, "Enver–Stalin." The explosion of a bomb in the Soviet Legation in Tirana (February 1951) prompted a wave of terrorism conducted personally by Shehu against former members of nationalist parties as well as against some more outspoken critics.[29] These were the days when a Party member advocating a modicum of moderation was suspected of being an anti–party element.

Jakova, a leader of the Shkodër Group and a founder of the Party (he was a carpenter by trade) had been, like Shehu, harassed by Xoxe and his men. Afater Xoxe's demise, he replaced his adversary as the Party's Organizational Secretary and was for a short period (June 1950–February 1951) Vice–Premier and Minister of the Interior. Jakova disgraced himself by trying to win over to the Party adversary elements by conciliatory methods. He was accused of being sympathetic to reactionary individuals and groups and especially the Catholic clergy who had borne the brunt of the religious persecution (Jakova was born a Catholic). His thesis that the class struggle was dying out in the country met with vigorous opposition from Hoxha and Shehu. He was dropped as Organizational Secretary and a Politburo member (Plenum of February 1951).[30] His associate Heba, Chief of the Directory of Cadres, was expelled from the Central Committee, together with Konomi, the Minister of Justice, punished for having been lenient in administering justice to class enemies.

The improvement of Yugoslav–Soviet relations after Stalin's death set in motion a wave of opposition inside the Party, led by Tuk Jakova and Bedri Spahiu. The proletarian Jakova reiterated his thesis of the extinction of the class struggle and demanded the rehabilitation of purged comrades. He was supported by Spahiu, a Politburo member and a high-ranking Party leader (he had been Public Prosecutor in the Special Court presiding over Xoxe, and later was Public Prosecutor in the trial that sentenced Xoxe to death). Spahiu clashed vehemently with Hoxha at the Plenum of June 1955. The Plenum expelled Jakova from the Central Committee but Spahiu from both the Central Committee and the Party.

Khrushchev's denunciation of Stalin at the 20th Congress of the CPSU rekindled the flames of the opposition. The dissidents came out into the open at the Party Conference for the City of Tirana (April 1956). They criticized the ruling élite for their autocratic methods, their contempt for the masses, their failure to redress the economic situation, and they pressed hard for the rehabilitation of Xoxe, Jakova, Spahiu and other purged Party members. Intervening personally, Hoxha succeeded in quelling the rebellion. Twenty–seven Party members were arrested and tried. Two prominent Party members, Liri Gega, a member of the first Politburo, and general Dali Ndreu, her husband, were arrested while "attempting to cross the [Albanian–Yugoslav] border."[31] They were both shot—the three of them, to be precise, Liri being, according to Khrushchev,[32] pregnant. In May 1957, General Panajot Plaku, former Deputy Minister of Defense, defected to Yugoslavia. Khrushchev offered him political asylum.

Soviet–Albanian relations began to deteriorate after Stalin's death. The leadership's idolatry of the Soviet dictator had won him over to the cause of Albania's territorial integrity which had been threatened by its neighbors. Forgetful of what he had once told Milovan Djilas, i.e., that Yugoslavia could "gobble up" Albania with his own blessing,[33] the Dictator found Albanian virulent attacks against Titoism very much to his taste. And the Albanian leadership felt secure under his large wings. It is indicative that Albania, alarmed by Khrushchev's rapprochement with Tito, joined the Warsaw Pact only in 1955. Khrushchev's denunciation of Stalin the next year added to the leadership's worries. The signing in 1957 of an agreement for the building of a Soviet naval base in the island of Sazan facing Vlorë reassured them momentarily. At about the same time they intensified their relations with China, which were resented by the Soviet leadership. An Albanian delegation visited China (June 1960) when the latter had made public its dispute with the Soviet Union. Khrushchev reacted by pointing to the Greek claims to Southern Albania. This led to Hoxha's denunciation of Khrushchev and the Soviet leadership at the November 1960 Moscow Meeting of Communist and Workers' Parties. Khrushchev suspended a shipment of grain which was badly nooded by the Albanian population and threatened to dismantle the Sazan base. Hoxha countered by threatening to destroy the vessels there. After embittered negotiations, an agreement was reached: the greater part of the submarines were allowed to leave, while the rest, as well as part of the military equipment, were left to the Albanians.

The purging mechanism was again set to work. In 1960, a conspiracy was discovered. Its leaders were Moscow–trained Rear Admiral Teme Sejko and Tahir Demi, former delegate to the COMECON. Five of the plotters were executed (May 1961). The show trial revealed that they had been in touch with Greek and Yugoslav officials as well as with the American Sixth Fleet. In September 1960, Liri Belishova and Koço Tashko were expelled from the Party and probably arrested, accused of hatching another plot. Belishova, Spiru's widow, had become a member of the Politburo after her husband's rehabilitation. She was the number 1 woman in the Party hierarchy and led important diplomatic missions (including the above-mentioned delegation to China). Tashko, a Comintern man who had been commissioned to organize the Albanian Communist Party, was discarded from the leadership when the Party was organized by the CPY. After the split with Yugoslavia, Tashko chaired the Party's Central Auditing Committee. Neither he nor Belishova made a secret of their loyalty to the Soviet Union. In 1961, Maqo Çomo, Belishova's second husband, was dismissed from his functions as Minister of Agriculture.

3. The Chinese Hegemony (1962–1978)

Unlike the split with Yugoslavia which shook the CPA to its very foundations, the rift with the Soviet Union caused no serious perturbations, an indication that the Albanian Communists were not particularly attached to the homeland of socialism. Once the Belishova–Tashko group disappeared from the political scene, no spectacular purges occurred for a period of eleven years. The Sino–Albanian alliance was unlikely to cause serious ideological ruffles, the Albanians being uninformed about the internal strife in the Communist Party of China and the Chinese uninterested in the PLA's ideological quarrels. The Hoxha–Shehu tandem maintained full control of the situation, despite the country's precarious economic condition following the Soviet Union's discontinuation of economic and technical aid. Beginning with the Third Five–Year Plan (1961–65), Albania adopted a policy of austerity, though assisted to some extent by China with credits and experts. Little improvement occurred during the Fourth Five–Year Plan (1966–1970), despite a Chinese loan of some 200 million dollars,[34] as well as stern measures taken to reduce bureaucracy, lower the salaries of better paid workers, and employ women in productive work.

The stress exerted on the population by the "further revolution-ization of the Party and the life of the country,"[35] was highlighted by the Cultural Revolution (1966–69), an imitation of some aspects of the Chinese Cultural Revolution. Bureaucrats were a main target; ranks and insignia were abolished and commisars were reinstated in the army, and intellectuals were sent to work in the countryside for a period of time.

China's switch to a friendly policy towards the United States re-proposed the question of doctrinal purity. Party members and the intelligentsia dared express opinions. The days of the revolution were long gone by, and a new generation had grown up, some of them with higher education obtained in more advanced socialist countries. This younger generation would not profess the same loyalty to the ideals of the revolution as their elders (hence the emphasis on "revo-lutionization"). The Youth Organization began to express discontent. Unorthodox customs spread among youngsters. At the same time a taste for new ways of expression in literature and the arts developed, backed by the mass media. Hoxha had in the meantime cultivated a propensity for writing and his nostrils had become sensitive to literary rot.[36] In the 4th Plenum (June 1973), he took up the cudgel against "liberalism," which he describes as "an expression of ideological and political opportunism, renunciation of the consistent class struggle . . . and acceptance of peaceful coexistence with the enemy ideology." The Party's axe this time fell on Fadil Paçrami and Todi Lubonja.

A crony of Spiru, Paçrami had become editor–in–chief of the Party organ *Zëri i Popullit* [The People's Voice] when only in his twenties. He carried important functions in the Party and in the government. In his mature years he turned to writing plays. These were suddenly found to be polluted with liberalism. Lubonja, Direc-tor of the Albanian Radio–Television, had seconded the contagion. The purge spread to the Youth Organization particularly affected and infected—"long hair, extravagant dress, screaming jungle music . . ."[37] It was reshuffled. So was the direction of the League of

Albanian Writers and Artists.

The cultural purge went on after the 4th Plenum. The 5th and 6th Plenums exuded the military purge. To call generals liberals will not do, another name had to be found which, due to the many stripes of their (former) insignia, had to be a string of names: "saboteurs," "counterrevolutionary revisionists," "plotters," "traitors." Such were found to be Beqir Balluku, Minister of Defense, Petrit Dume, Chief of General Staff, and Hito Çako, Chief of the Political Directory of the Army. They were charged with plotting to seize power through a military putsch. To that purpose, they had diffused in the army literature inspired by the Chou En-lai doctrine that "Albania could not be defended against external aggression, especially Soviet aggression, except by applying the tactics of partisan guerrilla warfare."[38] This was not exactly what Hoxha had been repeatedly stressing, i.e., that "every citizen must be a soldier and every soldier a citizen."[39] According to this tenet, "the key element in national defense and victory is man rather than weapons, the revolutionary consciousness of the 'citizen army' rather than military technology."[40] Apparently, Balluku and his staff wanted to build a modern army restricted in number but well-trained and disciplined and whose first loyalty was to the General Staff. The reinstatement of commissars in the army disrupted their plans. Their resistance to the Party's interference with their duties was interpreted as an attempt to set the Army against the Party. The issue at stake was who would command the army: the bygone generals, Hoxha and Shehu, or those actually in charge. A former metalworker from Tirana who had studied in the Voroshilov Military Academy and had served as Minister of Defense from 1954 to 1974, Lieutenant General Balluku could become another Xoxe if a pro-Soviet or a pro-Yugoslav tide should occur. He and his associates were found guilty of "distributing the documents and the materials of the Party and the works of Comrade Enver Hoxha, sent to the Army, in very limited numbers."[41] The proletarian "arch-traitor" was punished "by the laws of the dictatorship of the proletariat." His associates were also executed.

Did the Balluku group really conspire against the Hoxha-Shehu monopoly of power? A military putsch in a Stalinist regime is highly improbable. Their resistance seems to have been motivated by purely military defense concerns. The alliance with China was not a military one, like the alliances with Yugoslavia and the Soviet Union, though the Chinese leaders had more than once declared their readiness to come to Albania's rescue in case of aggression. Consequently, the Albanian military leaders had been expecting some form of military alliance. This seems to be the main reason for the recurrent visits to China by Balluku (1964, 1967, and 1972) and by Dume (1973). The Chinese kept supplying the Albanians with military equipment and experts. But that was all. After Albania's withdrawal from the Warsaw Pact (1968), the country was left alone to defend itself. Unable to change the course of foreign policy, the military leaders must have tried, one thinks, to strengthen the power of the army. This was perceived as a threat to Hoxha. Hence his reaction, and his precaution as well. The 1976 Constitution of the Socialist People's Republic of Albania states that the First Secretary of the Party is also Commander-in-Chief of the Army.

The cultural and military purges, cultural and military relating pretty much like thesis and antithesis, were to lead to the economic purge, their synthesis. This time the traitors were Abdyl Këllezi, Koço Theodosi and Kiço Ngjela, respectively, the Chairman of the Planning Commission, the Minister of Industry and Mining, and the Minister of Trade. Këllezi and Theodosi were Politburo members, Ngjela a member of the Central Committee. Their crimes? Sundry and divers: introduction of self-management and capitalistic methods, encouragement of bureaucratic and technocratic trends, waste in funds and materials, sabotage in industry and agriculture,[42] trade used as liaison with enemies. "This group, like the others, had been engaged in clandestine activity for years," one reads in the *History of the Party*, which further specifies:

> Both the group of B. Balluku and the group of A. Këllezi and Company relied on the aid of the Chinese leadership which incited the traitorous counter-revolutionary activity of these groups.[43]

"The Smashing of the enemy group,"[44] took place in the 7th Plenum (May 1975). On June 3, 1975, Adil Çarçani, then First Deputy Premier and now Premier of Albania, signed a five-year pact with China for a long-term credit without interest. The *History of the Party* does not mention the signing of the pact, which was, however, made public in the Party's organ, *Zëri i Popullit* (July 4, 1973).[45] At about the same time that an Albanian leader was conducting talks with Chinese leaders for economic aid to his country, the Albanian Plenum of the Central Committee was "smashing" the group of traitors who had tried to wreck the Albanian economy "rel[ying] on the aid of the Chinese leadership." The Albanians have a proverb that is a suitable comment to acts such as these: "I gave you bread, and you throw stones at me." It was the Chinese who in 1960, when the Soviets suspended their shipment of grain, fed the Albanian people with wheat purchased in Canada and paid for in hard currency.[46] And they continued their supplies of wheat until the Albanians, with help from Chinese experts and upon insistent Chinese advice, were able to produce enough grain to feed their country's population (1976), after making available for agriculture 200,000 hectares of drained land.[47]

According to articles in Party organs and reports of Party leaders, including Shehu's report on the Fifth Five–Year Plan,[48] the Fourth Five–Year Plan was a failure. The reasons for it were both internal and external, i.e., related to the leadership's unrelenting policy of centralization on the one hand and, on the other, to their increasing ideological alienation from China, resulting in decreasing Chinese economic aid. The quote from the *History of the Party* accuses both the military and the economic leaders for their "reliance" on Chinese aid. This means, as made clear by the literature of the period, that they suffered from lack of "self–reliance," they were defeatists, not confident enough in the energies of the Albanian people to resist foreign military or economic aggression. Self–reliance motivates the break first with the Soviet Union and then with China. The concept has an illustrious parentage: Stalin's theory of socialism in one country, and Mussolini's thesis of autarchy. The economic planners, just like the military chiefs, rejected the concept entailing isolationism. In 1968, the Party instructed its members to push for "working class control," a half–way decentralizing measure devised to increase productivity. It is possible that the economic planners implemented that instruction in the sense of Yugoslav self–management, as a cure for the economic asthenia resulting from rigid pyramidal centralization. No less damaging was the dwindling of the Chinese aid in response to Albanian criticism of China's new line. In these circumstances little could be done to restore the economy to health. Këllezi and his associates were scapegoats for the failure of a policy, the authors of which were determined to bleed white both the Party and the country for the dubious honor of immortalizing themselves as Stalin's epigones.

4. Ideo–political Self–Isolation

The tripartite purge (1933–36) was comparable to the Titoite purge (1948–1951) in its range and duration. It involved vital sectors of the Albanian government: industry and agriculture (Pirro Dodbiba, Minister of Agriculture and candidate Politburo member, was fired in 1976), education and mass media (Thoma Deliana, Minister of Education and Culture, was dismissed in that same year), literature and the arts, and the armes forces. The purge witnessed the reappearance of pro–Western trend among the intellectuals and the youth. The pendulum began to swing back, the eastward drive having exhausted its possibilities.

In 1976, a commercial agreement with Greece was signed. Trade relations with Yugoslavia, Italy, and other European countries were intensified in the years following China's cut–off of credits and aid (July 1978). Yet Albania's total ideological and political isolation could not fail to worry those directly responsible for the country's defense and foreign policy. After Balluku's liquidation, the Ministry of Defense was assumed by Shehu who, in 1978, passed it over to his brother–in–law, Kadri Hazbiu, the executant of the tripartite purge in his capacity as Minister of the Interior. Now that the internal enemies had been wiped out, Hoxha could devote himself to writing books in which he took care of the external enemies.[49]

One reads in the *History of the Party*:

> The party combatted any trace of the narrow concept of defense, which reduced it only to drilling and other military problems, a concept which had been cultivated by the traitors B. Balluku and company for their hostile aims. It became even more clear that the better the economic plans are fulfilled, the sounder the socialist order, the stronger the dictatorship of the proletariat and the Party–people unity and the better the people are prepared for the political, ideological, cultural, educational, and technical aspect, the stronger the defense of the country. . . . The Homeland is defended with arms on the basis of the military art of people's war.[50]

In this text, a sound internal situation is said to rest with the dictatorship of the proletariat exercised against those who sabotage the fulfillment of economic plans, while the defense of the country from external enemies is assured by ideological cohesion and, to a minor degree, by "external support," i.e., "the international Marxist–Leninist Movement."[51] But what about external aggression? Here Hoxha's answer is the "people's war," fought according to military art learned in "free military schools, according to the teachings of the great Lenin."[52]

In his 1919 address to the peoples of the East, Lenin praises the "revolutionary enthusiasm . . . accompanied by a powerful inner cohesion" of the Red Army, which was organized and led to victory by Trotsky during the Civil War:

> It will show them [the peoples of the East] that weak as they may be, and invincible as may seem the power of the European oppressors, who in the struggle employ all the marvels of technology and of military art—nevertheless a revolutionary war waged by oppressed peoples, if it really succeeds in arousing the millions of working and exploited people, harbours such potentialities, such miracles, that the emancipation of the peoples of the East is now quite practicable . . .
> [53]

Hoxha's concept of defense is rooted in this theory, which was formulated when Kolchak was ruling over Siberia. Lenin's theory proved to be right during the Civil War, at a time when the fighting was done with guns. Will that theory be practicable in our atomic age? Elsewhere, Lenin rejects outdated forms of fighting:

> Frequently the lackeys of the bourgeoisie reproached us for having launched a "Red Guard" attack on capital. . . . The Red Guards fought in the noble and supreme historical cause of liberating the working and exploited people from the yoke of the exploiters. . . . Does that mean that a "Red Guard" attack on capital is always appropriate, under all circumstances . . . ? We must know how to change our methods of fighting the enemy to suit changes in the situation. . . . We shall not be so foolish, however, as to put "Red Guard" methods in the forefront at a time when the period in which the Red Guard attacks were necessary has, in the main, drawn to a close (and to a victorious close)
> . . . .[54]

This seems to have been Balluku's position. Hoxha takes him to task for his planned strategy of abandoning the coast as indefensible and retreating to the mountainous interior of the country. Yet Balluku's strategy is supported by another Lenin text:

> . . . We demand that everybody adopt a serious attitude towards defense of the country. And adopting a serious attitude towards defense of the country means thoroughly preparing for it, and strictly calculating the balance of forces. If our forces are obviously small, the best means of defense is retreat into the interior of the country . . . .[55]

Hoxha's thesis that the homeland should be defended by the entire people, the People's Army being "only a part of the armed people,"[56] was presented at the 12th Plenum (July 1971). The Sixth Congress of the PLA sanctioned Hoxha's thesis while also stressing "the leadership of the Party in the Army."[57] With the adoption of these theses, entailing the militarization of the whole population and the Party's full control of the Army, the defense of the country fell back on methods practiced during the October Revolution and the Civil war as well as by the Albanian Partisans during their own civil war. Nostalgia for the days when Hoxha was Commander-in-Chief of the National Liberation War? His reference to Lenin misses Lenin's point that methods must adjust to changed situations. The "free" military schools he propounds as the means for military education of the masses have more affinities with fascist paramilitary training (pictures of young people of both sexes brandishing guns adorn Albanian magazines just as air raid bunkers decorate the Albanian landscape) than with Leninist war practices. A better reference is Campanella. Compare Hoxha's sentence, "The consolidation of the free military schools is making military training an intrinsic [my emphasis] part of the life and activity of every working [person],"[58] with the following excerpt from *The City of the Sun*:

> In addition there are the athletes who provide military training for all the people. . . . Beginning at the age of twelve, youths are taught to strike, to overcome the enemy by craft; to use the sword, the spear, the bow; to ride, pursue, retreat, and maintain military formation. The women are also taught these skills . . . in case of an assault they can defend the walls. . . . Every two months there is a military review, and every day there are exercises either on horseback in the countryside or within the walls. There is also a daily lesson in the art of war.[59]

Reaction to Hoxha's primitive conception of defense by Balluku and his staff was bound to occur. What was Shehu's position in this internecine struggle? The fact that he, as Premier, let his Minister of Defense go ahead with plans for resisting the interference of the Party in army affairs speaks for acquiescence. A professional soldier himself, Shehu could not possibly be happy with Hoxha's policy, while at the same time looking askance at his Minister of Defense as representing a potential rival. His assumption of Balluku's duties after his demise corraborates the hypothesis. Yet once become Minister of Defense himself, he must have begun, one thinks, to question the wisdom of a policy which had isolated Albania from the rest of the world.

Chou En-lai had once advised the Albania leaders to intensify relations with Yugoslavia and Romania. Did Shehu make moves in that direction? Did he take steps for the readmission of Albania into the Warsaw Pact? Hoxha's accusation of him as a triple agent, at the service of Yugoslavia, the Soviet Union and the United States, points in that direction. The day before he committed suicide, Shehu is reported to have received a Romanian official. And after the liquidation of his associates in the cabinet, including his Minister of Foreign Affairs, rumors have circulated that the Prime Minister intended to "Romanize" Albania.

In *The Titoites* Shehu is labelled "a superagent," having been recruited by the U. S. Intelligence Agency while attending the American Vocational School in Tirana. He later studied at the Military Academy of Naples and became an army officer, fought with the International Brigades in Spain as acting commandant of a battalion, and spent three years in a French concentration camp before returning to Albania in 1943. It was Shehu who organized and commanded the First Partisan Brigade, saved Hoxha and his staff from a German encirclement, and liberated Tirana from the German troops. After the liberation, he went to Moscow to study in the Voroshilof Academy. Hoxha called him back to resist the Yugoslav pressure and made him Chief of the Staff of the armed forces. We have seen how he stood up for Hoxha when the latter was threatened by Xoxe. It was Shehu who, together with Jakova, reportedly arrested Xoxe in his office, and subsequently had him tried and shot. And when Hoxha clashed with Khrushchev, who, in a moment of anger, likened Hoxha to MacMillan, Shehu is reported to have said to the Soviet leader: "Take that word back and put it in your pocket!"[60]

How then did it come about that this man turned against his old ally and friend? According to the story as told in *The Titoites*, the tripartite plot was masterminded by Shehu who "pulled the strings behind the scenes." His plan to liquidate Hoxha years later was thus a sequel to the previous attempt. His scheme was germane to the plans of the tripartite traitors: he wanted to "liberalize" the Party, thus leading it to its own demise. To that effect, he had one of his sons get engaged to a girl of a bourgeois and enemy family. The Politburo foiled his strategem by unanimously condemning the engagement. This sealed Shehu's fate who, in despair, took his life (December 18, 1982). Investigation of his suicide revealed that Shehu intended to kill Hoxha, conspiring with his wife, Fiqret Shehu, Director of the V. I. Lenin Party School, and with his nephew, Feçor Shehu, Minister of Defense, Nesti Nase, Minister of Foreign Affairs, and Llambi Ziçishti, Minister of Public Health. Hazbiu, Feçor Shehu and Ziçishti are reported (no official communiqué as yet) to have been put to death, and the other two sentenced to long prison terms. How many more have been purged is a matter of conjecture. The list may be long, considering that the purge involves personnel from four ministries and the Security apparatus, the latter the fief of the Shehu–Hazbiu clan for thirty–three years.

Since ministers, army chiefs and important officials are Central Committee members as a rule, it can be stated that the Party apparatus has undergone a complete overhaul with the purge of the governmental sectors that had been spared from the tripartite purge. This must be the meaning of the rejuvenation of the Albanian leadership, a concept referred frequently by Hoxha in recent years. As it appears now in retrospect, the dispute was about whether Albania could continue to be the prison–house of Stalinism, or open up to the world.

In the past Hoxha seems not to have been opposed to some kind of overture. In his *Reflections on China*, excerpts from his political diary and covering almost the whole span of Sino–Albanian relations (1962–1977), there is a note, "The Foreign Policy of China—A Policy of Self–Isolation." In that note he criticizes the Chinese trend of foreign policy during the Cultural Revolution:

> Their general tactic is: "Struggle with all, hostility with all." Such a tactic is extremely sectarian and leads only to the course, "either with me or against me;" "if you do not think and act as I say or as I act, then you are against me."[61]

Prophetic words, applying to Hoxha himself. But these were

written in 1967, when Albania was flirting with the Chinese idea of cultural revolution. After the tripartite purge, the Sino–Albanian relations went from bad to worse, and in 1978 China denounced the alliance. Hoxha responded with the publication of his *Imperialism and Revolution* (1978), the second part of which is a frontal attack against "Chinese social–imperialism." Following came his libels against Titoism, Khruschevite social–imperialism and Eurocommunism, which forestalled eventual attempts to take Albania out of its isolation. Hoxha wanted Albania to remain the country whose brand of Stalinism was to be the model to be imitated by all other socialist countries, with him as the prophet of pure, atheistic, Hoxhan Marxism–Leninism.

Reflections on China shows that Hoxha soon realized that Chinese Marxism–Leninism was quite different from his dogmatic Stalinism. In a note, "The Chinese Are Moving Towards Conciliation with the Khrushchevites" (July 2, 1962), Hoxha finds fault with China's readiness to publicize Khrushchev's statement that "if China is attacked, then the Soviet Union will defend China."[62] Ironically enough, Hoxha later adopted Khrushchev's formula, repeating that, if Yugoslavia is attacked, then Albania will defend Yugoslavia.

While publicly praising the great ally for its staunch defense of the purity of Marxism–Leninism, Hoxha was rebuking its leaderhsip for their "unprincipled line" in his own diary.[63] When Nixon visited China, Hoxha denounced "the scandalous and disgraceful propaganda and demagogy which Peking is making about the rabid fascist . . . Peking, which claims to be the world center of Marxism–Leninism."[64] That privilege belonged to Tirana alone. The conviction that Hoxha had superseded Mao as the greatest living theoretician of Marxism–Leninism is already present in that text. In a later note one reads:

> Nearly a month has passed since the day our article, "The Theory and Practice of the Revolution," was published and its echo is still very powerful. Now not only it is being given by all the news agencies of the world and commented on by various circles, but it is being dealt with extensively by major world newspapers and the comments are in our favor.[65]

Sober Party members could remember that Stalin signed a pact of non–aggression with Hitler in 1937 and, shortly afterwards, the Soviet Union fought against Nazi Germany as an ally of the United

States and Great Britain. A pact or an alliance with ideological enemies in the national interest was a Maoist no less than a Stalinist "unprincipled" practice. Nor was Lenin principled when he compromised on a milder form of capitalism (the NEP). And was Albania's treaty with the fascist Greece of the Colonels a principled treaty? Hoxha knows well, without having to read Machiavelli, that politics has little to do with moral principles. Indeed Hoxha could teach the Italian a lesson, something the history of the Albanian purges demonstrates *ad nauseam*.

As to the much maligned Chinese policy in Hoxha's *Reflections on China*, the overwhelming majority of the Albanian leadership seems to have been content with it so long as Chinese credits replenished the Albanian treasury and Chinese wheat filled the Albanian barns. For if China did not feel like entering into a military alliance with Albania, at least it had no intention of gobbling it up, as Yugoslavia had tried to do, or of turning the country into a European Cuba, as the Soviet leaders had probably thought.

In the light of what has been said, it would seem that the tripartite purge was engineered by Hoxha as a "revolutionizing" measure to cure Albanian Stalinism of the Chinese "opportunism" with, which he himself had inoculated the Party's body through his parody of the Chinese Cultural Revolution. He could try any experiment he wanted at the time, his personality cult having reached a degree comparable to that of his master. Unlike Stalin, however, he had no firm grasp on the government, which was in Shehu's hands. Hoxha's strategy was to start with a peripheral purge, aimed at ideological deviations, for which he was directly responsible as First Secretary of the Party. He tactfully refrained from attacking Shehu's government. And when the next year he assailed and demolished—in a two–stage operation—the military establishment, he had Shehu replace Balluku, thus giving the impression that he had nothing against his Premier. Once the army purge was accomplished, he turned his heavy battery against the government's economy sector, liquidating the chief planner, two ministers and (a year later) the Minister of Agriculture. This amounted to blaming on the Prime Minister the faults of his Cabinet members, condemned as traitors. He thus undermined Shehu's influence in the Party and in the country, but prudently forbore demoting him, aware that the Shehu–Hazbiu faction was firmly entrenched in the Ministry of the Interior and in the Security apparatus.

No reliable information from the impenetrable Stalinist fortress

had leaked out to explain what really happened between the two
leaders. Hoxha's account in *The Titoites* that the disagreement was
caused by a wedding engagement is ludicrous. The engagement was
only the match that ignited an antagonism begun with the tripartite
purge and exacerbated by differences regarding Albania's attitude
towards Yugoslavia, the barometer of Albanian politics.

Expectations that Yugoslavia would disintegrate after Tito's death
were rife in many circles. In the Spring of 1981, student riots occurred
in Prishtina, capital of Kosova, and in other cities of the Autonomous
Province. Albania protested against the brutal repression. Yugoslavia
accused Albania of having incited the riots. Albania's position regarding the Kosova problem, as specified in three successive articles
published in the Party daily, *Zëri i popullit*,[66] was that Albania would
continue to sustain the legitimate rights of the Albanian population
in Yugoslavia, including Kosova's right to republic status, while abstaining from territorial claims. This is to say that Albania does not
seek to annex Kosova, while wanting it to be made a republic. But
what will Albania do if Kosova, having been granted republic status,
requests to join the mother country? And if the union occurs, can the
country continue to be ruled as it now is? Concessions will have to be
made to the Kosovars, who were spared collectivization and who are
also religious, thus bringing to an end the collectivistic and atheistic
Albanian socialism. Would Hoxha accept sacrificing the purity of his
ideology for the sake of national unity, the goal that has haunted Albanians ever since Kosova and other parts of Yugoslavia and Greece
mostly inhabited by Albanians were left out of the "Greater Albania"
of the pre–independence Albanian patriots?

Questions such as these must certainly have been discussed and
debated in the Party forums. We know Hoxha's answer. Shehu's
position can be surmised, considering that he was a professional officer
turned stateman, not a rigid ideologist like Hoxha. Of the two he
was, no doubt, the more nationalistic, alien to Hoxha's doctrinary
postures of internationalism. Hoxha accuses him of being a Yugoslav
agent, in collusion with the Yugoslav Embassy in Tirana through
his nephew, Feçor Shehu, who transmitted to his uncle the following
UDB ultimatum: "Enver Hoxha must be killed at all costs, even in
the Politburo meeting, even if Shehu himself is killed."[67] Hoxha then
quotes a Yugoslav newspaper stating that a gunfight between the two
sides erupted at the meeting, during which Shehu was killed. The
two versions of his death are worth one another. The message they

both convey is an attempt on Shehu's part to come to some sort of understanding with Yugoslavia, possibly playing the Kosova card. But a rapprochement with Yugoslavia is anathema to Hoxha, and that explains the rage of his language.

5. Purging the Purgers

The history of the CPY–PLA is to a great extent the history of its purges. Consideration of the phenomenon sheds light on the Party's nature and the ideology informing it, purges being always explained in ideological terms, even when they are outcomes of bare power struggle.

The Albanian purges have affected Party dissenters, individuals or groups and factions and, exceptionally (the Titoite case) the Party as a whole. In collective purges, the names of only representative figures have been made public, while the group or faction has been given a discrediting label such as "opportunist," "saboteur," "Titoite," "Trotskyite," "Khrushchevite," "anti–party," "enemy," "traitor," "agent of imperialism," "foreign agent," etc. The descriptions fit the recipients loosely, often being completely gratuitous and even Orwellian ("war is peace"). With a few exceptions, such as the case of the Xoxe pro-Yugoslav faction, or the Belishova–Tashko pro–Soviet group, those who were purged were nationalistic communists just like Hoxha and Shehu but who, unlike them, resented foreign supervision, be it Yugoslav or Soviet. It is highly significant that during Albania's alliance with China, which did not interfere with PLA problems, no purges occurred for a period of eleven years.

Chronology shows that purges were diarrhetic during the Yugoslav tutelage. After the extensive Titoite housecleaning, there was a two–year pause (1952–54) before another wave of purges began, first against dissenting leaders (Jakova, Spahiu, Gega) and later, when Albanian–Soviet relations deteriorated, against pro–Soviet leaders (Belishova, Tashko). A shorter interval (1976–82) occurred after the sweeping tripartite purge (1973–76). The following table, in which only conspicuous Party leaders appear (almost all Central Committee and Politburo members), provides a general picture.

The table shows that the purges have been continuous from the foundation of the Party until the end of the Soviet patronage period (with a two–year interval following Stalin's death) for a comprehensive period of twenty years. During this period of time the greater part of the core leadership was destroyed, first by the Hoxha–Xoxe

Party Purges in Albania

Period	Year	Individuals, groups, and factions	Ideological trend
Yugoslav Tutelage (1941–48)	1943	Sadik Premte, Anastas Lulo	unclear
	1943	Ymer Dishnica	pro–West
	1944	Mustafa Gjinishi	pro–West
	1946	Sejfulla Malëshova	pro–West
	1947	Nako Spiru	independent
	1948		
Soviet Patronage (1949–60)	1949	Koçi Xoxe, Pandi Kristo, Nesti Kerenxhi, Kristo Themelko	pro–Yugoslav
	1950	Abedin Shehu, Niazi Islami	pro–Yugoslav
	1950	Gjin Marku, Beqir Ndou	unclear
	1951	Tuk Jakova, Theodor Heba, Manol Konomi	independent
	1952	Nexhip Vinçani	unclear
	1953–54		
	1955	Tuk Jakova, Bedri Spahiu	independent
	1956	Tirana Section Group	mixed
	1956	Lira Gega, Dali Ndreu	pro–Soviet
	1957	Panajot Plaku	pro–Yugoslav
	1959	Teme Sejko, Tahir Demi	independent
	1960	Koço Tashko, Liri Belishova	pro–Soviet
	1961	Maqo Çomo	pro–Soviet
Chinese Hegemony (1961–78)	1962–71		
	1973	Fadil Paçrami, Todi Lubonja	pro–West
	1974	Beqir Balluku, Petrit Dume, Hito Çako	independent
	1975	Abyl Këllezi, Koço Theodosi, Kiço Ngjela	independent
	1975	Pirro Dodbiba, Thoma Deliana	Unclear
Isolation (1978–)	1977–82		
	1982–83	Mehmet Shehu, Fiqret Shehu, Feçor Shehu, Kadri Hazbiu, Nesti Nase, Llambi Ziçishti	independent
	1983	Haxhi Lleshi	independent

duumvirate and then by the Hoxha–Shehu tandem. The tripartite purge liquidated most of the rest. The purge of the Shehu faction has reduced the core leadership to Hoxha and his wife, Ramiz Alia, Adil Çarçani and perhaps one or two others, some of the old guard members having died (Hysni Kapo, Gogo Nushi), and others having retired or been demoted (Spiro Koleka, Haxhi Lleshi). The process can be described as *progressive enucleation and deproletarization.* Proportionately with other classes and social groups, it is the proletarian core that has been harder hit: three of the Party founders and members of the seven–person Provisional Central Committee: Hoxe, Jakova, and Themelko as well as two Party builders, Kristo and Balluku. Such leadership enucleation and deproletarization is unique among European Marxist–Leninist parties.

Another distinctive feature of the Albanian purges is their *fierceness.* An example is the Titoite housecleaning, which involved the expulsion of a quarter of the Party membership and more than half of its leadership. Titoite purges occurred in all other European socialist countries, but they were less comprehensive. We shall briefly review the Balkan countries. The size of the Rumanian purge of 1950 (25 percent of the Party membership) comes close to the Albanian figure. Yet that purge, which occurred after the unification of communists and social democrats, aimed at raising the number of workers at the expense of petty–bourgeois elements in the Party.[68] In 1952, under Soviet pressure, Lukas, Pauker and Georgescu fell from power. Two years later, Patraşcanu was executed (arrested in 1948, he was rehabilitated in 1968).[69] In Bulgaria, the hanging of Petkov in 1948 was not a Party purge, he being the leader of the Agrarian Party. The same holds true for Lulchev, the socialist leader, jailed with his group of seven deputies.[70] Kostov, the major scapegoat for Bulgarian Titoism, was indeed executed while seven of his followers were given life sentences (1948–49); Yugov managed to survive by recanting—he occupied key positions in the government afterwards.[71] As to Yugoslavia, the massive anti–Stalin purge strengthened the Party's cohesion instead of loosening it. Of the main dissenters, Hebrang died in jail, and Jovanović was shot while trying to escape to Romania.[72]

Another characteristic of the Albanian purges is that all those directly responsible for the purges, i.e., the Ministers of the Interior: Lleshi (1944–45), Xoxe (1945–48), Kerenxhi (1949),Mehmet Shehu (1949–50), Jakova (1950–51), Mehmet Shehu (1951–54), Hazbiu (1954–78), Feçor Shehu (1978–82), have all been purged, without exception.

The purge of the purgers, an absolute rule in Albania, has manifested itself only sporadically in the other socialist countries of Europe (Rajk in Hungary, Yugov in Bulgaria, Ranković in Yugoslavia). The pattern is of course the Soviet Union (Yagoda, Yezhov, Beria). But whereas only three USSR Security chiefs have been purged and executed ever since the October Revolution, in Albania all eight ministers of the Interior have been purged and four of them executed or induced to commit suicide. This is an absolute record, comparable to other such records identifying the uniqueness of socialist Albania, the first atheistic state in world history and the country where Marxism–Leninism is pure 100 percent.

The analysis leads to the conclusion that Albanian Party purges are an endemic phenomenon of *ideological hemophilia* which is cured by professional hemophilic purgers who end up being purged themselves.

And how are we to describe the Party's ideology?

We can say it is Stalinism, Albanian style.

The CPA was born Stalinist because the CPY was Stalinist at the time, and it was under CPY tutelage that the CPA was founded and began to function. Of the various communist groups and circles existing then in Albania, Tito's emissaries, Miladin Popović, and Dušan Mugoša, managed to bring together the Shkodër Group, the Korçë Group and the Youth Group, excluding Trotyskites and other non-Stalinist elements. One such was, for instance, Zef Mala, leader of the Shkodër Group, a philosophy student and an orthodox marxist who thought that proletarian revolution makes sense where a proletarian class exists (it did not in Albania, the proletarian Jakova thought). Among the thirteen representatives who founded the Party, only two had some knowledge about the theory of Marxism: Koço Tashko and Qemal Stafa. Tashko, the Comintern representative, resented the presence of the Yugoslav comrades. These found Hoxha to be much more flexible as well as an able organizer. Stafa, a university student with a better theoretical preparation, was murdered by fascists in 1942. The rest were proletarian activists or youths who knew of Marxist theory little more than its rudiments. The one who was conversant with the theory and who had also experienced its Stalinist practice, Malëshova, arrived too late to change the situation, then dominated by Hoxha as Secretary General. The reader knows what happened during the war and immediately after. Instigated by his Yugoslav mentors, the proletarian Xoxe initiated the class struggle by jailing and hanging intellectuals and technicians who were to him, a tinsmith, the natural allies of the bourgeoisie. This is how Albanian Stalinism began its career, led by a Stalinist Party under Stalinist Yugoslav control. In the virgin forest of Albanian socialism, Xoxe blazed a bloody trail which Shehu and Hazbiu later pursued to Hoxha's gratification. The ideology did not change in substance, it only changed names. Albanian Stalinism resisted Khrushchev's pressure of de–Stalinization while gradually receiving a Maoist veneer. This crumbled away in time. *Reflections on China* includes many a critical note on Mao's Cultural Revolution. Yet the author carefully avoids mentioning his own Cultural Revolution, thus silently denying its Maoist paternity.

6. The Internal Factor

In 1975, Hoxha was still singing hymns to Chairman Mao, who had at the time lined up with the United States. His opportunism was dictated by economic reasons, which are likewise basic for explaining Albania's boisterous affairs with her two former partners. But since the Albanian party purges have been invariably contingent on the relations between the CPA—PLA and the Communist Parties of first Yugoslavia, then the Soviet Union and ultimately China, one would be led to infer that the main cause for the purges was ideological, prompted by the leadership's zeal to preserve the purity of Albanian Marxism–Leninism from alien influences.

Hoxha would, of course, accept this interpretation, tacitly assuming that leadership and his person are one and the same. His stress, however, is—we saw an example in his concept of national defense—on the internal rather than the external factor. The following excerpt is indicative on this point:

> The Chinese comrades talk a great deal about the class struggle in the Party, but in fact they are not purging the Party, which is the fortress of the revolution, from within, but are encircling it from outside with people who are not organized in a party of the vanguard. . . . The working class and the peasantry do not appear anywhere in this experiment.[73]

In this text, "purging the Party . . . from within" means waging class war in the form of dictatorship of the proletariat (the working class and the peasantry) against that part of the party which is af-

fected by petty–bourgeois and bourgeois ideology and which therefore
needs to be purged. We have seen where this leads: to the purging of
the purgers and the dictatorship of the Purger.

The internal factor concept reappears in another text which deals
with the founding of the Party:

> We know that Marxism–Leninism always regards the inter-
> nal cause, the internal factor, as the main determining fac-
> tor in the birth and evolution of every phenomenon. The
> process and birth of a communist party can never be an ex-
> ception to this law, hence, the process of the founding of the
> Communist Party cannot be an exception to it, either.[74]

Hoxha's concept of the internal factor is a time–honored one
and goes back to Aristotle (his entelechy). The question of whether
the external or the internal factor is determinant for the "birth and
evolution" of a phenomenon reminds one of the question of which
comes first, the chicken or the egg. Aristotle was for the egg. But I
doubt Marx shared that opinion, if for no other reason than because
the poor devil could not afford to eat many chickens when he was
writing *Kapital.*

We will not argue the cogency of the syllogism with which Hoxha
refutes the thesis that the CPA was founded by the Yugoslavs. And
we shall accept also the other syllogism that, since the Party was
not founded by the Yugoslavs (and Russians and Chinese were then
missing from the picture), the founders must have been the Albanians
themselves. The question is where are these founders now? According
to the *History of the Party,* there were fifteen founders,[75] two of them
being Yugoslavs. Of the remaining thirteen, only four are mentioned:
Enver Hoxha, Pilo Peristeri, Qemal Stafa, and Vasil Shanto. The last
two were killed by the fascists before the liberation, while Peristeri,
another tinsmith from Korçë, played no role in the top leadership.
This leaves Hoxha a lonely star in what used to be a constellation.
And if we add to the number of the purged founders: Tashko, Xoxe,
Lulo, Premte, Çitaku, Jakova, Themelko; the number of the purged
builders: Dishnica, Gjinishi, Malëshova, Spiru, Kristo, Spahiu, Gega,
Belishova, Balluku, Shehu, Hazbiu, one is left with the conclusion
that Hoxha alone on the one scale of the balance weighs more than
all the rest on the other.

Such being the case and taking the lead from Hoxha's doctrine
that the main determinant is the internal factor, the inference to be

made is that the main cause for the Party purges must be sought in Hoxha's entelechy, his *Wille zur Macht*. To realize this one needs only read the *History of the Party*, the Albanian counterpart of Stalin's *Short Course* of the history of the Bolshevik Party. It begins with a description of the communist groups before the Party's foundation. Hoxha is first mentioned (he joined the Korçë Group shortly before the Italian occupation of the country) towards the end of the first chapter, in a section exclusively devoted to him. From that point on, however, his name structures the text. It appears rather sparingly in the second and third chapters, which deal with the Party's activity during the period of the Yugoslav tutelage that saw Xoxe emerge as the real helmsman. But beginning with the fourth chapter, which focuses on the Party's struggle to industrialize the country, Hoxha's name and the Party become increasingly interchangeable terms. The *History of the Party* is indeed the record of his achievements, supported by citations from his reports and speeches. In vain one looks for his closest collaborators to be given some credit. They are never mentioned, except for one or two who are dead. Those who are named are invariably dissenters, branded as plotters and traitors. One expects that at least Shehu, his ally and Premier for twenty-seven years, would crop up somewhere. But not even he does. As everyone knows who is somewhat familiar with the Albanian Liberation War, it was Shehu who routed the nationalists, and it was he who, as commander of the First Army Corps, drove the Nazi troops from the capital. How does the *History of the Party* describe that battle?

> The units of the National Liberation Army were now engaged in the final operations against the German troops in Albania and in Kosova. Of these operations the most important was that for the liberation of Tirana. The order of the Commander–in–Chief was to wipe out the enemy, to stop the plunder and destruction of the city by the Germans and to liberate Tirana at all costs. The operation was to be led by the Command of the 1st Army Corps.[76]

The merit goes to the Commander–in–Chief who gave the order, not to the commander who found and won the battle. Not only is Shehu's name omitted, but even his personality is denied, the word referring to him being "command," an abstract noun.

The bible of Albanian Marxism–Leninism swarms with shams such as this. The impression one gets from reading Hoxha's works is

the same: history is being continuously reinvented to please the one
who detains its license. Things that never happened are presented as
facts, while facts are concealed or disguised, mutilated or otherwise
altered   wreckage of truth floating in a sea of falsehood. Looking for
a modicum of honesty in works such as these is a desperate enterprise.

The purges are a major theme in the *History of the Party*; they
constitute Hoxha's title of glory as the guardian and arbiter of the
ideology of the Party. To that effect, the victims, ghostly apparitions
wrested from the limbo of shame and misery where they have been
hurled, are made to parade before the throne of the victor their judge,
hidden in his aureole. The *History of the Party* exalts him as such,
approaching his books reverently like sacred scriptures. His name
is pronounced in formulaic clauses such as "Comrade Enver Hoxha
teaches" ("says," "explains"), "the teaching of Comrade Hoxha," preceding or following sentences in the form of maxims, often in association with the Central Committee as equiponderant with the latter.
The following are all found in Chapter VIII, 6, pp. 522–25:

> Special attention has been paid to providing the control
> group with ideo–political training and expertise. According
> to the instructions of the Central Committee and the teach-
> ings of Comrade Enver Hoxha, their training is ideological
> and political . . .

> "The cadre . . . first of all, must be educated in the school
> of the working class," teaches Comrade Enver Hoxha.

> "The cadres have their place, their role," pointed out Com-
> rade Enver Hoxha, "however, they do not impose their law
> on the Party, but the Party and the class impose the law on
> them."

> Comrade Enver Hoxha says, "The party must immediately
> and unhesitatingly bring down from their high horse and
> break the noses and bones . . ." of cadres with the kulak,
> bureaucrat or liberal mentality . . .

The lawmaker's injunction to his subjects to blindly obey his
law cannot be clearer. And if Hoxha has succeeded in reducing the
Party to worshipping him as the Prophet of Marxism–Leninism, we
can now explain the phenomenon of Party purges in conformity with
his thesis of the predominance of the internal factor: the Party purges
are a phenomenon of *Hoxhan phagocytosis.*

Those who were purged, in groups or individually, suffered their fate because they dared to disobey or scorn Hoxha's orders. Some of them, while having no qualms about expropriating the rich bourgeois and the big landowners, objected to jailing them and then harassing their families. Others who were in agreement with curbing the influence of organized religion would not condone the extermination of clerics, scoffing at the idea that Albania be made the first atheistic state in the world. No one would hesitate to distribute the confiscated land to the poor peasants. But to persecute a peasant "with less than 3 hectares [about seven acres] of land, 1 head of cattle and less than 10 sheep,"[77] seemed preposterous. "In 1960 there were some 1,500 kulak households, or less than 1 percent of the overall number of the peasant households. The kulaks had lost their former economic base," they had "disappeared in general as a class."[78] According to Marxism, class is defined by its economic base. But if this was lost, as the test spells out, can their persecution, which raged until they were annihilated, be justified? They were annihilated as a class that has ceased to be a class. Is this Marxism?

It is, of course, Stalinism, precisely Hoxhan Stalinism. When Malëshova protested against the killing without due process of former army officers by Shehu's partisans in the first days of the liberated capital, Hoxha justified the terroristic acts by saying:

> When we appealed to them to go to the mountains and fight the occupier together with us, they didn't budge from their comfortable shelters. Now they are "repenting" too late, and we have to settle account with the criminals.[79]

Criminals because they did not join the partisans? Malëshova is quoted as having replied: "You have lost the heart of a communist who values another man's life and thinks deeply before he decides to wipe out someone who might be corrected and serve the country."[80] A communist with a heart must have sounded ludicrous to Hoxha, which seems to be his reason for quoting Malëshova's reply.

7. Hoxhan Messianism

While Albanian Stalinism is not entirely a product of Hoxha, the ideology inspiring the PLA is completely his own. Party leaders and the intelligentsia only repeat or paraphrase what he says or writes. Albanian Marxism–Leninism remains as its nadir because any attempt to lift it above that level would immediately be taxed with revisionism.

Hoxha's status as the official representative and monopolizer of the PLA ideology dates from the post–Stalin era, when he began to oppose Khrushchev's process of de–Stalinization. He was able to capitalize on Stalin's cult to build up his own personality cult. At the time he joined Mao in challenging the de–Stalinization movement, Hoxha had achieved his objective of becoming the Albanian Stalin. Maoist ideas infiltrated his thoughts without indenting their Stalinist substratum. He merely parodied the Chinese Cultural Revolution, the ideo–political situation in Albania being very different from the situation in China. Mao launched the Red Guards movement because Party control was eluding him. This, however, was not the case with Hoxha, who dominated the Party. Behind his promotion of the Albanian Cultural Revolution lay his scheme to capitalize on Mao's doctrine, then popular with the extreme left. The sixties witnessed the flood of the student protest movement, which from the United States (the 1964–65 Berkeley Free Speech Movement) spread over many European countries (the French May of 1968). Mao's Red Guards were mostly pupils and students (hence the name of Cultural Revolution). Hoxha made good use of the student and in general intellectual discontent in his homeland in order to further his personality cult. This he did by encouraging attacks against the Party bureaucracy, thus casting himself in the role of the enlightened revolutionary leader. When Mao began to lose favor with the left because of his coming to terms with American imperialism, Hoxha saw his chance to promote himself to the longed for position of Commander-in–Chief of the forces of World Revolution, with Tirana as the Mecca of Marxism–Leninism. The cultural purge of 1973 cleared the ground of the weeds of liberalism grown during the diversified climate of the Cultural Revolution. And if the military purge had a Soviet pattern (Balluku's catastrophe parallels Zhukov's fall), it was meant to have ideological impact, just as did the cultural and the economic purge. One reads in the *History of the Party*:

> The struggle against the enemy groups of conspirators and saboteurs, like the struggle against earlier traitors, was, *first of all* [my emphasis], an ideological struggle as the entire class struggle waged in the ranks of the Party is.

We already know from *Reflections on China* that class struggle is carried not only outside but also inside the Party. This is to say that dissenters are class enemies. This is another Hoxhan development of Marxism, class being no longer defined by its economic basis, but by ideology. According to Marx and Engels, ideology is a phenomenon of the superstructure, indeed the common denominator of all superstructures, one can say. According to Hoxha's doctrine, a Party member becomes a class enemy by merely being a dissenter, despite the fact that he or she may belong to the proletarian class. The subversion of Marxism is total; Hoxhan Marxism–Leninism has stood Marx on his head.

We understand why, in *Reflections on China*, Hoxha criticizes Maoism as neglecting to practice class struggle within the Party and to purge it "from within." Another text in the *History of the Party* is a categorical rejection of Mao's doctrine of nonantogonistic contradictions arising within the Party and which can be solved without resorting to violence:

> The revolution, the dictatorship of the proletariat, cannot fail to use violence against the enemies of the Party, the people and socialism. The contradictions between us and class enemies cannot be resolved in any other way. To try to resolve these contradictions as contradictions among the working masses, between the various aspects of the socialist order, are resolved, means to fall into idealism and class conciliation. The purging of enemy elements from the Party, its struggle to smash their anti–party and anti–socialist activity, have further tempered the Party ideologically and politically as the vanguard of the working class and leader of the people.[81]

Mao's thesis of nonviolent solution of Party conflict is rejected in the name of Stalinian terrorism. The passage summarizes Hoxha's theory of revolution, his legacy to world socialism.

One looks in vain in his books for any original thought that would qualify their author as a theoretician. Hoxha's ideas come from the Stalinist baggage (seldom directly from Lenin) and are interspersed with ideas current in the left literature of the time. The logic is loose, with frequent non sequiturs and even contradictions, the language coarse and vituperative at best, the style (Hoxha himself prompts me to comment on his style, he having authored a volume of literary criticism) a repetitious display of ideological platitudes interwoven with cheap journalistic clichés. Hoxha writes as he preaches, his "theo-retical" books being germane to his prolix reports and much more exciting speeches (he is a skilled speaker). Lacking sufficient intellec-tual vigor to devise theories, he enunciates theses that are antitheses as a rule, i.e., refutations of adversary theses. There is a method in this. He hits the adversary right on the head with sledge hammer arguments, and without bothering to analyze his thesis, which he presents in a sketchy and usually distorted manner. Then he makes away with the thesis by producing one of his trump cards such as relentless class struggle, dictatorship of the proletariat, impossibility of peaceful coexistence between the socialist and the bourgeois order, proletarian internationalism, and the like. No attempt is made to supersede the antithesis into a synthesis. His definition of dialectic is sophomoric:

> Marxist–Leninist dialectics teaches us that there is no limit
> to development, that nothing stops changing. In this process
> of unceasing developments towards the future, quantitative
> and qualitative changes occur.

Heraclitus plus Engels, juxtaposed. And here is his refutation of Mao's theory of the three worlds, concerning the second world:

> In the countries of the so–called second world there is a large
> and powerful proletariat, which is exploited to the bone,
> which is kept down by crushing laws, the army, the police,
> the trade unions, by all the weapons of the dictatorship of
> the bourgeoisie.[82]

Here the trump card of the dictatorship of the bourgeoise concludes a sentence in which the police and the trade unions are put on the same level while the dictatorship of the bourgeoisie applies indifferently to all industrialized countries, to Japan as well as to Sweden. Else-where we read that the Emperor Hirohito is a "fascist dictator" just as Mussolini and Hitler were.[83] Santiago Carillo is "a bastard of revi-sionist bastardy,"[84] while "Aragon, André Stil, and André Wurmser not only changed their coats, but even sold their souls and their hides to revisionism."[85]

Hoxha's ideological daltonism, a consequence of his bone–dry dogmatism, knows no degrees of transition, let alone shades, only black–and–white. Other examples:

> The two imperialist superpowers represent *to the same de-*
> *gree* [my emphasis] the main enemy and danger of socialism.[86]

> On the one side stands the capitalist–imperialist bourgeoisie,
> which is the most ferocious, deceitful, and bloodthirsty class
> known to history. On the other side stands the proletariat,
> the class totally dispossessed of means of production, ruth-
> lessly oppressed and exploited by the bourgeoisie, which is at
> the same time the most advanced class of the society which
> *thinks, creates, works and produces,* but does not enjoy the
> fruits of its toil [emphasis added].[87]

Marx wrote that the proletarians will be able to perform these divers
activities when they cease to be proletarians in the society of the future which is communism. Thinking and creating presupposes leisure
time and some comfort, which "oppressed and exploited" proletarians do not have. This other revolutionizing doctrine of Hoxha supersedes Marx pretty much as Mohammed supersedes Jesus Christ.
In his Stalinist ideology there is indeed a novel element, peculiar to
him: messianism. But since this novelty may prove too much for the
reader, I shall preface discussion with a digression.

In his book on Tito, Dedijer reports a conversation in 1946 between Stalin and the Yugoslav delegation headed by Kardelj. To
Stalin's question as to who and what kind of a communist leader
Hoxha was, Kardelj answered that he was "good and honest on the
whole, although he ha[d] certain characteristics of a petty bourgeois
intellectual."[88] Such was also Stalin's opinion: "He is a petty bourgeois, inclined towards nationalism? Yes, we think so, too."[89] In
his article on "Left–Wing Childishness and Petty–Bourgeois Mentality," Lenin describes the language of the ultras as "defense of petty-
bourgeois sloppiness that is sometimes concealed by 'Left' slogans.'
"[90]

Can this description be applied to Hoxha?

During the wartime period, Hoxha was Secretary General of the
Party, Commander–in–Chief of the National Liberation Army and
designated Premier of Albania. After the Liberation, he was Premier,
Minister of Foreign Affairs, Minister of Defense and Commander-
in–Chief of the Armed Forces, besides being, of course, Secretary
General of the Party. Such accumulation of power (would Hoxha call
it democratic centralization?) is rather similar to accumulation of
capital.

Consider his idea of a pure Marxism–Leninism. It contradicts
his own definition of dialectics as Heraclitean becoming. Heraclitus
illustrated his metaphysical concept by saying that one cannot wash

one's hands twice in the same water. Indeed, if I wash my hands in a basin of fresh water, the water won't be the same after my act of washing because some of the dirt on my hands will have rendered the water less pure. Has any lasting religious or political movement remained as it started, pure? In his parable of the Grand Inquisitor, Dostoyevsky has depicted what would happen to Jesus were he to come back in our times. And Marxism is of course different from what we read in Marx's works, if for no other reason than because Marx was one and Marxisms are many. Purity is a religious and at best a poetic concept which has absolutely no place in 'dirty' politics. Those who associate purity with the latter are either hypocrites or troubled souls longing for origins, for the otherworldly home. True, there are also those who believe in the Kingdom of God on earth, and these are millenarians, waiting for the Messiah, or the Christ, or the Mahdi, to come back and deliver them from suffering. And I do not know whether Ayatollah Khomeini thinks of himself as a Mahdi. But a Sunni Mahdi, Muhammed Ahmed (1844–1885), fought a war of liberation in Sudan, where he established a theocratic regime. He fought to purify Islam. Closer to our times, Hitler provoked a world war, seeking to purify the German race. It makes little difference whether he believed in God or not, he certainly believed in the purity of the German race—and in the obscenity of the Jewish race, which he purged, very religiously indeed, through a modern equivalent of the pyre.

In one way or another, these people and others, too, who had a Savior's vocation, were convinced of being unique, chosen by God, or destiny, or even by themselves (again, it makes little difference from a practical point of view) to lead a tribe or a nation, a sect or a religion, and at times the whole of humankind, to what they thought to be the terrestrial paradise.

In the last several years Hoxha has devoted himself to writing, becoming remote, like Stalin in the last period of his life. Remoteness from the public adds a transcendent dimension to the personality cult. In *The Great Winter* (1977), a representative novel by the most representative Albanian writer, Ismail Kadare, Hoxha is portrayed as the Savior of the Albanian nation from Khrushchevik aggression, towering Olympus–like above the other members of the Albanian delegation facing Khrushchev.

Hoxha 'saved' Albania by daring to defy the Soviet colossus. Later he challenged Mao himself. A suitable analogy is David fighting Goliath. David felled the giant because he "trusted in the Lord without wavering" (Psalm 26:1). Hoxha humiliated Khrushchev supported by what angel, what faith? Compare Stalin's idea of socialism in one country with Hoxha's ideal of Albania as the chosen land of socialism. Both seem to derive from the Jewish belief in one and only one true God, which was adopted, with due modifications, by the other two monotheistic religions, Christianity and Islam. In *The Holy Family*, Marx criticizes the "theological critic" Bruno Bauer for his concept of atheism: "atheism, the last stage of theism, the negative recognition of God."[91] And in the *Manuscripts of 1844*, Marx writes that

> atheism, which is the denial of this unreality [of nature and man], no longer has any meaning, for atheism is a negation of God, through which negation it asserts the existence of man. But socialism as such no longer needs such mediation.

Yet Hoxha proclaimed Albania the first atheistic state in the world, thus outdoing even Stalin, who prudently restrained himself from taking that step. Hoxha's promotion of his "negative" religion was actively seconded by Shehu. Is it only a coincidence that Hoxha (Albanian 'hoxha' has the same sound and meaning as it English counterpart 'hodja') is the son of a mullah, and Shehu the son of a 'sheh' (English 'sheik')? I shall end with an anecdote. At some time there were in the Central Committee, besides Hoxha and Shehu and their wives, people such as Mihal Prifti ('prift,' an Orthodox priest), Manush Myftiu ('mufti,' Moslem religious head of a district), and Haxhi Lleshi ('hadji' is one who has made a pilgrimage to Mecca). An Italian comrade who happened to be in Tirana was curious to know whether names such as these had a meaning. And when an Albanian comrade explained to him what they meant, he is reported to have exclaimed: *"La santa famiglia!"*

VII. THE OTHER ALBANIA: A BALKAN
PERSPECTIVE*

Kosova has been in the limelight in the last two years. The Spring 1981 demonstrations and riots in Prishtina and other cities, followed by the Federal troops' drastic repression, have called attention to the 'autonomous province.' There is another autonomous province in the Socialist Federal Republic of Yugoslavia, Voivodina, the two provinces being integral parts of the Socialist Republic of Serbia. Their official description is the same, their differences being striking in two respects. Whereas Voivodina is a rich province, richer than the rest of Serbia, Kosova's economy is poorer than Serbia's and the poorest in Yugoslavia. The March 1981 student protest in Prishtina was sparked by undernourishment at the University's cafeteria and by space stricture in the dormitories, with student sharing beds by shifts. The high rate of unemployment among university graduates was an additional cause for the riots. The main cause, however, was the pent-up feeling of frustration, universal among the Kosovars, at not having their province promoted to republic status. And here we come to the other important difference between the two provinces. Voivodina is populated in greater part by Serbs (54.5 percent), whereas Serbs, Montenegrins, and other Slavic and Turkish ethnics make up less than 20 percent of Kosova's population, the remainder being Albanians. And since Kosova's population (1,584,558, i.e., 7.8 percent of Yugoslavia's entire population, according to the 1981 census) is scarcely smaller than the population of the province of Macedonia, and much larger than that of the Republic of Montenegro, the Kosovars feel strongly that the status of their province

---

* Published in *Studies on Kosova*, prepared for publication by Arshi Pipa. East European Monographs, No. 155. Boulder, 1984. Distributed by Columbia University Press.

should be raised to that of a republic.[1] The Yugoslav's refusal of this demand is interpreted by ethnic Albanians as discrimination against them. Their lower socio–economic status makes them the proletarian ethnics of socialist Yugoslavia, their second–class citizenship is felt as a yoke. These sentiments are shared by their leaders to a great extent, witness the extensive purges in the Party and the government after the riots.[2]

Serbian reaction to Kosovar nationalism is predictable. The Serbs fear that once republic status is granted to Kosova, the province would secede and join the People's Socialist Republic of Albania. Kosova's secession would weaken the Yugoslav Federation while also jeopardizing its national security. Serbs and Kosovars have been sworn enemies in the past, and Yugoslav–Albanian relations have been bad for more than a generation. A Greater Albania including Kosova would be a greater danger for Yugoslavia. The severe punitive measures against the supporters and even sympathizers of the demonstrations are motivated by precisely that fear.[3] Many of those sentenced to long prison terms were accused of irredentism, instigated by the Albanian government. Tirana has rejected the charge.[4]

Kosova was made an 'autonomous region' under the name of Kosmet (Kos[ova]–Met[ohija]) in 1945. Its autonomy was nominal for a long time, and it continued to be so even after Kosova was promoted to an 'autonomous province' in 1963. The Kosovars began to feel at home in the province only after Alexandar Ranković, notorious for his Albanophobia, was expelled from the Party. In 1968 demonstrators in Prishtina voiced the demand that Kosova be made a republic. From that time on, Kosova's dependence on Serbia has gradually diminished. The 1974 Constitution accorded the autonomous province rights that are almost the same as those exercised by the six federal republics. Kosova has her own administration and legislature, her territorial army, police, and courts. The language in the schools is predominantly Albanian, and the Kosovars can even fly their flag, which is the same as the Albanian flag. The Serbs feel they have been more than generous to them. Granting the province republic status would be tantamount to inviting the Kosovars to secede, they think. And Serbia would not permit secession. The Serbs consider Kosova Serbian territory, though the population of the province is only 13.2 percent Serbian (1981) census).

1. Historical Survey

According to Yugoslav historians, it was Stefan Nemanja (1168–1196), the Rašian founder of the first Serbian dynasty, who first conquered Kosova.[5] Albanian as well as some foreign historians maintain that Serbs settled in Kosova towards the end of the thirteenth century and that Kosova was still essentially Albanian in the fourteenth and fifteenth centuries.[6] When Stefan Dušan proclaimed himself Emperor of Serbs and Greeks, he founded the independent Patriarchate of Serbia in Peć (Pejë in Albanian). The treasures of Serbian religious art, the churches of Gračanica and Dećan (the Emperor was buried in the latter), are found in Kosovar territory. And it was in Kosovo Polje (Blackbird Field) that the memorable battle between Turks and Slavs (including Albanians, according to Albanian historians) took place in 1389, a date which marks the beginning of the Turkish domination of the Balkans. Serbian and Albanian princes surrendered or were defeated; Kosova became a Turkish province in the fourteenth century.

The Croat historian Milan Šufflay advanced the thesis of a Serbo–Albanian symbiosis in the Middle Ages.[7] Šufflay's thesis is confirmed by documents such as the 1416 Venetian Cadaster of Shkodër,[8] the 1455 Turkish *defter* ('register' [of landed property]) of the Kosova region,[9] and the 1485 Turkish *defter* of the Shkodër region.[10] In all three documents many landowners have Albanian names, usually with Slavic suffixes. To Serb historians these people were Serbs. Albanian historians maintain they were Orthodox or Catholic Albanians whose names had been Slavicized during the reign of the Serbian kings. These Albanians were autochthone descendants of the Dardanians, an Illyrian tribe who, according to the Greek geographer Strabo, lived in an area (capital Niš, Lat. *Naissus*) bordering on Thracia.[11] Study of the Albanian language has led some Albanologists to hold precisely that area as the primitive homeland of the Albanians.[12] Serb historians deny the existence of Albanians in "Stara Serbia" (Old Serbia, another name for Kosova) before the Turkish occupation of the Balkans. According to them, Albanians colonized Kosova and other parts of Yugoslavia with the strong support of the Turks, whose religion they were quick to embrace (today Kosovars are Moslem, except for a limited number of Catholics). Catholic ecclesiastical reports are proof that at least some Albanian Catholics lived in Kosova at the beginning of the seventeenth century.[13] During the 1690 Austro–Turkish war, a great number of Serbs who had sided with the Austrians left their lands, which were then occupied by Albanians, Yugoslav historians say. Albanian historians counter that Albanians too fought the Turks, migrating together with Slavs into Hungary when the Austrian army was defeated. Another Serbian exodus occurred during the 1737 Austro–Turkish War. In general Albanian historians do not deny that some Albanians occupied Serbian lands (the North–Albanians provenience of many Kosovars is attested by their family names). But they tend to minimize the degree of the colonization, while hinting that, after all, these Albanian immigrants occupied lands once belonging to their Illyrian kin, the Dardanians.

In the first half of the nineteenth century, Kosova was overwhelmingly populated by Albanians, who had also firmly entrenched themselves in the Novipazar region, reaching as far as Niš in the North. It was in Kosova that the nationalist movement for autonomy began. After the Turkish defeat by the Russians in 1878, the Great Powers convened in Berlin to moderate the Russian designs to increase the territories of Russia's protégés with lands carved from Turkish possessions inhabited wholly or in part by Albanians. The Albanians at that time were living in the four *vilayets* (governorships) constituting the greater part of European Turkey. The Vilayet of Shkodër was entirely inhabited by Albanians.[14] The percentage of Albanians in the Vilayet of Kosova was 60 percent in 1910, the rest being Serbs, Bulgarians, and Turks.[15] The Vilayet of Monastir (Bitolje), including Central and part of South Albania, had a typically Balkan population, i.e., it was composed of Albanians, Bulgarians, Greeks, Aromunians, Turks, and Jews, the Albanians having an absolute majority (58 percent in 1910).[16] The Vilayet of Yannina, including part of Southern Albania and Epirus, was inhabited mostly by Albanians (62 percent in 1910), the rest being Greeks, Aromunians, Jews, and Gypsies.[17] The Congress of Berlin assigned parts of the three former vilayets to Montenegro, Serbia, as well as Bulgaria. The cession of the Plavë and Guci (Plava and Gusinje) districts to Montenegro sparked the movement known as the League of Prizren, from the city in Kosova where the Albanian representatives met (1878). Under the leadership of Abdyl Frashëri, a South–Albanian diplomat, the League resolved to create fighting units for the defense of the Albanian territories assigned to the South Slavs. It summoned the Albanians, regardless of regional or confessional differences, to unite for the creation of an autonomous Albania comprising the four vilayets—later called Greater Albania—within the frame of the Ottoman Empire. The autonomy

was restricted to an Albanian administration with Albanian schools
and an Albanian army commanded by Turkish officers. The Turks,
who had at the outset favored the League, reacted against it when
the League opposed a compromise solution, accepted by the Turks,
to barter the Plavë and Guci districts for other North–Albanian districts. The North–Albanians revolted. Turkey jailed the League's
principal leaders and proceeded to disband it.

The Turkish defeat by the Balkan allies in the Balkan wars resulted in the further dismemberment of Ottoman Albania by the vic-
tors. The 1913 Treaty of London recognized an independent Albania
with an area roughly the same as the present one (10,629 square
miles, about the size of the Vilayet of Kosova) and with a population that was less than half of the Albanian population of the four
vilayets (close to two million in 1912). The Conference of Versailles
debated the question whether even this truncated Albania was to exist as an independent state. The greater part of the Yannina Vilayet
went to Greece. To the newly formed Kingdom of Yugoslavia were
assigned the greater part of Kosova, the Albanian territories east of
the Drin River in present–day Macedonia, and the Albanian coastal
zone incorporated by Montenegro after the Congress of Berlin. The
Kosovars rose up in revolt. The Serbian army crushed it.[18]

In the period between the two world wars, the Yugoslav government tried to colonize Kosova with Serbs and Montenegrins, by
legal as well as illegal means. The plan was to clear Kosova of the
Albanians. It failed, though many Kosovar families emigrated to Albania and Turkey. When, during World War II, Yugoslavia collapsed
(1941) and most of the Albanian territories merged with the Italian-
occupied Kingdom of Albania, the Albanians living in those territories
greeted the Italians as liberators. Anti–fascist resistance in Kosova
and the peripheral Albanian regions was consequently weak.[19] After
Yugoslavia's liberation from the Nazi–fascist troops by the Partisans,
reprisals took place against Albanian collaborators as well as individuals who had inflicted vexations on the Slav population. Soon
the reprisals degenerated into a persecution of the Albanian population. The Kosovars rose up in arms. Their insurrection was ruthlessly
crushed by the Partisans. The Autonomous Region of Kosmet was
born by Caesarian section.

This brief excursus on the history of Kosova is not meant to
prove anything. It merely purports to make the reader aware of the
complexity of the Kosova problem. Invoking history does not help to

solve it. History deals with the past, and the past cannot be erased. On the other hand, ignoring history is unwise, for history explains the present and orients it towards the future. To ask when the Serbs occupied Kosova and who was inhabiting it previously is a legitimate historiographical question. But answering such questions will not solve the problems besetting Kosova today. Calling Kosova Serbian because the Serbian nation was born there has its counterpart in calling Kosova Albanian because it was formerly inhabited by primitive Dardanians.[20] A reasonable way to avoid such pitfalls would be to shelve both "*Stara Serbia*" and "Greater Albania." One term is no better than the other. The four vilayets constituting the *Arnautluk* (Albaniandom) of the Ottoman Empire were administrative divisions corresponding to its political system, which was based on religion, not nationality. And to resort to Old Serbia as a counterweight for Greater Albania is to search for allies among conjured phantasms. Both Old Serbia and the Ottoman Empire are gone, and going back to them to prop up political arguments is to play politics with history.

The question is to be reversed. Kosova's location at a juncture where the road joining the Pannonian Basin to the Aegean Sea crosses the old road from the Adriatic to Constantinople makes Kosova a "turn-table" between Belgrade and Salonika on the one hand and Tirana and Sofia on the other.[21] Considering Kosova's rich agricultural and industrial potential, one can surmise that the chances for the province to become a major factor in the Balkans are as bright for the future as they are dark today. The Balkan vocation of Kosova is favored by its unique ambivalent nature as an overwhelmingly Albanian province within the framework of the Yugoslav Federation.

The Albanian leaders have repeatedly declared that Albania has no territorial claims on Kosova. This is not mere rhetoric, considering the important differences in ideology and political system between the two. An attempt by Albania to englobe Kosova would be a suicidal act. Albanian politics has been limited to cultural politics. The adoption in 1968 of the Tosk literary Albanian by the Gheg–speaking Kosovars has paved the way for ideological penetration through export of Tirana–printed textbooks and teaching personnel.[22] Because of Kosova's less advanced level of education, the cultural exchange between Kosova and Albania has been mostly unilateral, to the advantage of the stronger party. It is interesting to note by the way that it was an Italian of Albanian origin who propounded the original Marxist theory that a successful revolution by a subaltern class presupposes its cultural hegemony over the ruling class. That the Yugoslav leaders have permitted the Albanian cultural penetration of Kosova can be seen as a compliment to their accommodating attitude, unmindful of Gramsci's lesson. The state of siege is still in force more than two years after it was instituted.

2. Double Dependence

Dependent on Albania culturally, Kosova has relied heavily on Federal assistance for its troubled economy. The history of the autonomous province, marked as it is by this double dependence, has hardly been autonomous, while being very much provincial. The question is how to get rid of this double dependence, which is the only way for Kosova to obtain the full autonomy it has unsuccessfully pursued until now. The rest of this article will be devoted to reflections on methods for achieving the desired goal. We shall begin with the easier question, how to eliminate cultural dependence.

Here the answer is cultural differentiation. So long as the Kosovars will not differentiate themselves culturally from their Albanian brothers, their chances of obtaining republic status will be minimal. Differentiation does not mean discontinuation of cultural exchange. But the exchange should be, to deserve its name, on a parity basis, with the Kosovars as donors no less than recipients. Of course they should continue to develop their Albanian culture. But their contribution to the latter will be more effective if they elaborate on those national traits that are peculiar or more or less specific to them in fields such as language, folklore, ethnology, and history. Their own variety of Gheg presents distinct phonetic features not found in other Gheg dialects.[23] Their literary tradition goes back to the most important of the earliest Albanian writers, Pjetër Bogdani (1630–1688). A patriot and an erudite, this Catholic bishop produced a model of literary Albanian, a first *koine* of North–Albanian dialects. Elaborating on that literary tradition would free the Kosovars from mimicking a language unsuited to them.[24] Their bilingualism is an asset for studying—not discarding, as they have been doing—the Serbocroatian epic songs sung by Albanian bards.[25] An eminent Kosovar folklorist, Shtjefën Gjeçov, did not eliminate from his Albanian name its Slavic suffix. In the field of history, one expects Kosovar scholars to study in depth the League of Prizren, a capital Kosovar achievement. But Kosovars and peripheral Albanians played a major role in shaping not only modern Albanian history, but also the history of the dying Ottoman

Empire. Ibrahim Temo was a pioneer of the Young Turk movement,[26] which had among its influential members people like Nexhip Draga, Ahmed Nyazi,[27] and Dervish Hima.[28] It was the Kosovar movement of protest against Austrian interference that led to the proclamation of the Constitution which brought the Young Turks to power in July 1908.[29] And when Young Turk nationalism alienated the Albanians, the general insurrection planned by the Albanian leaders began in Kosova. In 1912, Hasan Prishtina, a foremost Kosovar leader, proposed that the Bulgaro–Macedonian leaders join the insurrection and create together an "autonomous Albanian–Macedonian state."[30] Led by him, the Kosovar insurgents gathered in Prishtina in July of that year demanded—and obtained—the dissolution of the Turkish Parliament. The occupation of Skopje (Shkup) by the Kosovar insurgents in August of that same year brought down the Young Turk government.[31] The Kosovar insurrection which paved the way for the victory of the Balkan allies over the Turks during the First Balkan War (October 1912) also created the conditions for the proclamation of Albania's independence (November 1912). Kosova has played a major role in shaping the Balkan map as it stands today to its own disadvantage. It is the responsibility of Kosovar historiography to explain this phenomenon and draw lessons from it.

Considerations such as these suggest that the Kosovars have much to gain by developing their own brand of Albanian culture, adding to it a Balkan dimension. This will make them visible in the European cultural scene. International recognition of their culture will immensely help their cause. Good work has been done in this direction by organizing Albanological seminars and language courses for foreigners at the University of Prishtina. Unfortunately, the same cannot be said for their cultural outreach activities. If the province is not yet sufficiently prepared for instructional exchange with other countries, contacts can be established through their scholarly publications and literature. The information and propaganda services are disorganized. In the United States, for instance, no distribution agency exists for Kosovar publications—Tirana has more than one. Not even the Library of Congress receives all their important publications.[32] To compile a decent bibliography of Kosovar scholarly and literary output, one has to travel to Europe.[33] Sizable Kosovar contingents live in Turkey, the United States, and Australia. They would like to know about what has been achieved in their homeland. Have their cultural needs been met?

When even university students are poorly fed and lodged, one can imagine the plight of the economy in the province. Kosova's social productivity is by far the lowest in the Yugoslav Federation: $795 per capita income compared with $2,635 as the Yugoslav average (1979). Kosova remains a province loosely attached to the rest of the Federation, almost an appendage. The problem of integration has been a main concern of both the provincial and the central government. It has often been pointed out that not all the blame for Kosova's lag rests with the Kosovars. Foreign experts have named Serbocentrism as one main cause. Another major cause is the Federation's policy of discrimination: Until the end of the 1950s, Kosova did not receive financial grants from the Federation like the other undeveloped areas. It has also been noted that lack of expertise diminishes Kosova's negotiating power with Serbia and the other republics. The primacy of basic industry (and thermoelectric), which dates from the period of the centralized economy, has not been seriously questioned, and no alternative has been proposed.[34] In 1944–48, Albania's economic subservience to Yugoslavia, a main factor for the planned annexation of Albania, was mostly a question of economic naïveté on the part of the Albanian leaders. It seems that the Kosovars have not profited from the lesson. They continue to invest in basic industries the funds allocated to Kosova by the Federal Fund for the Development of Undeveloped areas (88 percent for 1966–1970, 66 for 1971–1980).[35] These funds constitute nearly two–thirds of Kosova investments; part of them could be invested elsewhere. But one should know where and how to invest; and adequate cadres to run the economy are lacking. In 1982, the Department of Economics at the University of Prishtina was still at the very bottom of the scale as to the number of students.[36] Of course numbers alone are not a sure criterion for judgment. Yet considering what has been said and will be specified in the following paragraph, one wonders whether quality corresponds to quantity in this case. The bolstering of a nationally respected Department of Economics is an absolute priority for Kosova.

It can be safely stated that economic progress will not be possible until a process of economic education begins, involving large strata of the population. First of all this means determination to change the obsolete agricultural mode of production in the private sector (89.5 percent of arable land producing 75 percent of the total agricultural income).[37] Due to the province's high rate of unemployment (27 percent of Yugoslavia's unemployed, and only 178,000 employed in a

population of more than one and a half million), as well as to the high
rate of demographic growth (26 per 1,000 population compared to 8.6
for the Yugoslav average), the labor force in the private sector has increased about 10 percent from 1948 to 1978—in the rest of Yugoslavia
it has decreased about 16 percent in the same period.[38] The anomaly
is a result of agriculture's absorbing unemployment without substan-
tially adding to productivity. A great deal of human energy which
could be profitably used in industry is thus wasted. But industry itself
has been stagnating. Kosova's industrial output amounts to only 2.2
percent of the total federal output, whereas the province's population
represents 7.8 percent of the total Yugoslav population. The industry
is concentrated in two giant conglomerates. Trepča in Titova Mitrovica combines mining, metallurgy, and chemicals; Kosova in Obilić
uses lignite to generate energy while also producing fertilizers. The
processing industry is represented by a plant for shock absorbers in
Prishtina, another in Uroševac which makes steel tubes, and a third
in Suva Reka producing rubber conveyers. Now basic industry does
not create new jobs as processing industries do. The latter also bring
money, finished goods being an important source of income. Lacking such income, Kosova must resort to aid in the form of Federal
Development Funds. But whereas the underdeveloped republics use
these funds to supplement investment funds generated by their more
industrial establishments, Kosova invests the greater part of the Federal funds in basic industries. True, Kosova's share of those funds
has been proportionately higher than the shares of the undeveloped
republics. The Federation has been generous to its poorest unit. But
generosity in this case turns out to be a form of exploitation. Since
70 percent of Kosova's industry is of the basic type, the profits accrue
to those members of the Federation that use Kosova's minerals and
energy to generate goods and machinery. The Federal Development
Funds are, moreover, subject to repayment, although after a long
term and with minimal interest. Furthermore, the salaries of Kosovar
workers are lower than those of the average Yugoslav worker: $180
per month compared with $235. The situation is similar to that in
semicolonial countries exploited by foreign capital. The analogy becomes obvious if we add to the picture the illiteracy rate in Kosova:
31.5 percent, compared to 15.2 percent in all Yugoslavia.[39]

3. Suggestions

What can be done to remedy this deplorable situation? Expertise in the economic sector is of course a first requisite. Lack of it, however, is not totally the Kosovars' fault. The Kingdom of Yugoslavia did not allow them to have even elementary Albanian schools. Now they have their own university. But do they have enough vocational schools? They have built a modern library in Prishtina, of which they are deservedly proud. But they have long emphasized humanistic education, and now they are short of engineers and technicians. The sooner they acquire expertise in the various economic sectors, the closer they will be to freeing themselves from economic dependence.

But expertise alone will not solve the problem. A transformation of the still medieval mode of production in the countryside is badly needed and, together with it, a change in the Kosovar way of life, governed by traditional mores and outdated customs. The emancipation to be achieved is social no less than economic, and concerns first the still patriarchal family life, in which women are deprived of fundamental rights. They are kept secluded at home when they do not work in the fields, get minimal education, and are totally subordinate to male authority. In extended families, economics permitting, women live in a separate wing of the house. The emancipation of women is the first and foremost task for the Kosovars in achieving full emancipation. A community denying half of its members access to full education can never be a civilized community. It is also imperative that women be admitted to work in factories and plants. By exercising their talents in professions and participating in productive work, they will improve the economy of their families and begin to play a role in social life.

Cultural differentiation and economic expertise coupled with social emancipation will lead to self–determination. Since the Kosovars are the only large non–Slavic ethnic community in the Federation, it is extremely important that ethnic assertiveness not offend the national feelings of other ethnics, and Serbs in particular. The way to avoid trouble is to abide by internationalistic sentiments.

The history of the Balkans in modern times has been a sequence of battles and wars, instigated by immoderate ambitions for domination and fanned by nationalism and outright chauvinism. Differences of language and religious traditions and customs have been overemphasized in order to allow social groups and classes that used nationalism as a smoke screen to satisfy their drive for power and their greed. The victims thereof have invariably been the Balkan peoples, be they Slavs or Greeks, Albanians or Turks. Ethnic and cultural differences exist; they cannot be denied. But there exists something else too, which brings these peoples together: a common layer of culture, the sediment of first Byzantine and then Turkish domination. And underneath that layer lies the abjection of whole populations who suffered from them.

Stressing these cultural and socio–economic elements ought to be a concern for all who care for the future of humanity. In the troubled times in which we live, the globe risks being shattered to pieces by another world war whose main arena will most likely be Europe, just as it was in the two previous world wars. And here Kosova comes into the picture again. For besides being geographically located in the heart of the Balkans, Kosova bridges Yugoslavia and Albania through three limitrophe republics: Montenegro, Serbia, and Macedonia. Administratively a component of the Yugoslav Federation but ethnically a piece of the Albanian homeland to an overwhelming degree, Kosova is in an ideal position to bring the two countries together instead of separating them. The international conjuncture favors an initiative in this direction, Yugoslavia and Albania being the only two Balkan countries not aligned with either of the two military blocs. The declaration of the Albanian leadership that Albania would join Yugoslavia in resisting an invasion gives Kosova's leaders strong leverage for diplomatic moves toward their own goal, the province's geo–political situation lending itself to the role of a catalyst for Balkan integration. Precedents are not lacking.[40] And if Kosova will pledge itself to that worthy pursuit, it will elicit international support. Serbs themselves will be won over to its cause. For if Serbia has produced a Vasa Čubrilović,[41] it has also given birth to people like Dimitrije Tucović.[42] A Yugoslav–Albanian rapprochement would constitute an important factor for shifting the balance of power in the Balkans from the politics of war to those of nonalignment. Countries such as Greece and Romania which have shown fluctuations in their stance as members of their respective blocs could be attracted to the idea of a pact of nonagression signed by the four Balkan countries, a decisive first step for establishing peace in the Balkans.

VIII. HOXHA'S THEORY OF CAUSATIVE ATTRACTION*

The year is 1777, and the action takes place in Crimea. He is the son of the Grand Vizier, she a beautiful rayah. The young prince falls in love with the girl and begins to court her—the citizens begin to gossip. In vain the Grand Vizier tries to dissuade his son from wooing the maiden. In the meantime the Khan of Crimea has discovered that his vizier, during a diplomatic trip to Paris, has paid a secret visit to Diderot. The Khan suspects his vizier to be contaminated by republican ideas. And when he learns that the vizier's son intends to marry the rayah girl, he has the vizier arrested as an agent of the Encyclopédie. The evidence of his high treason: the projected marriage of his son to the despicable rayah. The morganatic marriage would open the door to infiltration of republican and atheistic ideas that will corrupt the youth, thus undermining the Khanate's social and religious order and eventually bringing the abhorrent rayahs to power.

This is not exactly what Hoxha relates in the epilogue of his latest book, *The Titoites. Historical Notes* (1982). In that part of his book, he accuses his Premier, Mehmet Shehu, of having conspired to split the Party of Labour of Albania (PLA) and to kill him. Shehu's plan for splitting the Party was to have one of his sons marry a woman of a declassed family. His plan failed because the Party acted promptly and the engagement was broken off. As a result, Shehu shot himself to death while one of his sons, an engineer, electrocuted himself.[1] Shehu's wife and another of his sons were arrested. Their imprisonment was followed by that of two other Shehu relatives: the

---

* Published in *Telos* 61, Fall 1984, as a review of Enver Hoxha, *The Titoites* (IMLSCC, Tirana, 1982).

former Minister of the Interior and the former Minister of Defense. Later two other ministers as well as other high-ranking officials were arrested.

The story of Shehu's suicide is the subject of the volume's latest chapter, "In Open Struggle with the Titoites." The previous chapters deal with the period 1941–48, i.e., from the foundation of the Communist Party of Albania under the close supervision of the Communist Party of Yugoslavia until the CPA broke loose from the CPY. The last chapter begins with a review of "the thirty-five years that have passed from the time when the Titoite betrayal was publicly denounced and unmasked" (567) and then focuses on the Shehu episode. The volume was apparently already written when Shehu committed suicide (December 17, 1981). A last moment addition, in fact an appendage, the chapter functions as an epilogue.

Yugoslav leaders, Albanian nationalists, and even purged Albanian communists[2] have stated that the CPA is a creation of the CPY. Hoxha begins his work by refuting that thesis. What he writes, however, is unconvincing. Not only was the CPA founded with the leading assistance of the CPY, but it grew and consolidated itself under the elder party's tutorship, to the point of becoming, after Albania's liberation from the Nazi troops, a mere appendage of the CPY. This Hoxha is at pains to admit. Since he was during that period the General Secretary of the Party and the Commander-in-Chief of the Army (and designated Premier of Albania even before the country's liberation), he tries to justify his capitulation by laying the blame on influential comrades in the Political Bureau. He accuses them of plotting to dethrone him. To this end, they became "secret agents" of Tito and his regime, who viewed Hoxha as the main obstacle to their achieving their sinister plan, the annexation of Albania as the seventh republic of the Yugoslav Federation.

The Titoites intends to be a narrative, based on memories and occasional notes, of Hoxha's unrelenting struggle against he Yugoslav representatives in the CPA and the Albanian government, working together with their Albanian "stooges" to enslave Albania under Tito's rule. The list of the Yugoslav representatives is long. It begins with Dušan Mugoša and Miladin Popović, the CPY delegates who were instrumental in founding the CPA while also acting as de facto members of its Central Committee for almost two years. Hoxha admits that at this time the Albanian communists "lacked experience" (17) in organizational matters and suffered from an "inadequate ideo-political level" (335). Yet he denies the Yugoslav's decisive role in the CPA's leadership. Except for Popović, Hoxha's mentor, whom he praises as a real friend of Albania and a true internationalist, all the others were enemies, most of them Great–Serbian chauvinists with an endemic hatred for everything Albanian. Such were Blažo Jovanović, the official Yugoslav delegate at the CC of the PCA, and especially Svetozar Vukmanović–Tempo, Tito's "roving ambassador," intent upon creating a Balkan Federation. Colonel Velimir Stojnić, chief of the Yugoslav Military Mission, organized the first plot against Hoxha at the Party's 2nd Plenum (The Berat Plenum, November 1944). Two Yugoslav representatives after the liberation, the "cunning" "diplomat of Albanian origin" Josip Djerdja and the "ill–famed" Slavo Zlatić, were responsible for the second and major plot, intended to liquidate not only Hoxha but Albania as well. Zlatić was assisted by Sergej Kraigher, the person in charge of operating the "economic union" between the two countries. General Kuprešanin pressed hard on the Albanian military chiefs to let a Yugoslav division be stationed in the Korçë district, allegedly to defend the Albanian border from an impending attack by the Greek army. The move was tantamount to a Yugoslavian military occupation of Albania. At the same time Koča Popović, the Chief of the Yugoslav General Staff, and Vukmanović–Tempo, its Political Director, were eagerly working for the creation of a joint Yugoslav–Albanian military command, thus eliminating Hoxha as Commander–in–Chief of the Albanian army. Backed by Mehmet Shehu, then the Chief of the Albanian General Staff, Hoxha managed to foil the Yugoslav maneuver by writing to Stalin, who disapproved of it. As a result, Hoxha survived, whereas Shehu was dismissed for his "anti–Yugoslavism" (439). This does not preclude Hoxha from branding Shehu, at the end of the volume, as the chief Titoist agent and even an imperialist "superagent," the one who presided over the tripartite—cultural, military, economic-revisionist conspiracy during the period 1973–75. Eventually Shehu tried to liquidate his ally, with whom he had been guiding Albania on the socialist road, first as minister of the Interior (1948–1954) and then as Prime Minister (1954–1981), a period of no less than thirty–three years.

This is the content of the book. The narrative is spiced with anecdotes that add to the portrayal of the characters. Hoxha has a knack for colorful epithets and idiomatic expressions. The Yugoslavs are recipients of a great deal of muckraking, which is principally directed, however, at Albanian opponents and rivals. As rivals Hoxha deigns to consider only three: Sejfulla Malëshova, Nako Spiru, and Koçi Xoxe. But while with the first two Hoxha exercises some restraint (they were, after all, intellectuals like himself), he has utter contempt for the proletarian Xoxe, a "you might say illiterate" (158) tinsmith, "swarthy, short podgy, with bulging eyes like those of a frog" (449)—"his pseudonym was Trashi [the Fat], our ex–quartermaster at [the village of] Panarit" (458). Hoxha calls him, according to the circumstances, a "gawk" (347), a "tragicomic clown" (370), a "plucked rooster" (556), and portrays him "drinking with the Yugoslav comrades until four in the morning [–] but he had lasted to the end like a man and had not disgraced us" (318).

Ismail Kadare has made a name for himself by writing historical novels in which historical truth relates to fiction in the same way as starch to the jelly it helps to solidify. Hoxha does not have to bother even that much about historical truth, he being the one who makes history, and who can therefore act as both writer and underwriter— *vetë shkruaj vetë vulos*, as the Albanian saying goes.

Here is Hoxha's necrology of his longtime friend and collaborator:

From the investigations following the suicide of Mehmet Shehu and from the documents in the possession of the Party, it results that Mehmet Shehu was an agent recruited by the Americans from the time he attended Fultz's school [the American Vocational School] in Tirana[3] [from which he graduated in 1932]. On Fultz's orders, Mehmet Shehu went to study in a military school in Italy, on the orders of the American secret service he was sent to Spain to penetrate into the ranks of the International Brigades. The aim of the American secret service was to provide its agent with the 'aura' of an 'internationalist fighter' so he could be used for long–term aims in Albania later. After the defeat of the anti–fascist war in Spain, Mehmet Shehu went to a refugee camp in France where he stayed for three years, at a time when many of his comrades escaped from it. In the camp he was recruited as an agent of the British Intelligence Service also. He was taken out of the camp by an officer of the German Gestapo and one of the Italian SIM [Italian Secret Service], passed through Italy, where he was held two months and was then handed over in Durrës to the Albanian notorious spy in the pay of the Italian secret service Man Kukaleshi, who released him after twenty days, and

Mehmet Shehu went to Mallakastër and linked up with the organization of our Party there. During the National Liberation War, Mehmet Shehu and his wife Fiqret Sanxhaktari were recruited as agents of the Yugoslavs, too, by Dušan Mugoša. (596–97)

It was Shehu's wife who visited various capitals of Europe to consult CIA representatives about Shehu's plans to physically liquidate Hoxha. Having obtained their approval, Shehu was to have gone about implementing his plan in this way:

In this context Mehmet Shehu arranged the engagement of his son to the daughter of a family in the circle of which there were 6 or 7 war criminals, including the notorious agent of the CIA Arshi Pipa. Such an engagement could not fail to attract the attention of the public. And it was done precisely with the aim of attracting public attention and causing a sensation. If it were accepted by the Party, it would lead to splits and liberalism among others, too, in the party, the Youth Organization, etc. If it were not accepted by the Party, measures would be taken against Mehmet Shehu, not imprisonment, of course, but demotion, removal from his position or even expulsion from the Party. This would cause a sensation and the Yugoslavs would use it, as they needed it for propaganda purposes to discredit the leadership of the Party of Labour of Albania and especially Enver Hoxha, who, as they have repeated over and over again, is 'eliminating' his collaborators, as Stalin did. (624)

Let us now look at the paragraph cited above. Based on an engagement that would naturally lead to marriage, the sentiments of the paragraph are structured around the concept of mixed marriage. The son of a communist leader wedded to the daughter of a declassed family is a case of miscegenation, class here substituting for race. This miscegenation will "lead to splits and liberalism" in the Party. How so? The polluted blood of the bride will first infect that of her husband and then the two together will pollute the Party's collective body, which will eventually fall apart and disintegrate. And the remedy? Quarantine of the whole family and family circle, the *pater familias'* suicide proving that the disease had already affected his brain.

Hoxha's concept of liberalism takes its lead from contagious diseases:[4] plague, leprosy, syphilis. *Syphilis sive morbus gallicus* fits the picture better. A veneral disease, it is usually transmitted through sexual contact, and it decomposes the tissues of the body, eventually reaching the brain. Apparently, waves of the sexual frenzy flooding the West have been washing up on the shores of Albania. A representative work of Albanian literature is much more specific.

In Kadare's novel, *The Great Winter*,[5] the main character, a journalist and a candidate for membership in the Party, is engaged to a girl who is the daughter of a vice–minister. But whereas the young man is a Party hardliner, his fiancée is more interested in buying dresses for the forthcoming wedding and furnishings for the anticipated home. The journalist, who knows Russian well, accompanies, as interpreter, the Albanian delegation, headed by Hoxha, which attends the 1960 meeting in Moscow of the representatives of the communist and workers' parties. It was at that meeting that Hoxha gave the memorable speech that marks the break of Albania with the Soviet Union. The journalist was an eyewitness to what happened. But he dares not say a word before the Political Bureau decides to announce the break. His muteness has deleterious effects on his fiancée, as she suspects that he has become enamored of a Russian girl. Worrying about her daughter's depression, the girl's mother visits the journalist's boss and tells him that her prospective son–in–law intends to break off the engagement. In the meeting of the Party organization that follows, the Party secretary requests an explanation for the journalist's changed attitude toward his fiancée. He refuses angrily, on the grounds that his relation with her is his own business. Since "a communist cannot hide anything from his organization"(358), his application for full membership in the Party is shelved. Meanwhile, his fiancée has taken to drink. In a moment of laxity, she gives herself to her teacher of French, the son of a "declassed" family. Two negative examples in Party ethics on the part of the novel's main characters is too much for socialist realism to take. Kadare saves the situation with a redeeming episode. The novel ends with a chapter in which the journalist's younger brother, a teenager who has been indulging in dating girls as well as attending dancing and drinking parties, is rid of these bourgeois symptoms as he joins the army.

Hoxha's account of the engagement in the epilogue of his book presents striking affinities with the engagement episode in the novel. He must have read Kadare's epic, which is an apotheosis of Hoxha (the episode where the Albanian leader confronts Soviet leaders, inflicting on Khrushchev a stinging defeat, is central to the novel). It was first published in 1973, the year when the Party conducted its offensive against "liberalism" in literature and the arts, which resulted in a sweeping purge. Kadare transfers the novel's temporal frame and cultural habitat to the Khrushchev era.

A reading of *The Great Winter* as a social document portraying the lifestyle of Albanian society at the time the novel was written and rewritten (the revised edition of 1977 appeared after the liquidiation of two more revisionistic trends, one in the army in 1974, and the other in the government's economic sector in 1975) confirms that the "liberalism" Hoxha imputes to Shehu's intentions was a rather widespread phenomenon in the PLA in the seventies. The level-headed Party members must have been turning a deaf ear to the virulent bombast against all sorts of revisionism from the mouth of one who believed himself to be the very incarnation of Marxism–Leninism. Party members who had read Lenin's *Left-Wing communism, an Infantile Disease*, must have realized that Hoxha's ultra-leftism showed symptoms of the polar opposite of infantilism. In this context it seems reasonable to think of Shehu as leading an opposition faction, not for a more liberal policy entailing a weakening of the Party's role, as Hoxha would like us to believe, but for a reactivation of Albania's international politics. The country's total isolation, a phenomenon unique on the globe, in which Albania found herself after the break with China, made imperative a reassessment of its foreign policy. It fell upon Shehu, as head of the Albanian government, to cope with that problem. We do not know how he approached it. What we know is that, in the past, Shehu had been, on a par with Hoxha, champion of an Albanian brand of socialism distinct from all other varieties. The downfall of Koçi Xoxe, marking the end of Yugoslav hegemony in the CPA, was mostly due to Shehu. And he was, in his capacity as Premier of Albania, no less adamant than Hoxha about freeing the country from Soviet control. Yet such evidence, to be found in many a book by Hoxha,[6] does not prevent him from branding Shehu as agent of both the Yugoslav UDB and the Soviet KGB. As the "superagent" he was, Shehu had been able to make a fool of everyone in the Party, including its First Secretary, for a period of almost forty years. The diabolic aim of this former student of Futlz was to liberalize and split the Party, which is tantamount to destroying it, a liberalized and split Marxist–Leninist party necessarily leading to its own demise.[7] Shehu's strategy toward that end was to have one of his sons marry a woman of bourgeois origin and related to war criminals.

The marriage would have led to the *embourgeoisement* of the Party and, as a consequence, to the reinstatement of the class system in socialist Albania.

What is class, according to Marxism? It is a basically economic concept, defined by the possession of the means of production and the human relations resulting therefrom. Capitalism is a social system in which the means of production are owned by a class, the bourgeoisie, which exploits the rest of the society. Socialism abolishes the bourgeois system by expropriating capitalists and constituting itself into a proletarian state in the form of a dictatorship. This has in fact occurred in Albania, where the means of production are owned and supervised by a state that is entirely controlled by the Party. Such being the situation, does it make sense to maintain, as Hoxha does, that an engagement can become a propellant for reversing a historical process that has long since taken place? It is more than a third of a century since the Party wiped out all possible opposition from the privileged classes and groups of old. These people may well resent the Party for having expropriated and humiliated them. Yet in the 99.99 percent police state that is Albania today (as measured by poll statistics), they cannot even express their resentment, except perhaps in their dreams. Raising the ghost of their return to power will fool no one. For ever since they were liquidated, the only opponents have been dissident Party members. The splits in the Party have all occurred because of a power struggle among Party leaders. The official *History of the Party of Labour of Albania* presents that power struggle in the guise of ideological conflicts between Hoxha's pure Marxism–Leninism and the deviationism–revisionism of his opponents. Yet nowhere in that text, which could not have been written without the approval of the First Secretary of the Party, does one come across a single case in which family relations concerning Party leaders caused crises such as the one Hoxha portrays in his book. His argument is indeed an offense to the Party. For only a rotten party can be split by an engagement, albeit the engagement of a communist prince to a modern Cinderella. Hoxha's saying qualifies for a collection of proverbial jokes.

The French edition of the *History of the Party of Labour of Albania* contains a chapter on Hoxha as a theoretician of Marxism. The authors analyze various revisionistic outgrowths—Titoism, Soviet social–imperialism, Maoism, Eurocommunism—as described by Hoxha in his works. Yet Hoxha never defines his own brand of social-

ism, except negatively, i.e., by rejecting all other existing variants.
He lumps them together under the common denominator of revisionism, while remaining silent about his own revisionism for good
reason: his isolationist and utterly nationalistic Marxism–Leninism
is in flagrant contradiction to two main tenets of Marxism, socialist
solidarity and proletarian internationalism. He was in the process of
writing *The Titoites* when the French edition of the *History of the
Party* appeared.[8] I shall supply my own analysis of Hoxha's latest
work, limiting myself to its epilogue.

Hoxha has enriched Marxism–Leninism with a very modern theory, which smacks of Fourier (his theory of attraction) as well as of the
American practice of advertising. The author's thesis is that Shehu
wanted to split and liberalize the Party by having his son marry a
woman of a declassed family related to war criminals. Shehu's first
move was to "arrange" their engagement, which was bound to "cause
a sensation." And this, in turn, "would lead to splits and liberalism"
in the Party, if accepted by it. If not, Shehu's political career would
be doomed. But this would still "cause a sensation," which the Yugoslavs would then use to discredit the PLA and especially Hoxha for
his Stalinist methods.

The either/or argument revolves around the concept of sensation.
If Shehu succeeded, this would be because of his ability to "attract
the attention of the public" by means of an engagement "causing a
sensation." If he failed, this would be because of the Party's acting
to forestall his planned sensation, leaving him with the surrogate satisfaction of seeing his failure made into a sensation by his patrons.
Sensation works both ways with a conceptual frame that can be described as causative attraction. In the first alternative, we are faced
with a chain reaction set in motion by an engagement endowed with
magic. The chain is composed of several links: engagement attracting public attention causing sensation leading to Party splits involving
liberalism resulting in Party liquidation. Is the reader getting dizzy
from the chain reaction? Let me explain how the theory works in
practice.

A handsome young couple is naturally attractive, though not
necessarily sensational. "To attract the attention of the public," the
couple needs a striking setting. A picture advertising a new brand of
car with a young couple in bathing suits can serve as an illustration.
Such a picture per se is not particularly striking and can hardly "cause
a sensation." For the latter to occur, the persons in the picture must

be unusual: he should be a well-known public figure, she a beauty queen. Now, have this picture published in a prestigious magazine. It will certainly cause a sensation and many people will rush to buy the car. This, of course, is capitalist practice. Hoxha is applying to the PLA a capitalist pattern, which he traces back to Shehu's capitalist mind. Shehu's stratagem to have his son marry a woman carrying in her blood the degenerate genes of war criminals become U. S. citizens bears, of course, a CIA stamp. The moment a picture of the newlyweds appeared in Albanian magazines (Shehu would see to that) the radiance of the couple would reflect upon him, thus bringing to an end Hoxha's long monopoly as a public and publicity figure.[9] The newspapers and magazines of the capitalist world, including, of course, Yugoslavia, would widely publicize the picture, thus helping their agent obfuscate the figure of his rival.

The trouble with Hoxha's theoretical jewel is that it contradicts the narrative in which it is set. He does not tell us when the engagement took place and when it was broken off. But even if it did not last long, due to the prompt intervention of the Party, it occurred anyway. The question arises: How is it that such a sensational event was not even mentioned in the capitalist press, which thrives, as is well known, on sensations? Hoxha himself tells us that "Shehu arranged the engagement . . . with the aim of attracting public attention and causing a sensation." If so, one would expect Shehu to have communicated the sensational news to his patrons, the CIA and the UDB, which would have been only too glad to spread it. The news could have been easily transmitted by Shehu's wife, Fiqret Shehu, who, Hoxha writes, consulted various CIA representatives during her European trip. He also writes that Feçor Shehu, Minister of the Interior, was in close touch with the Yugoslav Embassy in Tirana. Was it not in the interest of the Yugoslavs to let the world know that Hoxha and Shehu had clashed on a question directly regarding Shehu's family? Hoxha himself states that the Yugoslavs "would use" the sensational news of Shehu's political disgrace, "as they needed it for their propaganda purposes to discredit the leadership of the Party of Labour of Albania and especially Enver Hoxha." In the same way they would, one thinks, use the split caused by the engagement, featuring, say, a soap opera on the wranglings in the Politburo about such a paramount ideological issue.

If anything stands out clearly in what Hoxha tells us in his narrative, it is the exact opposite of what he writes, i.e., that Shehu

did not want to attract public attention and cause a sensation. It
is Hoxha himself who, with a spectacular piece of news about a plot
against him under the cover of a romantic engagement, has managed
to attract public attention and cause a sensation through reports in
the international press.

What the author has to say in his memoirs is certainly more
credible as fiction. Perhaps he should write fiction to be credible at
all. From memoirs such as this to historical novels such as Kadare's
the distance is small. Yet Hoxha's real vocation seems to be writing
detective stories. The epilogue in question reads well as such; witness
the following excerpts (625–27):

> On the eve of the meeting of the Political Bureau, at which
> the grave political mistake [the engagement] was to be dis-
> cussed, the Yugoslav Embassy in Tirana, acting on orders
> which it had received from Belgrade, sent its agent and con-
> tact man Feçor Shehu to transmit the "ultimatum" of the
> UDB that "Enver Hoxha must be killed at all costs, even
> in the meeting, even if Mehmet Shehu himself is killed."
> So hard–pressured were the UDB, the Great–Serbian and
> Titoite clique with the situation in Kosova, so gloomy seemed
> the future, that they decided to "destroy" their trump card,
> their superagent, provided only that something spectacular
> would occur which would "shake socialist Albania and the
> Party of Labour of Albania to their foundations"! At ten
> o'clock that night, on December 16, 1981, Feçor Shehu went
> to Mehmet Shehu's home and transmitted the order of their
> secret center. On December 17, the discussion commenced
> in the meeting of the Political Bureau. All comrades, old and
> new, took part in the discussion, and resolutely condemned
> Mehmet Shehu's act of engaging his son to a girl in whose
> family there were 6 or 7 war criminals. . . . At the end
> of the discussion of the first day, I said to Mehmet Shehu:
> "Reflect deeply all night and tomorrow tell us in the Polit-
> ical Bureau from what motives you have proceeded. Your
> alibi for the engagement does not hold water, something
> else has impelled you to this reprehensible act." What I
> said alarmed Mehmet Shehu, he suspected that the crime
> he was preparing might have been discovered. . . . Appar-
> ently he judged matters in this way: "I am as good as dead,
> the best thing is to save what I can," and decided to act

like his friend Nako Spiru, to kill himself, thinking that the
Party would bury this 'statesman,' this 'legendary leader,'
this 'partisan and fighter in Spain' with honours. . . . Together with his wife he flushed the poison down the WC. .
. . Fiqret Shehu, as the agent she was (she who trembled
and wept over nothing), agreed to the suicide of her husband cooly and cynically, provided only that their 'historic'
past and she and her sons were saved. However, they had
reckoned their account without the innkeeper. As soon as
they informed me about Mehmet Shehu's final act, within
moments I proposed that his suicide be condemned, that he
had acted as an enemy, and the Political Bureau expressed
it unanimous condemnation of the act of this enemy. . . .
He was buried like a dog.[10]

I shall spare the reader comments on this diatribe, the language
of a mind run amok with insatiable revenge. A trial following the un-
precedented purge might reveal more details such as those just read,
but not the truth of what happened. The bolshevik leaders who
were publicly tried by Stalin in the thirties confessed to having been
traitors to the Party and even agents of imperialist countries. They
did so to spare themselves further torture and to save their families.
Saving her sons is a phrase Hoxha attributes to Fiqret Shehu in the
cited excerpts. Family ties continue to be strong in socialist Albania, despite the Party's efforts to have family cohesion superseded
by Party loyalty. Because of family ties, when a person commits a
Party crime, his or her family shares the consequences. The sins of
the fathers are visited on their children, as in biblical times. Persecution that reaches this point takes on a tribal character, similar to
the vendetta once practiced by North–Albanian tribes. First exercised against reactionary and declassed families, revenge, grown into
a habit, shifts over to comrades and their families. A case in point is
Hoxha's revenge against Shehu. The dictator's rage does not stop at
his target, but from an individual extends to his family and from his
family to his kinfolk, constrictor–like. Such emphasis laid on kinship
in matters regarding the Party degrades the latter—one is reminded
of Engels' words about "the decisive role that kinship plays in the
social order of all peoples in the state of savagery and barbarism."[11]

One must add, to be fair to savages and barbarians, that their
vendetta is less cruel by far than a Stalinist vendetta. They kill,
but they do not torture. In a Stalinist regime, invidious revenge

tends to nestle in that sector of the Party which performs police functions, the Security apparatus. When Albania recovered its independence, the dreaded Albanian Security became the fief of Koçi Xoxe, Organizational Secretary of the Party and Minister of the Interior. After Xoxe's demise, the Minister of the Interior became Mehmet Shehu. Under his leadership, the Security apparatus was instrumental in ruthlessly enforcing the Party's collectivization policy. When Shehu moved to the Premiership, the previous position was assumed by Kadri Hazbiu, his brother-in-law. And when Hazbiu became Minister of Defense, the key position was occupeid by Feçor Shehu, Mehmet's nephew. Now, in record time, the clan has been purged by methods similar to those used by Stalin. Hoxha eliminated Malëshova in alliance with Xoxe, and sold out Spiru to Xoxe when the later controlled the Party, demanding Spiru's head. And when the break between Yugoslavia and the Soviet Union occurred, Hoxha allied himself with Shehu to purge Xoxe. The subsequent Party purges were carried out for Hoxha by Shehu, and later by Shehu's man, Hazbiu. Now the eliminators have been eliminated: the "innkeeper" need no longer fear a rival, Albania is all his, he shares power with none. Just like Stalin.

From 1948, when Xoxe fell from power, until 1982, when Hoxha clashed with Shehu, the two together ruled socialist Albania. But, whereas Shehu concentrated his efforts on consolidating his grip on the state machinery through the Security network, the more clever Hoxha devoted his energies to building a cult around his person. He achieved that aim through his charisma, his oratorial skill, his French manners, and, last but not least, his photogenic looks. Opportunistic and servile writers and artists helped create a halo around his figure. In his old age, he has produced a corpus of literary works in which he appears as a historian of the PLA, a memorialist, and chief ideologist of Albanian Marxism–Leninism. His ambition is to secure a seat in the Pantheon of Marxism–Leninism, alongside Stalin and Mao. He certainly will be remembered, and not only for his theory of causative attraction.

IX. HOXHA'S HERITAGE*

There has been widespread speculation as to whether, now that Enver Hoxha is dead, Albanian politics will move away from the orthodox Stalinism which has long been its chief characteristic.[1] Will an Albanian Khrushchev arise to bury the Hoxha myth? And if so, will this person be Ramiz Alia (the new party leader) himself, or somebody else? Will the change, if it comes, be sudden and explosive, or will it proceed slowly and without convulsions? Will it be superficial or affect the regime's very substance?

Everybody seems to believe that, whatever happens, the country's isolation must end. In that case, the options would be: to rejoin the Warsaw Pact, thus reentering the Soviet orbit of influence; to open simultaneously to both East and West, in alignment with Third World countries (which could entail a certain rapprochement with Yugoslavia and/or China); or to open to the West only. No such clear choice, however, would allow the Party of Labour of Albania (PLA) to remain unchanged. A new leadership would have to emerge—accompanied, as is usual in such cases, by a major purge. Minor purges may also occur as a consequence of less radical changes. So the question of evolution of the Albanian leadership is necessarily at the center of any discussion of the perspectives facing the country.

In other words, to answer the questions adumbrated above with some measure of conviction presupposes an understanding of the political, economic, and cultural situation created in the country by an authoritarian regime long dominated by the personality of Hoxha, the chief ideologist and artifex of Albanian–style socialism. Always very

---

* Published in *Labour Focus on Eastern Europe*, vol. 8, no. 2, May 1986, as an abridged version of "Ueber die Zukunft des albanischen Sozialismus," *Gegenstimmen* 21/6, Fall 1985.

great, his control became absolute after the sweeping purges of the seventies, which (in relative terms) compare in scope with Stalin's in the thirties. Like Stalin, Hoxha was able to eliminate, one after the other, all his real or potential rivals. The history of the PLA is thus marked by continuous and, in part, bloody purges. Whether a change in orientation will occur in the near future depends, ultimately, on whether the Stalinist carapace of the Party cracks under pressure from anti–Stalinist elements. A summary survey of Party purges will provide a point of departure for assessing the extent and depth of Hoxha's Stalinist legacy.

1. Through the Prism of the Purges

Initially tutored and organized by the Communist Party of Yugoslavia, the Communist Party of Albania (predecessor of the PLA) was reared in the Stalinist mold. But in 1948 the CPY broke with Moscow, whereas the CPA's relations with Stalin by contrast acquired a new dimension. Just prior to the Yugoslav–Soviet split, Mehmet Shehu had lost his position as Chief of the General Staff of the Albanian Army and Hoxha's own position as Party Secretary had become precarious: Albania had, in fact, appeared to be on the verge of joining Yugoslavia as the seventh republic of the federation. So when in 1948 Stalin accused the Yugoslav leadership of deviationism, Hoxha and Shehu seized the opportunity to denounce Albania's alliance with Yugoslavia and return to power. They managed to purge and then liquidate the pro–Yugoslav faction, with support from the Soviet Union and Stalin—who was impressed with their anti–Titoite zeal. He calmed their fears by guaranteeing the independence of Albania from Yugoslavia, as well as Albania's contested southern frontier with Greece.

These events made the Party leadership devotees of Stalin. When, after the latter's death, Khrushchev made his secret speech criticizing Stalin and his tradition, the Albanian leadership found themselves exposed to a similar critique within their own party. Khrushchev's attempt to bring Yugoslavia back into the Soviet bloc, moreover, was seen by Hoxha and Shehu as implying the removal of Soviet support for their continued leadership. So, taking advantage this time of the growing rift between the Soviet Union and China, they sided with the latter and branded the former as revisionist. A fresh purge of the Party followed.

A third wave of purges took place in the mid–seventies, when China established diplomatic links with the United States. Once again, a change in the external environment became the occasion for striking at the internal 'enemy': at all those who might now hope for a liberalization of cultural, political, or economic life and look forward to a more flexible foreign policy. The purges struck the 'liberal' intelligentsia and the leadership of the Youth Organization, followed by the Ministry of Defense and the General Staff of the Armed Forces (who were showing signs of reluctance to break with the country's one strong ally and military supplier). They went on to engulf those in charge of economic planning and industry, who—faced with economic problems growing out of a rigid policy of economic centralization—had experimented with methods of partial decentralization, thus making themselves liable to the charge of pro–Yugoslav deviationism.

In all these purges, lasting from 1973 to 1976, Shehu faithfully supported Hoxha. Yet they fatally weakened his position as Premier, involving as they did the dismissal of his cabinet colleagues one after another. Shehu's turn came only years later, in 1981. During the last years of his dictatorship, Hoxha saw new purges clean out the last governmental sectors that had so far escaped his wrath: the Ministries of the Interior and Foreign Affairs. Exactly how and why Shehu was eliminated remains a mystery; with his departure, however, the whole Party and state leadership was overhauled, with Hoxha now as the sole survivor from the old communist core.

2. Albanian Stalinism

Hoxha studiously copied Stalin in building up his dictatorship, with the difference that his rejection of all existing socialisms—which entailed total isolation for Albania—came at the very time when polycentrism began to flourish in the communist world. The method of using sweeping purges to establish an undisputed personal rule is particularly akin to Stalin's practice. Hoxha also emulated his master—this was a logical consequence—by writing a series of books aimed at establishing his own brand of 'Marxism–Leninism' as against all others.

All other forms of existing socialism were denounced in the name of the Albanian—i.e., Hoxha's—road to socialism. Only by purging dissident Party members—even more dangerous than the class enemy—could the Albanian Party become a model of this 'Marxism–Leninism.' And, while strenuously preaching socialist internationalism, Hoxha in fact severed all ties with it. *The History of the Party of Labour of Albania*, written under his close supervision, served the same function as the *History of the Communist Party of the USSR (Bolshevik)*—to provide the first atheistic state in the world with a New Testament.

In his *Philosophy of History*, Hegel defines as "historic individuals" those "whose particular aim involves those large issues which are the will of the World Mind." These people, Hegel adds, may be cruel at times, may trample down and crush their opponents. But, even in doing so, they have insight into the requirements of the time and strive to actualize them. They have, in other words, a sense of history. Could it be said that Hoxha had this sense of history? Did he try, in Marx's elaboration of Hegel's postulate, to answer questions that were raised because they could be solved? Has Hoxha's brand of socialism responded to the Albanian people's real needs?

3. Balkan Context and Albanian Specificity

Albanian socialism can be seen as the outcome of a combination of factors, in part common to all Balkan nations and in part peculiar to Albania. Among the common Balkan factors, two are especially important: the backward agrarian condition and the Byzantine–Ottoman heritage. We shall confine ourselves here, however, to the factors proper to Albania: the last Balkan country to achieve independence and the only Balkan country with a majority Moslem population.

With Orthodox and Catholics constituting one-third of the population and the rest subdivided into two Moslem faiths (Sunni and Bektashi), Albania has been a country of four religons inhabited by a population that remains 'pagan at heart.' This judgment of Fan Noli, an Orthodox bishop and former Prime Minister of Albania, is somewhat exaggerated; it is true, however, in the sense that the Albanians have always identified with their language rather than with a religion or state, as was the case with other Balkan nations. Religious differences were played down in the name of a common ethnicity—as expressed in the old slogan of Albanian nationalism that the favored religion of the Albanians is Albaniandom (a slogan that long survived the achievement of national independence, when it was re-adapted as the slogan of the mass media under Hoxha). Nationalism, which keeps the past alive, is thus one fundamental trait of Hoxha's brand of socialism.

The fact that Albania was the last Balkan nation to achieve independence is no less relevant for understanding Hoxha's heritage. Except for the short period 1920–24, during which Albania began functioning as a properly independent state, the country has never had a democratic regime allowing for the existence of more than one political party. The diversifying function of political parties had traditionally devolved on tribes, clans, and extended families, with nepotism as one of its main characteristics. This feature of the old pre–capitalist society remained a pillar of Hoxha's regime.

In the past, Albanian politics had been dominated by powerful feudal and tribal chiefs, men such as Esad Toptani, Ahmet Zogu ('King Zog'), or Shefqet Vërlaci. Enver Hoxha and Mehmet Shehu are their modern equivalents, with Party members playing the role of old retainers. The way Shehu terrorized the population from his fortress of the Security apparatus, first personally and then through members of his clan, is strikingly reminiscent of the manner in which an Ottoman lord treated his bonded peasantry. It was by such means, for example, that the Party leaders achieved the collectivization of the land.

As for Hoxha, he treated the Party as his fiefdom, shuffling and reshuffling the Central Committee and the Politburo like a pack of cards. A shrewd gambler and broker, he was one of the most unprincipled politicians of his time—albeit *principialnost* was a favorite word on his lips. Hoxha's rule, based on an absolute and exclusive monopoly of power, is yet another relic of the Albanian past, diverging increasingly from the aspirations and needs of the Albanian population as a whole.

4. The Balance Sheet

As the only interpreter of Marxism, monopolizing indeed the formulation of ideology in general, Hoxha was decisive in producing a cultural atmosphere totally dominated by a doctrinaire propaganda exalting nationalism. Linguistics, literature, history, geography, folklore, and ethnology have been cultivated, not only to give the people a sense of their own past, but also to spread and inculcate xenophobia, slavophobia, isolationism, ethnic compactness, and linguistic uniformity. The result has been a systematic falsification of history and of historical materialism.

Forty years of uninterrupted Stalinism have left scars on almost every aspect of Albanian life and culture. Albanian art is crudely

primitive (with the occasional exception of music); Albanian literature has remained with the prison-house of socialist realism; economics has been reduced to a 'science' of increasing percentages.
When Albanian leaders proudly declare that their economic growth
is due only to Albania's own efforts, and that Albania does not owe
a penny to anybody, this is simply not true: every time Albania has
shifted allegiance from one country to another, it has automatically
written off all debts to its former ally—the debt to China alone has
been calculated as amounting to $5 billion.[2]

This is not to argue that Hoxha's record has been completely
negative. There have been achievements in agriculture and industry;
diseases are under control; the social status of women has greatly improved; illiteracy has nearly disappeared. The question is whether it
was necessary to pay such a high price. When the Albanian leadership
tells the workers that exploitation does not exist in Albania because
the Albanian state is not a capitalist state, they circumvent the real
question of who controls the Party and the state—the question of
people's self-determination.

5. Prospects

What now that Hoxha has gone? It would seem that his image
is being allowed to fade, just like Stalin's at first. Hoxha killed and
persecuted many old comrades, including the old proletarian core of
the Party; he segregated the country from the world and from other
socialist states; he has left behind a highly embarrassing version of
'Marxism–Leninism.' But he was for too long the embodiment of the
Albanian Party of Labour for the Party simply to abandon him to
his deserved fate. Those who are now in power were, after all, his
disciples—and many have vested interests to protect.

Yet, however successful the purges in the past may have been,
it was surely impossible to purge all dissidents. It is conceivable,
moreover, that the process of rehabilitation of individuals may occur
in the relatively near future, which would signify the beginning of the
end of Albanian Stalinism. But the barometer of Albanian politics
has always been its attitude toward Yugoslavia. Hoxha and Shehu
assumed power in 1948, after a break with Yugoslavia. They broke
with the Soviet Union after Khrushchev tried to win Tito back into
the Soviet bloc (1961). They consummated the rupture with China
after Tito visited Peking (1977). The split between Hoxha and Shehu
followed upon the mass demonstrations of Kosova Albanians in 1981.

Yugoslavia has been a useful scapegoat: if the anti–Yugoslav attitude of Tirana were to change, that would be a strong sign that Albania is moving away from Stalinism.[3]

But where to? It cannot move towards the Soviet Union: the Albanian pro–Soviet faction was never strong (which is why its purge was a relatively minor affair). Nor will it move towards China—the alliance with China was the by–product of very special circumstances. It is unlikely to move towards the United States. It is also true that socialism has survived in Albania despite its terrorism; the Albanians have shown it a degree of forbearance they never extended to any other regime in the past. The question is whether Albanian socialism will be able to redeem itself.

X.   A BOOK ON HOXHA*

The work consists of selections from Hoxha's six books of memoirs: *Albania Challenges Khrushchev Revisionism* (1976), *Imperialism and Revolution* (1979, 2nd rev. ed.), *With Stalin* (1979), *Reflections on China* (2 vols., 1979), *Eurocommunism is Anti-Communism* (1980), and *The Anglo-American Threat to Albania* (1982). It has six chapters, the first of which is concerned with Hoxha's memoirs of the situation in Albania after the country's occupation by Italy (April 7, 1939); the last chapter contains Hoxha's comments on the mysterious death of Mehmet Shehu, the Albanian Premier (December 1981). Editorial explanatory notes (in smaller type) preceding excerpts, or inserted among them, provide chronological continuity and some unity to the selections "dealing almost exclusively with external relations" (Editor's Introduction). The introduction (pp. 1–17) also discusses briefly a few important internal problems, such as the economy, the position of women, and religion, which are not considered in any depth in the six books in question, because Hoxha's motivation for writing them was his ambition to imitate—one can say ape—the greatest exponents of Marxism as authors. The work includes a chronology of major political events, two appendixes (one on the Kosova question), biographical notes, and an index of mostly geographical and proper nouns.

1. Brutal Monster

The editor's judgment on Hoxha, developed in his introduction,

_____
* Published in *Labour Focus on Eastern Europe*, vol. 9, no. 1, March–June 1987, as "Hoxha, the 'Artful Albanian,' " a review of *The Artful Albanian: The Memoirs of Enver Hoxha*, ed. Jon Halliday (Chatto & Windus, London, 1986).

is found in a nutshell in the book's title, "artful" meaning both 'ingenious' and 'tricky.' The ambivalence of the term is varied in a series of oppositional pairs. Hoxha "writes about his enemies as real people even when the framework is that of a fairy tale," discusses "his own cult in a way that is <u>partly</u> disingenuous but also partly reflects the real situation," "applies blatant double standards" (twice), "combines his intelligence and power of observation with brutal frankness," "is both <u>unusually</u> frank and mendacious." His trickery is illustrated by many an example: He avails himself of "self–serving bombast and evasion," his "alleged ideological purity . . . serves as a convenient cloak for nationalism," he "fails to give due recognition to the sizeable sums of aid" given by the three communist countries that were Albania's allies, his "claim to have kept notes throughout his career" is dubious for the war period, and "there are gaps of up to nine months" in his *Reflections on China.* The author also praises Hoxha's ingenuity: his "power of observation" is "shrewd," he has an appreciation of "genuine love," excels the "crashingly boring" leaders of East European countries, is "far too intelligent" to be compared to "most other Third World leaders," is "well read," and "the range of reference in his memoirs is not what one would expect from a Balkan ex–Muslim Stalinist." Hoxha "was not just 'quite' cultured, he was very cultured."

The "artful" of the title could thus be read as "ingenious in trickery." Yet Halliday dwells on another aspect of Hoxha's character, his 'brutality.' "He shared Stalin's quality of brutality . . .," "almost delighting in his own brutality." "Hoxha's path to power, and <u>in</u> power, was littered with the corpses of his old foes, and his old friends." "Hoxha's brutality is reflected in the curious combination in his invective . . . a rather colloquial and even lively invective of Albanian tradition, and grafted on the top of this (like his Marxism–Leninism) the vicious but much stodgier tradition of Vyshinsky and the ritual communist–type denunciation of enemies."

The reader could ask at this point whether or not "stodgy" and "vicious" brutality can be reconciled with "far too intelligent" and "very cultured." The answer is suggested by the author's quoting (approvingly, it seems) a sentence in Khrushchev's memoirs, in which he called Hoxha and his then top colleagues, Shehu and Balluku, "worse than beasts—they're monsters." Halliday cites proof of Hoxha's brutality. Liri Gega, a former Politburo member, was "shot while pregnant" as a Yugoslav agent. Liri Belishova, another Politburo member and Nako Spiru's widow (he reportedly committed suicide) "was apparently strangled" because of her pro–Soviet stance. A passage from Hoxha's *Albania Challenges Khrushchev Revisionism* spells out Hoxha's "vicious" brutality. It is about General Panajot Plaku, who escaped to Yugoslavia to avoid the fate of Liri Gega and her husband, General Dali Ndreu:

> "He is a traitor," I said, "and if you accept him in your country we shall break off our friendship with you. If you admit him you must hand him over to us to hang him publicly."
>
> "You are like Stalin who killed people," said Khrushchev.
>
> 'Stalin killed traitors, and we kill them, too," I added. (206)

According to Webster's Third International Dictionary, a monster is "a legendary animal usually of great size and ferocity that has a form either partly brute and partly human, or compounded of elements from several brute forms." Since intelligence and culture are human attributes but brutality a characteristic of brutes, Hoxha would fit the former alternative. In other words, he is the modern incarnation of Machiavaelli's centaur.

2. Bohemian Intellectual

Halliday's title is thus euphemistic. What is meant is 'the Albanian monster,' more precisely, 'the handsome Albanian monster,' Hoxha being "very handsome, and very charming—to both women and men." Handsome indeed he was, and elegant, too, even in his military uniform, with his cap slightly tilted to one side. His civilian dress was impeccable, his trousers well–creased, his gilet showing under his jacket, and his Borsalino hat (the Italian variety of fedora) over his well–groomed head. Leigh White, an American correspondent who talked to Hoxha in the Fall of 1945, when diplomatic relations between Albania and the United States had not yet been broken, describes him as follows: "He is a large, ungainly man, with broad hips, narrow shoulders, and deceptively soft brown eyes. If he were not so fat, and if his body were more masculine, he would be extremely handsome" (*Balkan Caesar*, 1951, pp. 160–61). At the time Hoxha was indeed somewhat fat. Yet the correspondent exaggerates in portraying him as effeminate, perhaps because he was unfavorably impressed by his "well–manicured hands" (*ibid.*, p. 162).

Habits such as these could be (and have been) attributed to his French education. One must also consider that Hoxha joined commu-

nism later than other comrades, when he was past thirty. Until then
his life had been that of a middle–class bohemian intellectual. Having graduated from the French Lyceum of Korça, he obtained a state
scholarship to study natural sciences at Montpellier. He was there
from Fall 1930 to March 1934, according to the official Albanian Encyclopedic Dictionary (1985). Having lost his scholarship, probably
for not being in good academic standing, he goes to Paris, where he
lives on random jobs, "attends lectures at the Law School . . . and
establishes ties with the organ of the Central Committee of the French
Communist Party, *L'Humanité*." The official Albanian Encyclopedic
Dictionary has no words for Hoxha's alleged articles in *L'Humanité*.
How did this myth, routinely repeated (also by Halliday) come about?
Leigh White speaks of "articles attacking King Zog's government in
the radical Franco–Belgian press" (*Balkan Caesar*, p. 163). He could
not possibly have invented what he writes; he must have heard it from
Hoxha, one presumes. Then Hoxha moved from Paris to Brussels,
where he worked "as the only employee of the Albanian Consulate
in Belgium" (AED) (Halliday: "as private secretary to the Albanian
consul there"). He was fired from his job because of his "revolutionary
viewpoints" (AED). From the same source we learn that, upon his
return to Albania, Hoxha was first hired as "a temporary instructor"
of French and the Tirana Gymnasium, and then appointed as "professor" (read 'instructor') of French at the Korçë Lyceum. It is hard
to believe that a person fired as a "revolutionary" by the Albanian
government in the Spring 1936 could be hired as a regular teacher
in April 1937 in Korçë, then a hotbed of communist activity. These
were the years when the Minister of the Interior was Musa Juka, a
person most devoted to the King. It was he who "in November 1936
. . . organized the brutal persecution of communists and all progressive elements" (*History of the Party of Labour of Albania*, 1982, p.
37). Hoxha was not among the arrested. These were also the years
when civil war was raging in Spain, and quite a few Albanian communists were fighting in the International Brigades. One of them was
Mehmet Shehu, later Hoxha's collaborator and friend, and Premier of
Albania for no less than twenty–seven years, until he was pushed to
commit suicide when Hoxha accused him of being a traitor to the nation and an imperialist superagent. Shehu was no better than Hoxha
as a 'monster' of cruelty, to use Khrushchev's term. Yet, at about
the same time when Shehu was fighting fascism in Spain and later a
prisoner in a French concentration camp, Hoxha was teaching French

in King Zog's Albania. And perhaps it is not inopportune to add here
a note that tells the kind of teacher he was. A student of his at the
time, now a physician in the United States, has told me that during
examinations Hoxha would stand upon his desk to make sure that his
students did not cheat.

Halliday remarks that "enjoying invective," as he did, is "a dan-
gerous and common trait among middle–class intellectual Marxists."
To Stalin Hoxha was a downright "petit–bourgeois" (Milovan Djilas,
Conversations with Stalin, 1962, p. 146).

The second point I should like to make is what sort of Marxist
intellectual Hoxha was. He did not graduate from the University of
Montpellier, where he lived for more than three years–more then the
usual period of time needed for obtaining a *licence*. The official AED
does not say that he lost his scholarship because he wrote articles
against King Zog. And once back in Albania, there are no signs that
he wrote any articles in the progressive or left–oriented journals of the
time. As Secretary General of the Party (1941–1985) and Premier
(1944–1954), he had to present reports to the Central Committee
and the Party Congresses, to deliver speeches in political meetings
and cultural conventions, and occasionally to write articles in the
Party journals and newspapers. His collected works, which began to
be published in 1968 (46 volumes up until 1985), is a collection of this
kind of stuff. His first 'theoretical' work, *Imperialism and Revolution*
(1979), appeared ten years later; Hoxha was then seventy. The work,
considered as his 'theoretical' masterpiece, contains passages such as
the following:

> When we saw that the Cultural Revolution was not being
> led by the party but was a chaotic outburst following a call
> issued by Mao Tsetung, this did not seem to us to be a
> revolutionary stand. (390)

> Our party supported the Cultural Revolution because
> the victories of the revolution in China were in danger. (392)

> Of course, this Cultural Revolution was a hoax. (*ibid.*)

The work, a potpourri of 'theoretical' banalities, journalistic
clichés, and vituperative language, teems with double–dealings and
contradictions such as the one just quoted. In *The Titoites* (1982), his
'literary' masterpiece, he tells an amusing story. During the talks with
Yugoslav experts about the Yugoslav–Albanian Economic Convention, which included the equalization of the currencies, Nako Spiru,

the Albanian Minister of the Economy, found himself stranded, and called on Hoxha for help. Hoxha confesses—one of his few concessions to frankness—that at the time he knew no more than his Minister of the Economy did about economic problems. Therefore

". . . I completed a real course for the 'intensive assimilation' of problems of economy. For days and nights I read that literature from Marx, Engels, Lenin and Stalin that I could get hold of in French, which dealt with problems of the economy." [He then wrote to Spiru:] "Tell them that the different levels of economic development of the two countries do not provide possibilities for a fair and realistic equalization of our lek with dinar." (316–17)

3. Did He Read Marx?

The anecdote shows Hoxha's cultural level at about forty. He had to bother the founders of Marxism and Marxism–Leninism to come up with an answer he could have easily found by consulting a textbook manual of political economy. Had he read Marx previously? Probably not. Nor did he, as it seems, read him later. His minimal references to him in his 'theoretical' works are those of a freshman first exposed to an Introduction to Marxism course. It would seem that Hoxha is the kind of "Marxist intellectual" who has not read Marx. And if we grant that he read him in his old age, when he began to dabble in Marxist–Leninist theory, he certainly would not and could not understand him. Therefore to say, as Halliday does, that he was "well read," is more than an exaggeration, it simply is not true. He was in fact unread, something his appallingly shallow writings abundantly show. And because he was unread, he never learned how to read other people's writings, let alone to analyze them. In his *Eurocommunism Is Anti-Communism* (1980), there is a passage where he inveighs against the French Communist Party for keeping the working class from joining the May 1968 uprising. The target of his anger, however, is less "the pseudo–Marxist" Georges Marchais than Aragon, the communist poet. In his report to the 22nd Congress of the FCP, Marchais had included a poem by Aragon taken from *Elsa's Fool.* Hoxha cites the following lines:

. . . Will there always be prisons and torture
always massacres in the name of idols
a mantle of words cast over the corpses

a gag in the mouth and nailed hands?
But a day will come with orange colours . . .

Hoxha reads "idols" as meaning 'Marx, Engels, Lenin, and Stalin,'
and then, referring to "orange colours," he adds: "This is Aragon's
way of saying that he and his party have abandoned the red colour,
communism" (230). Hoxha, like the fighting bull in the arena, sees
only red. His zealots in Albania, who have lately discovered poetic
treasures in his memoirs, may wish, I suggest, to consider him also as
a literary 'critik.' Just as he is blind to colors other than red in his
abuse and insult, Hoxha is deaf to genuine love, too. A person whose
"path to power and in power was littered with the corpses of his old
foes, and his old friends," cannot possibly have an appreciation of
love.

4. An Inveterate Liar

While praising the editor of *The Artful Albanian* for his painstak-
ing compilation of Hoxha's memoirs in one volume, his elegantly comprehensive introduction, and his scholarly notes, I must disagree with
some of his oxymoronic characterizations, such as the one in which
the hero is described as "both unusually frank and mendacious." To
me Hoxha was only occasionally frank and mendacious as a rule. I
would call him, sparing understatements, an inveterate liar. Even
official Albanian scholarship, which is not famous for being objective,
has felt the need—now that he is dead—to correct his arrogance.
The Albanians have an epithet for people like Hoxha: *gjysmak*, 'half-
educated.' The word is usually applied to persons whose education
remains incomplete. This generates in many of them an inferiority
complex, which extremely selfish and unscrupulous *gjysmak* try hard
to overcome by posing as superior beings. A person of this ilk will
thus become a "good actor," as Halliday calls Hoxha, i.e., dishonest
("evasive"). And if these cultural and moral dwarfs happen to possess
a big voice ("he had the doggedness to go on and on until he wore his
opponents down"), they will, by dint of silencing other people, end
up believing they are giants. They thus lose all sense of measure, get
purblind to distinctions, speak and write in "black and white," while
their praxis becomes fraudulent and violent—and bloody, too, if they
manage to become dictators.

There are two reasons for Halliday's use of superlatives in describing Hoxha's intelligence and culture. One is prompted by his

comparing him to the "crashingly boring" leaders of East European communist countries. The other reason is more complex. As an educated citizen of a once–dominant nation that has developed a superiority complex manifest in the ironic twist of its language, Halliday is both fascinated and amused by this "Balkan ex–Muslim Stalinist" who managed to liquidate all his rivals while playing carom billiard with the destiny of the Albanian nation. Both reasons induce a portrayal of the hero larger than life. Had Halliday known Zog better, and compared the dictator to the king, he would have found that the Hoxha phenomenon is not unusual among Albanians. Esad Toptani is another example. The list, of course, could be longer.

This brings me to my last point. The author has consulted a considerable number of U.K. citizens who have known Hoxha personally or have been involved in Albanian politics. These persons may well have provided relevant information. But would it not have been opportune to consult the Albanian press in exile? Unilaterality is bound to lead to errors. One comes closer to truth by way of comparisons.

The cover of the book shows a smiling Hoxha in his old age, dressed impeccably as usual, except for wearing, instead of his Borsalino hat, a workers' cap, which seems to be cut from the same fine fabric as his jacket and vest. I would have preferred him with his Borsalino. Yet, looking closer at the picture, I discovered that the red badge on his jacket flap reads: "1 Maj" (May 1st). I concede that in this case irony works better than sarcasm.

XI.   STALIN AND HOXHA: THE MASTER AND THE APPRENTICE*

And I turn to our government with a request:
to double, treble the guards over that gravestone slab,
so that Stalin should not rise, and with Stalin—the past.
It seems to me to that coffin a telephone's connected:
to Enver Hoxha Stalin transmits his latest edicts.
To where else is that direct line linked up?

> —Yevgeny Yevtushenko[1]

No, Stalin was no tyrant, no despot. He was a man of
principle, he was just, modest and very kindly and considerate
towards people, the cadres, and his colleagues. . . . No mistake
of principle can be found in the works of this outstanding
Marxist–Leninist.

> —Enver Hoxha[2]

But the period which we call the personality–cult period
affected our laws. . . . This led to arbitrary rule and the reign
of lawlessness. Stalin and his close associates are responsible
for those methods of governing the country. Any attempts to
justify that lawlessness by political needs, international
tension or alleged exacerbation of class struggle in the
country are wrong.

> —Mikhail Gorbachev[3]

---

* Published in *Telos* 73, 1987–88.   Rept.   in *Dielli* [The Sun],
September 15, 1988.

Something is happening in the Soviet Union. One wonders whether it is a remodeling of the outdated Soviet system, or a real 'reconstruction,' the term used by its ambitious and somewhat pretentious champion. One can accept with less reservation the other parameter of his 'new thinking,' i.e., 'openness,' its main thrust being the reexamination and redefinition of the Stalin myth. In this perspective, *'glasnost'* is an attempt to retrieve the meaning of history which, during the Stalin era and also the Brezhnev period, was perverted into a narrative of gross falsification and forgeries of all sorts. An example may suffice. In 1970, the Moscow Progress Publishers issued *A Short History of the Communist Party of the Soviet Union* by a team of Soviet historians under the direction of B. N. Ponamarev. The book exalts Lenin as the architect of Soviet Communism while being completely silent about Stalin, whose name is not even mentioned (Brezhnev's is, by the way). We thus have a history of the Soviet Union without Stalin—one could as well speak of a house without a roof, or a car without a steering wheel.

While Stalin's cult merely waned during the 'thaw' interlude, due to Khrushchev's desecration of the dictator's icon, Gorbachev's initiative could lead to dumping it. Joining a campaign inaugurated by some radical historians, Gorbachev has accused Stalin of "violations of law [with] tragic consequences."[4] His daring move has met with considerable popular support in the Soviet Union, while being coldly received in the Warsaw Pact countries, whose leaderships perceive it as a threat to their power. One can surmise acerbic reactions by some more unpopular leaderships in those countries. Albania, let us recall, broke loose from the Soviet bloc when Khrushchev pressed on the Hoxha–Shehu tandem for reconciliation with Tito, felt by them as marking the end of their duumvirate and therefore pushing them to go over to China. Such adventuristic changing of sides is probably an extreme case, typical of politically immature leaderships. Nonetheless, if 'reconstruction' obtains in the Soviet Union, restructurings of parts of the Soviet empire are bound to occur.

Ever since it rejected Yugoslavia's tutelage, Albania has been moving in erratic eastward orbits, circling first one and then the other sun, and ending up swirling. Despite these twists and turns, Albania remains a Stalinist country, the only one in Europe where Stalin's memory continues to haunt the leaders' minds. The question arises: If the saga of Stalin as the builder of the greatness of the Soviet Union is liquidated there, what will happen to Hoxha, his 'heir' and the architect of Stalinist Albania?

Before answering this question, let us see whether Yevtushenko's description of Hoxha as Stalin's most faithful 'heir' is accurate.

In his book, *With Stalin*, published in 1979, i.e., in the same year as *Imperialism and Revolution*, Hoxha's most representative 'theoretical' work, he extols Stalin for "his stern and principled struggle for the defense, consistent implementation and further development of the ideas of Marx, Engels and Lenin" (6), "his great work without precedent in history" (12), and defends him from "slanders" such as "bloody tyrant" and "murderer" (14), while pointing out his "brilliant mind and pure soul" (16), his "exhilarating laugh that went right to one's heart" (146), "his voice so warm and inspiring" (219). Just as "before the body of Lenin, Stalin pledged that he would loyally follow his teachings" (10), when Stalin died, Hoxha, in the name of the Albanian people, "sign[ed] the Oath . . ."[5] to "carry out [his] instructions."[6]

And in general he kept his word. He gave priority to the industrialization of an overwhelmingly agrarian country while pushing hard for its thorough collectivization, achieved with methods similar to those used in the Soviet Union. He organized the army and the State Security apparatus according to strictly Stalinian patterns. He all but copied the Soviet school system, and imposed on literature and the arts the Stalinist dogma of 'socialist realism.' Stalin's theses on Soviet linguistics inform the language reform of the so-called 'unified literary Albanian.' Last but not least, Hoxha submitted the Party to a series of ruthless, typically Stalinian purges,[7] which led to his being glorified as the genius of the Albanian revolution and the father of modern Albania.

This is not to say that Hoxha imitated Stalin in everything Stalin did. Unlike Stalin, Hoxha dressed elegantly while also affecting French manners. Stalin's despotism was all grounded on terror, whereas Hoxha could charm people with his joviality and eloquence. On the other hand, he lacked his master's prudence and cool bearing, as made clear by his declaring Albania the first atheistic country in the history of humankind—Stalin would not commit that blunder. There are a few more differences between the two, but despite those differences, Hoxha was indeed Stalin's most faithful disciple in at least four respects.

Just like Stalin, Hoxha built his personality cult through consecutive Party purges mainly by playing his rivals against each other.

He first allied himself with Koçi Xoxe, then the Party's strongman, to eliminate Sejfulla Malëshova, the only Albanian communist leader with a Marxist theoretical background. He then pushed to suicide Nako Spiru, the talented young Minister of the Economy, whose head was wanted by Xoxe. Next Hoxha liquidated Xoxe by joining Mehmet Shehu, a popular military hero. He then had Shehu, first as Minister of the Interior and later as Premier, do the dirty job of repressing all kinds of dissidents and deviators, including the former Minister of Education, Fadil Paçrami, an innovative playwright much admired by the youth. Finally the dictator turned against his longtime faithful collaborator, accusing him of being a 'superagent' of imperialism (Shehu allegedly committed suicide). Hoxha's path to dictatorship, just like Stalin's is strewn with the corpses of his actual or potential rivals.

Like Stalin, Hoxha suffered from megalomania, the kind characteristic of mediocrities striving to cover up their inferiority complex by posing as superior beings. The Bolshevik leaders Stalin liquidated: Trotsky, Bukharin, Zinoviev, to name the most important among them, far outdid Stalin in statesmanship and creative power. Envious of their superiority of mind and culture, he tried hard to prove himself their equal as a Marxist theoretician while pretending to be the sole heir to Lenin, although Lenin's testament mentions Bukharin as such, while criticizing Stalin for his 'duress.' Driven by his ambition to be hailed as the theoretician of Marxism–Leninism (his name for Stalinism), the former seminarist wrote authoritatively on the Soviet economy and, in his capacity as commander–in–chief of the Soviet armed forces during World War II, dabbled in military theory. He even reached out to legislating over areas totally extraneous to his interests. It was Stalin who, together with Gorky, concocted the doctrine of 'socialist realism.' And it was Stalin who reformed Soviet linguistics by demolishing Marr's concept of language as a superstructural phenomenon with class character. Hoxha imitated his master by dabbling in all these areas and in others, too, such as history (he wrote several books of memoirs), education (he had taught French for some time), and also religion. Being no genius and also half–educated (he dropped out of university studies, and only in his old age read and wrote extensively), he would enunciate trite and half–baked judgments, but never a deep, let alone an original, thought.[8] His sporadic attempts to deal with Marxist theory show him poorly acquainted with even its basics—in this much inferior to

Stalin, who could sustain his arguments with pedantic logic couched
in catechistic style. Hoxha was so insignificant as a theoretician of
Marxism that his 'teachings' did not even invite elaboration by his
devotees, who have been merely uncritically parrotting him. And
since it was he who held the monopoly of Marxism–Leninism in his
country, Albanian Diamat (dialectical materialism) is of the lowest
quality, and Albania the only communist country in Eastern Europe
where Marxist theory is at zero level.

A 'bloody tyrant' as a statesman and a half–educated mediocrity
as an intellectual, Hoxha resembles Stalin also for his unprincipled
Byzantine–style Machiavellianism. After siding with the Bukharin-
led faction against the Trotsky–Zinoviev 'left' opposition, and once
he had liquidated the latter, Stalin shifted to the position of the 'left'
faction and then turned against his former allies on the 'right.' He
repeated this *volte-face* when he concluded a nonaggression pact with
Hitler after a relentless campaign against all kinds of fascism, branding as such social democracy itself. As the Commissar for the nationalities, Stalin defended the right of Soviet peoples to cultivate their
national languages, a position he later reversed when he proceeded to
Russify the Soviet Union, his justification being the Diamat principle
according to which what is valid today may be invalid tomorrow due
to circumstantial changes. Hoxha's *principialnost* was from Stalin's
blueprint. Under Hoxha's leadership during the 'national liberation
war,' the Albanian Communist Party concluded an alliance with the
nationalist Balli Kombëtar (National Front) and the royalist party
to resist and fight Italian fascism. Pressed by his Yugoslav mentors, Hoxha quickly denounced the alliance while blaming it on his
delegates. When the Yugoslavs found Xoxe more amenable to their
plan of annexing Albania, upon Xoxe's request and hoping to gain
Tito's confidence, Hoxha praised Tito in an article.[9] At the time,
this amounted to his consenting to the annexation plan. And when
Stalin denounced Tito, Hoxha promptly accused his ally as a traitor
to international communism while having Xoxe hanged as a traitor to
the Albanian nation. Hoxha played the same game with Khrushchev.
When the Soviet leader requested that Hoxha make peace with Tito,
Hoxha went over to Mao instead, branding Khrushchev as a 'social-
imperialist.' He extended that epithet to Mao when China came to
terms with the United States.

There was a time when this horsetrader of Marxism was ap-
plauded as the champion of 'pure' Marxism–Leninism by ill–informed

foreign acolytes, thus prompting Hoxha's Albanian devotees to hail him as the Messiah of world communism. Purism in politics is much more suspect than purism in language and poetry, 'pure art' being no more than a religion of art, with beauty substituting for deity. Stressing purity in politics is a disingenuous way of hiding its impurity. Now 'purity' has been a preferred label for the Albanian brand of Marxism–Leninism, which is nominally Marxist, minimally Leninist, and essentially Stalinist, with a smattering of Maoism. The adequate name for this new religion is Stalalbanianism, or simply Hoxhanism. It reached its apex with the apotheosis of its founder, following his death. Scholars vied with each other to glorify the hero as a great statesman, a military genius, an eminent Marxist and philosopher, an outstanding historian, and even a distinguished writer, applying such epithets as 'universal,' 'immortal,' 'eternal' to his mind or work.[10] Stalin's cult as the architect of the first socialist state in the history of humankind and the builder of the Soviet Union into a superpower is in the tradition of Russian messianism and the myth of the Third Rome. Hitler's charisma was grounded on the national feeling for revenge compounded with the myth of racial purity traced down to pagan times. Hoxha exploited the rising Albanian nationalism against the religious and regional differences of his people, a strategy formulated by a man of the Albanian Risorgimento, Pashko Vasa: "The Albanians' religion is Albaniandom."

This mixture of patriotism and religiosity was in his blood, his family belonging to the Bektashi sect, a Shia Sufi heretical sect particularly influential in Albania on account of its patriotic activity. *Reflections on the Middle East*[11] includes a sort of essay on the Arab civilization, in which one runs into sentences revealing Hoxha's Islamic *parti pris*: "In fact the Koran is more complete and purer than the Bible (Torah) of the Jews, the Christian Gospel, etc." (464). He greatly admires Mohammed: "While being a preacher of the Koranic law, Mohammed, at the same time, was also 'head of the state' " (483). "Mohammed was not an 'autocrat' . . . because [sic!] God was the only 'source of authority for both the leader [Mohammed] and for the people' " (484). Sentences such as these strongly suggest that Hoxha tends to identify with Mohammed, a projection of his own image as the founder of a new credo, Albanian atheism. Another passage praises Islam for its 'democracy': "Its democratic character was reinforced, also, by the liberation of people from the tyranny of different religions . . ."(486). Here Hoxha has in mind polytheistic religions as contrasted with monotheistic ones. But can a monotheistic religion be called democratic because it liberates peoples from polytheistic religions? This sounds like monopoly capitalism liberating the world from English and French colonialism. Can a person who utters such an enormity be a follower of Marx, for whom religion, any religion, is 'opiate for the people'? Elsewhere one finds: "Mohammedanism, or Islam, is a 'universal' monotheistic religion" (463), ". . . its monotheism expressed in the axiom, 'There is no god, but Allah, and Muhammed is his prophet' " (464). Leaving out Allah, and paraphrasing, one gets: Hoxhanism, or Stalalbanianism, is a universal mono[a]theistic religion, ". . . its mono[a]theism expressed in the axiom, 'There is no god but Hoxha is his prophet.' Here the parallel with the Georgian seminarist lies in each man's fanatic pursuit of absolute power. They would not relent before reaching it, using to that end old and new Machiavellian means: lies, slander, hypocrisy, perjury, treachery, as well as overbearing or cringing according to the case, generalized espionage, falsification of history, corruption of science, not to speak of jails, psychiatric confinement, gulags, torture of all kinds, and especially murder, be that the shooting of a pregnant woman once a Politburo member or the systematic extermination of millions of people, including old Party members and even Party founders.

Khrushchev dealt the first blow to Stalin's cult, while going only halfway in his de–Stalinization reform (it was Khrushchev who repressed the Polish protest in 1956 and then crushed the Hungarian revolution of the same year). Gorbachev seems committed to doing away with both Stalin and the Stalinist plague. How will *glasnost* affect Albania, where Stalin has survived, and Stalinism in its Hoxhan variant is very much alive? Some signs of a change seem promising. Albania has established diplomatic relations with the German Federal Republic and Canada, while intensifying commerce with East European communist countries. The volume of tourism has increased. And for the first time since Albania broke with Yugoslavia, non–Party people have been allowed to visit their Yugoslav relatives. Facts such as these imply a partial rejection of Hoxha's isolationistic politics. If the trend consolidates, Albania might soon follow the example of other East European countries as to foreign policy. What about internal policies? In his recent talks with Albanian leaders in Tirana, Genscher, the West German Foreign Minister, raised the question of human rights,[12] thus alluding to the fact that Albania is the only

European country that has not signed the Helsinki Pact. Now that Hoxha is gone, there is no reason for Albania to persist in being Europe's black sheep. Normal participation in international associations and conferences (one thinks especially of Third World and Balkan conferences) will erode the Hoxha cult. Once the Hoxha myth is debunked, the Hoxha cult will go down the drain.

The question is who will be the one to start the debunking campaign. The actual number one, a most faithful disciple of the master, hardly seems indicated for the job. The same can be said for the rest of the leadership. An initiative from the rank and file is to be excluded a priori, Stalinist unions having no more autonomy than fascist corporations. The students, perhaps? One think of the recent tumultuous demonstrations in China and South Korea, Albania being, according to some, more affinal to Third World than to European countries. One also remembers that the Albanian Cultural Revolution launched by Hoxha, emulating Mao, relied only in part on students, whose enthusiasm Hoxha distrusted.

My guess is that a student protest movement in Albania—not to be excluded considering that a precedent exists: the 1981 mass demonstrations by the Albanians in Yugoslavia requesting republic status for Kosova—could hardly take place without being instigated, or at least condoned, by those in power. The latter alternative seems more probable, in view of the long period of totalitarian rule in the country. In other words, Albania would follow the example of the current Chinese leadership which, having shelved Mao's legacy, has allowed a modicum of liberal reforms in the nation's economy, administration, and foreign policy. If so, the current Albanian leadership could manage to operate the shift in anodyne manner. Hoxha's name would still be mentioned for rhetoric's sake, while sounding more and more hollow. And one hopes a day will come when the new generation will feel embarrassed and even ashamed at having had parents who could revere a person such as Hoxha. And where his body lies, a nameless slab will read: *Sic transit gloria immundi.*

XII.   THE POLITICAL SITUATION OF THE ALBANIANS IN YUGOSLAVIA, WITH PARTICULAR ATTENTION TO THE KOSOVA PROBLEM*

The international press has more than once drawn attention to Yugoslavia's deteriorating economic and political situation. The Yugoslav crisis was the subject of a hearing of the European Parliament in Strasbourg on January 20, 1988. In a recent meeting of the foreign ministers of the European Community in Constance, there were warnings that Yugoslavia may be "close to economic collapse."[1] A major problem is the situation in Kosova, an 'Autonomous Province' within the framework of the Republic of Serbia.

The Kosova problem is basically an ethnic one. The Province is inhabited by a compact majority of Albanians (over one and a half million), with Serbs and Montenegrins as minorities (ca. 12 percent). The Kosovars (as the Albanian ethnics call themselves) are unhappy with the status of the Province, which is inferior to that of a republic and therefore involves lesser representative and participatory power. They resent Serbia's control and want the Province to be fully emancipated, claiming the right to have their own republic, just as Montenegrins and Macedonians do. Under the slogan '*Kosova Republikë!,*" violent demonstrations occurred during the Spring of 1981 in various cities, and especially in the Province's capital, Prishtinë (Priština). A drastic repression ensued. Far from putting an end to Kosovar unrest, the repression exacerbated Kosovar nationalism. The Albanian population grew openly hostile; students and intellectuals organized illegal groups, some of them of Stalinist inspiration. A wave of arrests and imprisonments followed. Unable to vent their anger against the authorities, most of whom are Kosovars, the Albanian population has occasionally resorted to acts of violence against

---

* Published in *East European Quarterly*, vol. 13, no. 2, June 1989.

local Serbs and Montenegrins. This has caused an uproar of protest, amplified and concerted by the mass media in the republics of Serbia, Montenegro, and Macedonia, where many Albanians live (in Macedonia, the Albanians, most of them Kosovars just like those in Kosova, make up more than 20 percent of the republic's population). Due mainly to the deteriorating economy of the Province ("in 1985 unemployment was 3.3 times the Yugoslav average"),[2] many Serbs have left Kosova. Their migration has been construed as "expulsion" by Serbian nationalism. In early 1986, a group of 206 Belgrade intellectuals signed a petition addressed to the respective Assemblies of Serbia and Federal Yugoslavia and including the signatures of the former editors of *Praxis International*, a respected socialist journal.[3] The petition accuses the Serbian and Federal leaderships of a passive attitude towards "the Albanian aggression in Kosova and Metohija," resulting in the "expulsion" of the Slav population—a "politics of national treason." It also indicts ethnic Albanians for "genocide in Kosova" while warning "its leaders and ideologues [that they] are leading it into a national adventure in which it can lose all."[4]

The document is only one in a series of forms of protest on the part of growing Serbian nationalism as a reaction to Kosovar nationalism. Faced with this situation, the Federal government decided to send a special police corps to Kosova in October 1987. So far the presence of this corps seems to have been a moderating factor. Yet the situation remains tense, due to the reiterated attempts by the new Serbian Party leadership to pressure the Kosovar leaders into renouncing some of the constitutional rights guaranteeing their autonomy.[5]

1. Stalinized Chauvinism?

Emigrations of Serbs and Montenegrins have in fact occurred, and in alarming numbers. Yet are they a consequence only of Kosovar pressure? According to Branko Horvat,

> in the first post–revolutionary period, i.e., up to 1965, there was no emigration of Serbs and Montenegrins from Kosova. The subsequent economic falling–behind [of the province] must have given a powerful impetus to emigration.[6]

Because of the high rate of unemployment in Kosova, on the one hand, and, on the other, the vexations undergone by Kosovars under the rule of Aleksandar Ranković, Vice President and Chief of Police of Federal Yugoslavia, migrations from Kosova and other Albanian–

inhabited districts have occurred, too. By the way, this is not the
first time that both Serbs and Albanians of Kosova have abandoned
their homelands. After the defeat suffered in 1737 by the Austrian
army, including Serbs and Albanians from the Këlmendi (Clementi)
tribe,[7] the latter settled in Banat.[8]

It is thus not only Serbs who have abandoned Kosova in the post-
war period, not to mention the exodus of Albanians from Kosova and
Macedonia in the prewar period under the pressure of the monarchist
regime. The leitmotif of a Serbian 'expulsion' from Kosova in the seventies and eighties conveys a one–sided view of the Kosova problem as
part of an anti–Albanian campaign of denigration. The language of
the following excerpts from the petition of the Belgrade intellectuals
speaks for itself:

> In the last twenty years, 200,000 people have been moved
> out of Kosova and Metohija, more than 700 settlements have
> been ethnically "purged," the emigration is continuing with
> unabated force, Kosova and Metohija are becoming "eth-
> nically pure," the aggression is crossing the borders of the
> Province [to Macedonia and Serbia].

> As is known from historical science, from still unextin-
> guishable memory, the expulsion of the Serb people from
> Kosova and Metohija has already been going on for three
> centuries. Only the protectors of the tyrants have been
> changed: the Ottoman Empire, the Habsburg Monarchy,
> Fascist Italy and Nazi Germany have been replaced by the
> Albanian state *and* the ruling institutions of Kosova [empha-
> sis added]. In place of forced Islamization and Fascism there
> is Stalinized chauvinism. The only novelty is the fusion of
> tribal hatred and genocide masked by Marxism.[9]

The petition describes the Kosovar leadership as an extension of
Albanian Stalinism. Is the charge justified?
Let us begin with some historical notes.
Eminent historians maintain that, before the Ottoman invasion
of the Balkans, Albanians and Serbs lived together in what is now
Kosova. Whereas the Serbs were Orthodox, the Albanians were var-
iously Orthodox and Catholics. The Turkish conquest brought in a
new confessional factor, Islam, which made proselytes among Kosova
residents. Turkish authorities promoted conversion to Islam by offer-
ing various allurements, including lands vacated by fugitive Serbs. It

was in this way that Albanians coming mostly from the Dukagjin region reached as far as Novipazar and Niš: witness their patronymics, which are in most cases the same as those of Albanians in the mother country. According to the Turkish census of 1910, the Albanians made up at the time up to 60 percent of the Kosova *vilayet* [governorship], the rest being Serbs, Turks, and Bulgarians.[10] After World War I, the vilayet's greater part was incorporated into the Kingdom of Yugoslavia. An Albanian revolt against the Serbian occupation in 1913 was crushed by the Serbian army. During World War II, following the fascist–Nazi dismemberment of Yugoslavia, Kosova—together with some Albanian regions of Macedonia and Montenegro—was united with Albania, then an Italian dominion. They were reunited with Yugoslavia at the end of the war. In 1944, another major revolt broke out in Kosova, repressed by the Yugoslav army. The constitution of 1946 describes Kosova as the "autonomous region of Kosova–Metohija" within the Republic of Serbia. The 1963 constitution promoted the 'region' to the status of a 'province.'

In 1966, Ranković, the Serbian leader who had harassed the Albanians of Yugoslavia for more than two decades, fell from power. In the ensuing relaxed political atmosphere, the Kosovars drew a breath of relief. They began to voice their discontent with being considered the pariah nation of the federation. In 1968, demonstrations occurred in Prishtina, in which the slogan "Kosova Republic!" made its appearance. The request was refused; yet the Kosovars obtained in return, as a compromise solution, the right to display the Albanian flag, have their own university, and use the Albanian language on a par with Serbocroatian. The flag Kosovars displayed was the same one flown in Albania. They also decided to discontinue the use of their traditional literary language, based on the mother country's Gheg (northern) dialect, in favor of the newly–adopted official Albanian literary language, based on the Tosk (southern) dialect. According to trusted oral reports, it was university students who forced on academia the adoption of the official Albanian. Since cultural exchanges between Albania and Kosova had already been established at the time, involving lectures of Tirana professors based on Tirana–printed books imbued with Stalinist ideology, it is quite possible that at least some of the students who pressed for the changing of the language were affected by that ideology—the slogan "Long live Enver Hoxha!" was voiced in the 1968 riots. How far it spread out in the following years up to the 1981 demonstrations, and how influential was that ideology

during the latter, is a matter of speculation. The constitution of 1974
gave the Province many of the same rights enjoyed by the republics,
without, however, granting it republic status, something hardly to be
expected after the Kosovar leadership had decided for the Albanian
flag and the official Albanian language. The denial of republic status,
implying the 'sovereignty' of a state, was a main factor in the ensuing unrest of the population, fomented by Tirana sympathizers. It is
more difficult to assess the position of the Kosovar leadership. Had
it also been affected by Stalinism, as the petition of the more than
two hundred Yugoslav intellectuals implies? The excessive harshness
of the punishments inflicted on ethnic Albanians involved in the 1981
demonstrations seems to disprove that accusation, unless one thinks
that by such harshness the leadership intended to allay any suspicion of its tacit support for them, a suspicion voiced by Serbs and
grounded in the adoption of the Albanian flag and the official Albanian language.

The irony is that while some Kosovars, because of their failure to
obtain what they most wanted, were turning their eyes towards Albania, the Tirana leadership was not at all disposed to help them realize
their goal, apart from launching far-flung sallies of rhetoric. Enver
Hoxha, then the indisputable master of the country, could not but be
cool to the Kosovars' desire, knowing well that a Republic of Kosova
within the framework of anti-Stalinist Yugoslavia, his mortal foe,
would tend to develop into a rival and adversary of Stalinist Albania.
The idea of two Albanians with strongly contrasting ideo-political
systems could not be alluring to him, considering what has happened
to the two Germanies, two Koreas, and two Vietnams. And of course
he knew well that 'socialist' countries could, just like bourgeois countries, wage war on each other, witness the frontier clashes between the
Soviet Union and Maoist China in the sixties. He also feared that,
were Kosova to join Albania, his dream of making Albania the world
center of Marxism-Leninism would come to a quick end, leaving him
as the scapegoat. For the overwhelmingly-Moslem Kosovars, who are
attached to their religion and can cultivate it in today's Yugoslavia,
would hardly stomach the Albanian drive for atheism. Nor would the
forced agricultural collectivization practiced in Albania be palatable
to Kosovar peasants, who constitute the great majority of the population and who own their own land (socialist Yugoslavia resorted
to agrarian reform instead of collectivization). Hoxha's personal interest for Kosova was to have Kosovars make trouble for Yugoslavia,

which he had begun to hate passionately on learning that Tito preferred the tinsmith Koçi Xoxe to him at the Party's helm.[11] Hoxha's anti–Yugoslavism, just like his anti–Sovietism later on, was, to a great extent, a vindictive drive to assuage his wounded pride. How much he cared for Kosova and the Kosovars can be gathered from his having the Albanian government lift not so much as a finger in their defense in such international forums as the United Nations European Commission on Human Rights. The advocacy of the Kosovar demand for republic status was limited to a series of unsigned articles, mostly published in the Party organ *Zëri i popullit* [The People's Voice], which were widely broadcast and then published in book form in various languages, but which, unlike interventions in international forums such as those just mentioned, were not binding on the Albanian government.

Since the Albanian government is not really interested in Kosova's promotion to a republic, let alone in its joining the mother country, one wonders why the government has strongly supported the Kosovar demand since the 1981 demonstrations. Only for the malign pleasure of causing problems for Serbia? Tirana's main purpose was to ingratiate with Kosovars the ideology of Albanian Stalinism. Through previous agreements for cultural exchange in areas such as tourism, sports, theater, films, radio–television, university teaching and academic meetings, begun at a time when Prishtina did not yet have its own university and textbooks had to be imported from Tirana, Albanian Stalinism has been able to affect a number of students and some of their teachers, prompting in them the illusion that Albania as a whole was behind the Kosovars, ready at need to come to their aid or rescue. Slogans such as "Long live Marxism–Leninism! Down with revisionism!" were displayed during the 1981 demonstrations, together with "Kosova Republic!" And we shall shortly see that the Stalinist influence was not limited to slogans alone.

2. Posing the Problem

Let us begin by noting that the assignment to Serbia and Montenegro by the London Conference (1913) and the Versailles Conference (1919) of Albanian–inhabited territories more than half the size of present–day Albania hardly changed the ethnic picture in those territories, despite the de–Albanization policy undertaken by the monarchist Yugoslav regime (1918–1941), consisting in clearing parts of Serbia (the Vranje district in particular) of Albanians by expatriating them to Turkey, as well as colonizing Kosova with ethnic Slavs. The ethnic picture remained more or less the same because of the Kosovars' high birthrate. Considered as intruders who did not belong in the South Slav kingdom, the Kosovars were treated with open hostility, often deprived of elementary civil and human rights. Such a behavior gave rise to an irredentist mood, which materialized when the Kingdom of Yugoslavia was destroyed by the fascist–Nazi aggression. The territories in question were annexed to Albania, to the elation of their Albanian inhabitants, who saw the foreign administrations as a change for the better in their dejected situation. The Italian occupation of Kosova and adjacent Albanian districts was not resisted by Kosovars. And when the Nazi troops occupied them, an Albanian unit of volunteers joined the SS troops. Now it was the turn of the Albanians to harass South Slavs, an affront avenged by the Yugoslav Partisans soon after the end of the war, when Kosovars rose in revolt. To the Albanians of Yugoslavia, Serbian communists were no better than Serbian royalists, the change of ideology not having resulted in a change of attitude towards them.

The roots of the Kosova problem lie with the deep–rooted Kosovar sentiment that "Kosova and the Dukagjin Plateau [Metohija] is a region predominantly inhabited by Albanians who, *now as always before, desire to unite with Albania*" [emphasis added]. The sentence is found in the resolution of communist Kosovars representing the Anti–fascist National Liberation Council of Kosova–Metohija, known as the Bujan resolution from the village in which it took place (Dec. 1943–Jan. 1944).[12] Any attempt at solving the problem must begin with considerations of how the three parties directly involved in the question: Serbia, Kosova, and Albania, have reacted to the idea of union.

The Serbian government clearly rejects the idea, which is also rejected by the Serbian population in general, as made manifest by several demonstrations, declarations, and petitions, including that of the more than two hundred Belgrade intellectuals. And we just argued that the Albanian leadership does not want the union, either, while one is not sure of what the Albanian population thinks of it, public opinion being nonexistent in Stalinist Albania. There remains the third party, Kosova. Serbian provincial leaders obviously do not want the union, a sentiment apparently shared by Kosovar leaders, who would otherwise risk being accused of national treason, especially now that the Serbian party leader, Slobodan Milošević, known not to be a friend of Kosovars, has defeated the moderate wing in the Party. What about the Kosovar public opinion? Unlike that in Serbia, it does not exist—just as in Albania. For a public opinion to exist, one residing with the civil society as distinct from and independent of the government, an intelligentsia is needed, one which dares question the government's actions and criticize its mistakes and misuses of power. Since this condition is still lacking in Kosova, it is difficult to know what the population thinks and how it feels about the question of union with Albania. Slogans and jokes are not enough to form an idea about such a major question.[13] On the improbable hypothesis that Kosova is granted republic status at the present historical stage, the results of a plebiscite on the question of unification would almost certainly be negative: the leadership would easily defeat the proposal by telling people, among other things, that they would be expropriated of their lands and other properties, while also being denied the right to worship. And Tirana would probably instruct its sympathizers not to vote for a proposal which entails changes of frontier with Yugoslavia, something Albania has consistently stated, moved to it less by its official commitment to respect the frontiers of other nations than by fear of provoking discussion of its own frontiers (the case of 'Northern Epirus' in particular). The conclusion that follows from these considerations is that in the present political and cultural climate in Kosova, the idea of union has no chance.

Nor has the idea of republic status, which in the minds of Serbs is strictly related to the former, though the two concepts are distinct and independent from each other. The request has not found favor among the republics of Yugoslavia. And while the Soviet Union has been silent, the United States, interested in having Yugoslavia maintain a neutrality friendly to the West, has looked on the Kosovar emancipation movement as a destabilizing factor, one jeopardizing Yugoslavia's territorial integrity. When Serbian intellectuals dare to accuse the Serbian government of condoning what they describe as a path to "national treason"; when they charge "the ruling institutions of Kosova" with "capitulation" to the Stalinist "Albanian state," thus paving the way for massive protests by Kosova's Serbian population; when the Serbian Minister of Defense calls the single-handed Paraćin barracks murder an "attack against the Yugoslav army";[14] and when a general is elected President of Serbia at a time when Serbian nationalism seems dead-set on depriving Kosova of the autonomy granted to

it by the constitution—in these circumstances, insistence on requesting republic status for the Province is clearly counterproductive.

Retrospective thinking leads to the same conclusion. When the
Partisans invaded Kosova in 1944, thus provoking the population's
mass rebellion, that rebellion was quelled in blood. When in Spring
1981 the Kosovar youth rioted in protest, they were met with tanks
and machine gun fire.[15] According to official sources, during the period 1981–1986, over 150,000 Kosovars have undergone police interrogation, about 50,000 of them being punished or reprimanded. Of this
number, about 7,000 have been jailed, including about 1,000 minors,
and 1,234 have been sentenced to terms up to twenty years. During
the same period, in Macedonia, where more than 400,000 Albanians
live, there have been more than 1,300 incarcerations.[16] The figures are
startling by European standards. According to the 1985 Amnesty International report on Yugoslavia, of the 594 political arrests made
there in 1982, 64 percent concerned ethnic Albanians. And during
the decade 1975–1985, of a Yugoslav total of thirty–five instances of
capital punishment, sixteen, i.e., almost 50 percent, were carried out
in Kosova alone.

3. A Case of Reconquest?

No one would object to people cherishing their memories of old,
cultivating treasures of the nation's history and folklore, revering
heroes whose deeds signalized their times, and worshipping saints
who issued from the suffering heart of the nation. Understandably
enough, Serbs must be fond of Kosova, which contains their most
beautiful churches, houses the see of the Serb Patriarchate, and takes
its name from the plain where that famous battle was fought which
marks the end of their glorious past. To Serbian nationalists Kosova
is their sacred land, much as Palestine is to Jews. Zionism succeeded
in expatriating half of the Arab population of Palestine while condemning the rest to the status of second–class citizens. Is Serbian
nationalism haunted by a like idea? Judging from what is happening
in Palestine today, a Serbian attempt to Slavicize Kosova would be
disastrous for both sides, exhausting them in a war of attrition with
no end in sight. And here history is again to be consulted. It tells us
that after a period of five or six centuries of Serb domination over the
older inhabitants of Kosova, the Serbs forfeited it to the Turks, who
ruled over it for almost as long a period. It also reminds one that
Albanians have been living in Kosova for at least three centuries, a

period long enough to justify them calling themselves Kosovars. How are we to define the concept of homeland? And to whom does the land belong? Vico explained *patria* as a neuter plural meaning the belongings of the fathers. According to the Gospel, the land belongs to God, like everything else created by Him, man being merely God's steward. According to Albanian state socialism, it belongs to the state, which then rents it to agricultural cooperatives. Yet common law recognizes occupancy of land for a relatively long period of time as a legitimate title of ownership. Perhaps one day humanity will agree on better criteria for ownership titles. As things now go, land changes hands pretty much as money does, though not as quickly. The attitude of Serbian nationalists to their sacred land may or may not be motivated by a desire of reconquest. Yet the harsh repressive measures against Kosovars have been such as to cause embarrassment to some American congressmen not previously known for sympathizing with the Kosovars' plight.[17] Violation of civil and human rights has been criticized not only by Amnesty International, but by Yugoslavs themselves. A petition (June 20, 1986) sent to the Presidencies of Yugoslavia, Serbia, and Kosova, and signed by eighteen members of the Committee for the Defense of the Freedom of Thought and Expressions, thirteen of whom are members of the Serbian Academy of Sciences, includes the following passages:

> Among the prisoners from Kosova are certainly also those who advocate hatred towards other peoples and who call for violence. . . . The committee . . . does not protect such prisoners. But, persecutions of Albanians, including many young people and even minors, for having read articles, daubed slogans or made utterances which call neither for violence nor for national or any kind of hatred, has become more frequent in Kosova. Proceedings against them have many illegal aspects, such as extortion of admission of guilt, fabrication of evidence and false testimonies.[18]

Branko Horvat has been even more explicit:

> "Kosova republic!" is in no way a counterrevolutionary slogan for which citizens should be liable to arrest. Rather it is a political demand which in a socialist country—and Yugoslavia is supposed to be such a country—is perfectly legitimate. Whether this demand is justified or not should be decided by political debate rather than police measures.[19]

Albanians are treated even worse in Macedonia. According to Amnesty International, two prisoners were killed by the guards of the Idrizovo prison because they disobeyed the order to enter solitary cells.[20] A recent article in a Swiss journal tells of a schoolteacher who was fired for wearing a red sweater and black slacks, red and black being the Albanian colors. Calling Skopje by the city's Albanian name 'Shkup' is punishable by a fine. Discrimination runs high. It begins in school, where students are taught more classes of Macedonian language than contemplated by the regulations. And whereas Macedonian pupils are failed only exceptionally in examinations for admission to secondary schools, the rate of failure for Albanians reaches 50 percent.[21] In Montenegro, Albanian is slowly disappearing from schools. Ulqin (Ulćin), once an overwhelmingly Albanian town, is now filled with Yugoslav villas, while Tivar (Bar) has been almost completely Slavicized. Whole Albanian villages in the Titograd district have been abandoned by their Albanian inhabitants. On top of all this, there have been cases of government–sponsored terrorism against Kosovar emigrés.[22]

An article recently published in a Zagreb journal concludes that "on the daily scene of Kosova, Serb nationalism is more aggressive, better organized and more active than Albanian nationalism, not least because it has won support in sections of the mass media."[23] The writer has visited the so–called Serb capital of Kosova, Kosovo–Polje, where frequent demonstrations of women took place. "It is difficult, if not impossible," he writes, "to believe that these demonstrations are quite as spontaneous as it is claimed." They resemble staged shows, with speakers succeeding one another in good order, amidst intervals of applause, shouts of approval, chanting, and slogans such as "An eye for an eye!" "To arms!" "We shall give up our lives but not Kosova!" The author, having made an inventory of the crimes imputed to Albanians, then proceeded to interview the secretary of the Department of Internal Affairs, who produced statistics which show that the crimes, numerically hardly relevant, were committed by Albanians and Slavs alike.[24] The writer notes that "the state apparatus has for a long time now been quite strict with the Albanians." They, in turn, have been cautious on their part not to provoke the other side, even to the point—so the joke runs—of moving away from a Serb entering a bus for fear of stepping on his foot. The author sees an impending danger of 'war and blood' in the ongoing strife between the two ethnic groups.

4. Critical Observations

What can be done to prevent that danger?

A first step would be for all parties to have the courage to admit errors, and then work hard to correct them after a sustained dialogue governed by mutual respect. The dialogue should lead to concrete proposals acceptable to both sides. Let us first consider the case of Serbia.

(a) Serbia's error has been to keep Kosova under its suzerainty. According to the official census of 1948, the Albanians in Kosova made up more than 60 percent of the province's population, the Serb minority accounting for 27.4 percent. As a socialist republic, Serbia was bound to respect the democratic and socialist principle of letting the population decide its own destiny. A plebiscite not held under the flashing of bayonets would have resulted in Kosova's joining Albania. This would not have upset Serbs, Albania being at the time a Yugoslav (one can even say a Serbian) protectorate. This did not happen because the Yugoslav leadership was then Stalinist, i.e., nonsocialist in essence, genuine socialism being internationalist, bound to the principle of popular self–determination.

But if the Yugoslav objective of Albania's unification with Kosova in one socialist federal Yugoslav republic failed to materialize due to Stalin's denunciation of Titoism, Serbia could still have granted Kosova the status of a republic, the status, namely, of neighboring Macedonia, a republic ethnically less compact than Kosova, including as it does Bulgarians, Serbs, Albanians, Greeks, and Turks. Serbian nationalism would not allow that much. And this was the second mistake. Hatred and phobia prevailed, soon to result, under Ranković's heavy–handed rule, in a policy of persecutions hardly dissimilar from the one implemented by the monarchic regime. After stating that the 1944 insurrection of Kosovars against the Serbian takeover was "the only instance of an armed rebellion against the Communist terror," an American student of the Yugoslav national question writes: "In dealing with them [the Albanians] the Communists were guilty of extreme measures which at times differed little from those by [fascist–Nazi] occupation authorities during the war."[25] He also writes:

In actual practice, between 1946 and 1966 Kosova

was under secret police control. Serbs and Montenegrins, not Albanians, played the dominant role in the administration and politics of the province.[26]

"After the riots of 1968," he further observes, "the opportunity to declare Kosova a republic was lost."[27] The 1974 constitution recognized Kosova as a federal unit in its own right, without, however, granting the province republic status.

Still another mistake was the overreaction to the demonstrations of Spring 1981, which caused consternation and protest in various European countries, and which were followed by drastic repressive measures, as described. In this case those responsible were not only the Serbian and Yugoslav authorities, but also

the provincial leadership [which] had, by the late 1970s, begun to look tolerantly on expressions of Albanian nationalism, and would not permit criticism of developments in the province on the part of other republics—for example, in the case of the 'Blue Book' of 1977 cataloguing Serbian grievances, which was suppressed, in part, due to the objections of the Kosova provincial leadership.[28]

The constitution of 1974, we said, granted Kosova almost the same rights enjoyed by the republics. One would think, considering the vexations suffered by Kosovars in the monarchic period and, more recently under Ranković's rule, that they would have been content. They were not. They resented their still being termed a 'nationality' rather than a 'nation,' the implication being that they were an inferior nation. In order not to feel that way, they had to have the province promoted to a republic. The Spring demonstrations of 1981 erupted with that main demand in view. One wonders whether the repression would have been less harsh had they been conducted with moderation and caution. One incentive for the crackdown was that among the demonstrators chanting "Kosova Republic!" were others holding placards bearing the slogans "Long Live Marxism–Lenism! Down with Revisionism!" and "Unification of All Albanian Lands!" The Stalinist Albanian ideology, bitterly antagonistic to Titoism, had already infiltrated part of the student body and also some professors. Kosovar leaders and cadres had been slow to realize that Tirana's interest in the cultural exchange programs between

Kosova and Albania had been to instill and propagate, under the cover of Albanian culture, the Albanian brand of Stalinism.

After religion, and often as its surrogate, nationalism has proved to be most contagious among new political formations in search of national identity. Kosova's identity has been divided between Serbia and Albania, nationalism causing division to become a chasm. Instead of a rapprochement, the would–be goal set by communists of both ethnic groups, a continued falling apart has occurred. The blame for the miscarriage lies with both, while once more proving vain the efforts of present–day socialism to live up to its internationalist ideal. Clearly humanity is not yet ripe for genuine socialism. When one sees the editors of *Praxis International* sign a document smacking of Serbian nationalism, one wonders whether the socialism of this *fin de siècle* has advanced much over that of its first decades, when French and German socialists were killing each other in the name of patriotism, a name less compromising than nationalism. We have commented on the failures of Serb nationalism. Let us now dwell shortly on the sore spots of Kosovar nationalism.

(b) In 1969, after the riots of 1968, Kosovars won the right to display their Albanian flag. It was the flag of Stalinist Albania: the red flag stamped with the black two–headed eagle surmounted by the pentagonal red star. The traditional Albanian flag does not have that star, which was added to parallel the pentagonal red star set by Yugoslav communists on their traditional blue–white–red flag at a time when the Albanian Communist Party was little more than the Yugoslavs' branch office. Yet in 1948, the Albanian Communist party—which, after its emancipation, had changed its name (but not its flag), becoming the Party of Labour of Albania—was at loggerheads with the League of the Communist Yugoslavs. Nevertheless, the supposedly anti–Stalinist Kosovar leadership adopted the flag of Stalinist Albania without a change. Undeterred, the Kosovar leaders, who were Yugoslav citizens, identified symbolically with a sworn foe of Yugoslavia. The significance of their move could not possibly go unnoticed by Yugoslavs, who drew the conclusion that, deep down, the Kosovar leaders wanted to unite with Albania, even Stalinist Albania. They must have felt that move as an act of defiance. Still, they let them proceed.

But the Kosovar leadership went much further: they also adopted the language of Stalinist Albania. Until that point they had been speaking and writing their own Gheg dialect, while producing a body of literature which, because of the more liberal climate obtaining in Yugoslavia, was considerably better than the irksome verbiage of Albanian socialist realism. That promising start was lost in the following years, when they began to write in the official 'unified literary Albanian,' a reformed variant of Tosk enriched with Toskicized Gheg vocabulary. Instead of cultivating their own literary dialect, which has a tradition initiated by a major Kosovar writer of early Albanian literature, Pjetër Bogdani (1630–1688), thus earning the merit of keeping alive the literary Gheg which the overwhelmingly–Tosk Albanian leadership had condemned to death, they resorted to the ready–made Tosk variant. A question only of intellectual slovenliness? The determining cause was, once more, their uncontrollable desire to identify with Albania, this time not merely symbolically. For language and thought are the two faces of a curved mirror. By using a certain language one absorbs the ideology imbuing it, just as by inhaling air heavy with tobacco smoke one absorbs the nicotine contained in it.   "In politics [language is an eminently political means of communication] to concede the language is to concede the case."[29] The Kosovar leaders conceded the case and cause. They invited on themselves the charge of Stalinism through the proxy of a Stalin–inspired language.[30] By adopting the official Albanian language, the Kosovar leaders made themselves even more liable to charges of Stalinism. Instead of differentiating themselves from it, which was the right thing to do in their circumstances, they have tended to identify with it. According to one account, they adopted the Tirana language to shield themselves from the slanderous charge that they were degenerate Albanians, unlike those of Albania proper. According to another version, they were afraid that they might have to undergo what had happened to Yugoslav Macedonians, who were incorporated into the republic of Macedonia, their West Bulgarian dialect being raised to the dignity of a new language, Macedonian, the language identifying the new republic as such. If so, the Kosovars' fear was unreasonable, for everyone knows that Albanian is a language with two main traditionally spoken and written dialects, Gheg and Tosk, something which cannot be said of Bulgarian. By adopting the Albanian Stalinist flag and the Albanian Stalin–inspired language, Kosovars have provided Serbian nationalism with two counts of indictment. Instead of distancing themselves from Albanian Stalinism, they have flirted with it. They have thus done exactly the opposite of what they ought to have done in order to have their republic.

How are we to explain this paradox?

When I left Albania in 1957, I spent, before entering the United States, a whole year in Sarajevo. There I made the acquaintance of several Kosovar and other Yugoslav Albanians who were then studying at the University of Sarajevo—the Kosovars did not yet have their own university. Two students accompanied me to the railway station one evening when I was going to Belgrade for my visa. Suddenly the platform was invaded by a group of young men speaking Albanian. They were escorting a fellow national— and nationalist—who had been liberated from prison that same day. I saw my friends join the group and embrace the young hero Albanian–style. He left, when the train started, amidst applause and loud greetings. I knew my friends were communists (they could not have obtained fellowships otherwise), and I had long suspected that their communism was lip service paid to the powers that be. So I was little surprised to see them behave as the other nationals did. This experience left me with the impression that, communists or noncommunists, Kosovars and Yugoslav Albanians in general are nationalists almost to a man. What counts for them is Albaniandom; that is the ideology in which they really believe, all others being layers of veneer.

The yearning of the Kosovars to identify with the Albanians of the motherland by adopting their flag and their language is a psychological reaction to their being looked down by Yugoslavs as an inferior race rather than another nation, not much unlike blacks are in the United States. They resent this treatment bitterly, and more so since their inferior socio–cultural condition is no fault of their own. Besides being persecuted in various ways in monarchic Yugoslavia, the Kosovars were denied even instruction in their own language. Communist Yugoslavs treated them more humanely, yet not quite as equals: their inferiority stigma has remained insofar as Kosova is persistently denied republic status, while the Albanians in Macedonia and Montenegro are kept on a short leash.

By the way, the inferiority complex thus inflicted on Kosovars

and other Yugoslav Albanians is far from being shared by the
Albanians of the mother country. Except for a five–year interval
of foreign occupation during World War II, which was resisted
by the population in general (witness the successful movement of
national liberation), the Albanians in the mother country have
been self–ruled. If they too have been suffering from something,
it is from a superiority complex which, during the dictatorship
of Hoxha, a megalomaniac of the worst kind, reached ludicrous
heights. To conflate the Albanian leadership "and" the Kosovar leadership under the rubric of 'Stalinized chauvinism,' the
accusation made by the Belgrade intellectuals' petition, is thus
completely off the mark. The Kosovar leadership has never been
an agency of Albanian Stalinism, as hinted at by the petition.
Also, the kind of Stalinism informing the behavior of the Kosovar
leadership was never the same as that adopted by the Yugoslav
Communist Party before Yugoslavia broke loose from the Soviet
orbit. And whereas the Yugoslav Communist Party afterwards
shook off Stalinism to a great extent, it clung in large part to
the Kosovar leadership. Their attitude towards noncommunist
and anticommunist fellow Albanians in exile can be taken to il-
lustrate the phenomenon. When Albania was a Yugoslav protectorate and Yugoslavia Stalin's darling, the Kosovar leaders were
bound, as the Albanian leaders were, to consider those exiles as
enemies, the very fact of their having left the country illegally being considered by Albanian Stalinists a treacherous act. Yet the
Kosovar leaders' hostile attitude towards Albanian exiles continued even after Albania became Yugoslavia's sworn foe. Among
those exiles there were historians and writers who had not been
involved in Albanian politics during the war, as well as others
whose only offense against Titoism was an occasional expression
of sympathy for Kosovars' plight. Strangely enough, these people
have been tabooed in Kosova just as they have in Albania, and
their books, from which Kosovars have much to learn, have been
banished from the schools and from public view.

The reason for this other paradox is that Kosovars, divided as
they are geographically between Yugoslavia and Albania (though
the great majority remain outside the Albanian frontiers), have
developed a split–personality state of mind, fluctuating between
devotion to Albania, as the ethnic Albanians they are, and loyalty
to Yugoslavia, as Yugoslav citizens.[31] That Albania is a Stalinist

country and, as such, an ideological foe to 'anti–Stalinist' Yugoslavia weighs less with them than their burning desire to be rid of Serbian rule.[32] Whereas the Kosovars reacted to the 1945 Partisan occupation with armed rebellion, one can safely assume that the leadership backed Yugoslavia's plan to unite Albania and Kosova as the seventh republic of the Federation. Such a plan would have delivered the leadership from Serbian servitude while bringing them on equal footing with their fellow Albanians. The plan fizzled out, to their great disappointment, one thinks, thus stirring up Ranković's Albanophobia. Kosovar Stalinism can be ultimately explained as a sedimentation of Kosovar enviousness of the freedom their brother Albanians enjoy in the mother country. What matters to Kosovars and Yugoslav Albanians in general is to get rid of Yugoslav dominance at almost any price—one thinks of their attitude towards the Italian troops as liberators.

(c) We have little to add to our criticism of the Albanian leadership. By championing the Kosovar demand for republic status, they have incited Kosovars to form illegal groups, some of them adopting Tirana's ideology, antagonistic to Yugoslav Titoism. This has prompted Serbs to accuse Kosovars of acting at Tirana's bidding and so to exert on them a severe repression. Yet the Albanian advocacy of the Kosovar demand has been limited to volleys of rhetorical noise. And when persecuted Kosovar members of illegal groups have sought shelter in Albania, they have been handed back to Yugoslav authorities (249 cases during the period 1981–1986). The Albanian Kosova policy has thus resulted in adding to Kosova's woes. The post–Hoxha leadership seems to have realized its futility. In the Balkan Conference held in Belgrade (February 24–26, 1988), the Albanian Minister of Foreign Affairs, Reis Malile, declared that the question of minorities is an internal one to be handled by the state in which they live.[33] The declaration suggests that Albania will no longer continue its Kosova advocacy policy. True, Malile adds that noninterference in other states' minority problems does not imply indifference to them on the part of a neighbor state. Yet this *mise au point* sounds more like an apology for the Hoxha leadership's rude interference in the problems of Kosova than an expression of the position of the post–Hoxha leadership, which has been slowly but steadily moving away from the self–reliance policy identified with Hoxha.[34]

5. Conclusions

The conclusions to be drawn from the preceding criticisms (beginning for continuity's sake with Albania) are as follows:

1. The post–Hoxha leadership seems to have realized the blunders made by the defunct leader. Humiliated by Tito,[35] Hoxha personalized the Kosova question by championing Kosovar rights while hurling vituperative language at Tito and Titoism. He thus made normal relations between Albania and Yugoslavia impossible. By the same token, he minimized the Kosovars' chances of participating with full rights in the Federation by using them as a poker for stirring up firebrands in the ongoing feud. During the Albanian Cultural Revolution of the late sixties, Hoxha had dreams of extending that revolution to Kosova through cultural exchange—this at a time when the Province, embarked on his own plan of opening a university in Prishtina, was in dire need of cultural aid. Hoxha seems to have wanted his brand of Marxism–Leninism to spread among Kosovars, hoping that, once that ideology had struck roots among them, they would first press for Kosova's republic status and then for secession from Yugoslavia and union with Albania. It is not accidental that the "Kosova Republic!" slogan first made its appearance in the 1968 demonstrations, when the Albanian Cultural Revolution was in full swing, together with other slogans, such as "Long Live Albania! Long Live Enver Hoxha!," Down with Traitors!," "One Nation, One State, One Party." The 1981 demonstrations, in which these slogans were reiterated, with the addition of some even more provocative ones, such as "Long Live Marxism–Leninism! Down with Revisionism!" and "No Dialogue with the Red Bourgeoisie!," instead of serving Hoxha's ambitious scheme doomed it, while at the same time bringing discredit on the older and not very efficient Kosovar leadership.

2. The new Kosovar leadership has learned its lesson only too well. They have inflicted drastic punishments on their own fellow-dissidents, often quite gratuitously, in order to allay the anger of Serbian nationalism. On the other hand, they have resisted the heavy pressure of the Serbian Communist League to give up some of the constitutional rights the Province has been exercising, remaining calm in the face of provocations and verbal attacks. To their credit, the population has adopted a like behavior. They

have accepted without a word the change of the flag, imposed on them, in a rather anodyne way, through a decree for changing the flags of other nationalities as well. But they have not yet had the courage to admit the blunder of immolating their own literary dialect in favor of the Tirana language. Their visceral passion for the mother country began to cool off only when they realized that the Albanian government, far from sympathizing with their liberation movement, was afraid of it.[36] We have already mentioned the various accounts purporting to explain the Kosovars' decision to adopt Tirana's official language. The 1974 constitution, which increased the Province's autonomy, strengthened their self–confidence to the point of prompting them to entertain hopes of liberalizing, through cultural exchange with Albania, the latter's autocratic regime. No doubt this sounds bizarre, for at the time the Kosovars were manifestly by far the weaker party. They must have known, one thinks, that in a cultural exchange it is the stronger party who gets the lion's share. Moreover, culture is exported chiefly through language, which is the most ideological means of communication. And Kosovars had been importing the Tirana language lock, stock, and barrel through literary works and textbooks overflowing with Albanian Stalinism. These publications were eliminated or purged after the 1981 events.[37] Ever since Kosovars adopted standard Albanian, their literature has undergone a descending curve.[38] Abandoning it would also be the best way to persuade Serbs that they are finally washing their hands clean of all residues of Stalinism.

3. In its turn, Serbia should seriously consider ending its policy of repression, which is in clear contradiction with the principles of human rights in the Helsinki document signed by Yugoslavia. The country's constitution does not rule out a demand of the Province for promotion to republic status. And even a demand to secede would not be unconstitutional, once Kosova is made a republic. Yet the possibilities for this are nil in the existing conditions, for even a single negative vote by one of the republics—Serbia—would defeat that demand. And previous discussion has sufficiently shown that the Albanian leadership does not want Kosova to join Albania. The union issue is entirely moot at this historical moment. So is the "Kosova Republic" demand, unacceptable to Yugoslavia in general. With Milošević now heading the Serbian League of Communists, and given his offensive aimed

at curtailing the Province's autonomy, preserving it is the utmost that the Kosovars can achieve.

The concrete question is whether the Serbian government, faced as it is with the tide of Serbian nationalism, is willing to contain it and let it subside. This can be done by refusing support to the nationalist anti–Kosovar campaign, while at the same time exacting strict guarantees for respect of the legitimate rights and sentiments of the Serbian and Montenegrin minorities from a Kosovar leadership committed to correcting errors made by previous leaders. An amnesty for all those who accept the federal and republican laws as specified in the constitution should follow, not excluding those who have favored or voiced the "Kosova Republic!" slogan. As already stated, there is nothing wrong with the slogan per se, when expressed quietly and through legal channels. Indeed, the Kosovar leadership itself should have long advocated that demand, thus preventing dissidents from making conspiratorial use of it. And if the Kosovar leadership dared not make that demand, the Kosovar intelligentsia should have, as representative of the *vox populi*. Unfortunately—and here we touch the sore point of the problem—at the time when the slogan first appeared, i.e., in the 1968 demonstrations, a Kosovar intelligentsia hardly existed. Yet through no fault of their own. Having been denied elementary human rights by monarchic Yugoslavia, the Kosovars had been lagging behind their neighbors for more than two decades when Yugoslavia began its existence as a socialist state. They advanced rapidly afterwards, but could not of course catch up with the Serbs, who had already formed their intelligentsia in the royalist period. When the Kosovars finally managed to lay the foundations of their university during that troublesome year of 1968, their burgeoning intelligentsia could hardly match the weight and prestige of the Serb intelligentsia, part of which, at least, as the petition of the more than two hundred Belgrade intellectuals shows, is still haunted by nostalgic memories of Stara Serbia. Had a Kosovar intelligentsia existed in 1968, blunders such as the adoption of the Stalinist Albanian flag and Stalin–inspired standard Albanian language would have been avoided, thus giving the Kosovar leadership much more political clout in dealing with their Serb controllers.

One point not yet made by this article is that the Serbian repression of the Kosovars has been by and large condoned by the other republics mostly because they have perceived Kosova as a possible extension of Stalinist Albania, Albanian Stalinism having managed to make proselytes among Kosovars, especially the younger generation. If this fear vanishes, the repression may cease. Then cultural relations between Kosova and Albania, which were cut off after the 1981 demonstrations, can be resumed. It is also quite possible, judging from recent developments in the Soviet Union, that Stalinism in Albania will lose its edge, dying away by degrees. This will create a favorable atmosphere for improved relations between Albania and Yugoslavia, with Kosova ceasing to function as a buffer–state. And if this happens, then the persistent demand of Kosovars to have their own republic could be granted. It is a legitimate demand, which cannot fail to generate persuasion and assent. Thus a day may well come when, with the recognition of the Republic of Kosova within the Federal Republic of Yugoslavia, the very name Yugoslavia, presently denoting only South Slavs, might be dropped for another name, one more fit to denote the community of peoples inhabiting the western part of the Balkan peninsula. Such a picture would imply the existence of two Albanian states. Whether the 'Other Albania' will eventually merge with the mother country is a matter of speculation, contingent on whether Yugoslavia will continue to exist as a federation. This article was written on the assumption that it will, so long at least as the equilibrium of the two superpowers in Europe remains unaltered. Yugoslavia's disintegration would destroy that equilibrium, something no one seems to want—not the United States, which looks on Yugoslavia as a neutral state friendly to the West and not the Soviet Union, which, as their withdrawal from Afghanistan indicates, seems not eager to expand its *imperium* at this historical conjuncture. As to Europe, all its countries, Albania apart, have, by signing the Helsinki agreement, committed themselves to not seeking changes of frontier.

XIII.   GLASNOST IN ALBANIA?*

Ever since Hoxha's death in April 1985, people have been expecting some sort of liberalization in Albania's politics. The expectations have not been entirely unfulfilled. Albania has established diplomatic relations with West Germany, Spain, and even Canada, a country closely related, both politically and linguistically, to the United States and the United Kingdom, two countries with whom Albania has no diplomatic relations. Tourist groups, including many American citizens, have visited Albania. Among them have been clergy who have had good things to say for the Albanian atheist regime.[1] Foreign policy has changed considerably, and internal policy shows improvement. The much-feared Albanian KGB has sheathed its claws; now people can talk, no longer afraid of being arrested for even verbal offenses.

1. Economic Problems

The economic situation was the major theme in Ramiz Alia's report to the Ninth Party Congress (November 1986). He did not try to cover up the failure of the 1980–85 quinquennial plan. Growth in agricultural production during this period was 13 percent, instead of the 30 percent target. Industrial output came out with a deficit of 10 percent, and the extraction of oil reached about half the expected 58–60 percent growth.[2] On the whole, the objectives of the 1981–85 quinquennial were reached only by half, while the growth of national income fell from 4.3 percent to 3 percent in the next period.[3] The 1986–1990 plan seems no more promising than the preceding one. The President of the Plan Committee, Niko Gjyzari, has reported the growth rate for 1986: social product, 5.1 percent (instead of the expected 9.5 percent); national income, 7.9 percent (instead of 10.6

---

* Published in *Telos* 79, Spring 1989

percent); industrial output, 6.4 percent (instead of 7.3 percent).[4] His report for 1987 presented no production figures and no growth rates, laying the blame on the harsh winter, the long drought, and the resulting penury of water and electricity.

According to the Swiss newspaper *Neue Zürcher Zeitung* (August 29, 1988), Albania remains an underdeveloped country, in spite of its rich mineral resources and rich electric power potential. Because of the ban on foreign loans and the shortage of foreign currency, foreign trade occurs mostly in the form of barter. Tourism is not encouraged, also for fear of alien ideological infiltration. The periodical quotes figures from a study made by the Hamburg Institute of Economic Research. Whereas two-thirds of the labor force are in the agricultural sector, its contribution to the national income is merely 20 percent, as compared to 55 percent in the industrial sector. While one-fourth of the labor force works in the extraction and processing of raw materials, manufacture is rather scant. The study warns that these figures must not be taken at face value due to lack of published data, and also because the statistical apparatus is rather poor.[6]

An article in the Greek periodical *Embistevtiko gramma* (October 21, 1987) states that the situation of the Albanian economy has prompted a secret report circulating in some ministries of the European Common Market.[6bis] The article points out that the demographic explosion in Albania is not matched by economic growth: the industrial equipment is to a great extent obsolete; agriculture is backward and lags behind; services are inadequate. In the long run, unable to solve her economic problem, and for want of any assistance from the countries of the European Common Market, Albania would have to end up resorting to the Soviet Union.

This assumption seems to have been proved wrong by the decision of the Albanian government to sign a technico-industrial treaty with West Germany (June 3, 1988). Writers of reports such as this should give at least the benefit of the doubt to a pertinent Hoxha slogan, repeated in various wordings: We will feed on grass rather than kneel down to capitalism. The saying is arrogant enough, but does contain a grain of truth: when one falls to one's knees, the mouth is in a better position to begin grazing.

A Belgian journalist who visited Albania recently has reported an oral exchange which can be taken as a better yardstick with which to measure the psychology of the Albanian leadership.

Question: Albania had one million people in 1944–45; now

it has three million. Before the [last] war, life expectancy
was merely 38 years, now it is 71. The country's area is
28,000 square kilometers, two–thirds of which are mountainous. Don't you think that in the long run you are going to
have problems?

Answer: We are not afraid, for we can increase our [national]
production so as to feed six million in 15—20 years.[7]

A bit of braggadocio, no doubt, for the data shows that the rate of
growth has continued to decrease during the last two quinquennial
plans. According to Michael Kaser, an English specialist on the Albanian economy, Albania's arable land amounts to 600,000 hectares.
On the assumption that the Albanians' high birthrate (70,000 per
year) will not slow down, at the end of the century one hectare of
arable land will have to support six–and–a–half people, something
hardly possible under present conditions of yield.[8]

A 1987 editorial in the Party daily *Zëri i popullit* [The Voice of
the People], laments the lack of spare parts for agricultural equipment.
Of the items to be furnished by the Tractor Factory in the first three
months of the year, 67 were delivered at 100 percent of projected
levels, 8 only in part, and 13 not at all. The Rubber Factory delivered
100 percent of only 2 of its 13 required items.[9] A later editorial in the
same newspaper (June 14, 1987) reports the Politburo's opinion that
oil extraction has been "unsatisfactory."

2. Defense and Security

Due to the obsolescence of agricultural machinery and the lack
of spare parts in industry, national productivity has decreased in almost all economic sectors. Exports have diminished, causing currency problems affecting all state sectors, including defense. After
Czechoslovakia's occupation by the Soviet army, the Albanian army
adopted the Chinese style of "people's war," based on guerilla warfare.
The government distributes arms to all those capable of bearing them
(one–third of the population) and gives them paramilitary training.
This militia is to be placed in bunkers, waiting for the assailant, while
the regular infantry attacks. According to a Greek source, the army
is 31,500 strong, 20,000 of that number being conscripts on two–year
service. Naval personnel number 3,300; those in the Air Force, 7,200.
A considerable part of the military's equipment is out of service. The
infantry has a total of 20 Soviet armored cars and about 80 Soviet

armored personnel carriers. The Air Force has 30 helicopters, 100 MiGs, and 20 Chinese planes, most of them useless. Useless, too, is some 40 percent of the Navy's equipment, which consists of 3 Soviet submarines, 12 Chinese torpedo boats, and quite a few Chinese patrol boats, as well as a flotilla of 7–8 minelayers. Modern anti–tank and air defenses, as well as coastal defenses, are lacking.[10] The same periodical states that the secret police is 5,000 strong, a sort of pretorian guard whose principal function was to protect the dictator from eventual *coups d'état* on the part of the armed forces.

The grip of the secret police has slackened since Hoxha's death. The leadership must have realized that police terror has negative effects on the population's morale, with baleful consequences for the economy and culture. Particularly significant in this respect are the election results for the National Assembly in March of 1987, in which voter participation was 100 percent, with not even one abstention. How such things are possible in Albania is explained by the Albanian Penal Code, in which class struggle is spelled out as the criterion governing Albanian justice.[11] Abortion is illegal, homosexuality is punished with ten years' imprisonment, and a prisoner unwilling to be reformed can be interned after having served his or her sentence.

Class struggle as the principle of justice, what does this mean in practice? It means servitude and infamy for whoever does not accept Albanian Marxism–Leninism. The principle is operative not only against class enemies, but also against Party dissidents, who end up—even those who had been Party leaders—as non–persons: in Hoxha's own words, as "garbage in the dustbin of history."

From this kind of social ethics, grounded on terror against all kinds of adversaries, a culture is born which could not but be one of cruelty and servility. We shall first examine some of its manifestations, beginning with education.

3. The Cultural Scenario

After my release from prison in 1956, I had great difficulty in making a living. Threatened with starvation, I decided to see Ramiz Alia, then Minister of Education, who had been my student at the Tirana Lyceum in 1943–44. The reception was urbane, and soon after I was appointed a teacher of Albanian in an elementary school. The reader in use was heavy with Party literature. And the grammar textbook was studded with excerpts from Hoxha's speeches, along with Party slogans. Grammar had to be taught by grafting these onto the pupils' tender brains. It was too much to take; my nerves were growing more and more on edge. And so as not to end up in a hospital, I quit.

The politics of language, begun in the elementary school with the prostitution of grammar to Stalinist ideology, was crowned with the pseudo–scientific masterpiece called "unified literary Albanian," which is in fact the language of the victorious Tosk communists imposed on the vanquished Ghegs. I explain the terms with an example. The periodical *Mësuesi* [The Educator] contains an article on undeserved good grades.[12] The author finds that the phenomenon is, luckily, not widespread. As examples of secondary schools that do not assign good grades unless deserved, he mentions those in three cities, Përmet, Korçë, and Gjirokastër, while taking the Kukës school as a contrary example. Now Kukës is located in North Albania where Gheg is spoken, whereas all three other cities are located in South Albania, where the Tosk dialect is used. I do not contest the veracity of the author's statements. But I wonder why schools in South Albania function better than those in the north. Is it because Tosks are more intelligent than Ghegs? The reason is that Tosks can speak and write without difficulty in "unified Albanian," which is structurally Tosk, whereas Ghegs find it hard to express themselves in a dialect that is not their own, literary Gheg having been suppressed.

Moving now to the level of higher education and post–graduate studies, what strikes one is the almost complete absence of criticism. In my capacity as bibliographer for Albanian literature in the *Modern Language Association Bibliography* (I apologize for once more using a personal example), I am expected to read works of literary criticism, reviews of literary and historical books, comments on doctoral dissertations, and cultural writings in general. The evaluations are always positive; nowhere do I find a note on what is deficient or wrong. One pays compliments to another, according to the well–known Latin adage, while at the same time never forgetting to pay tribute to Comrade Enver as the patron saint of Albanian scholarship. Reading such writings, one gets the impression that everything is as it should be in the best of all possible worlds.

That not everything is as it should be can be easily ascertained by going over what Party leaders say. In his speech to the Fifth Central Committee Plenum (March 2, 1988), Alia pointed out that the inveterate tendency to privilege quantity at the expense of quality informs even graduate studies: "In most of them scientific information, though more unified and concentrated, does not go beyond the level of courses taught in the last year of university studies."[13] Alia criticizes another tendency, the

> levelling out of values, a consequence of shallow criticism and overgeneralized judgments. . . . One only needs to read the Sunday edition of *Drita* [Light], where one runs into an interminable list of authors' names superlatively praised.[14]

The "levelling of values" is justified as an antidote to "elitism." But "socialist society must support individual creativity. . . . Art in particular is not made with patterns and prefabricated materials."[15]

What Alia calls "leveling of values," Foto Çami, the Politburo person in charge of culture, calls "mediocrity," a more pertinent term.[16] Mediocrity won't be overcome as long as there is no "qualitative rise," a phrase which has been sounded like a broken record by Party ideologists for a whole generation now. Çami makes no bones about the lack of quality: "Party criticism of negative manifestations in literature holds for all other cultural areas as well."[17] He underscores the low level of theater[18] and cinema, i.e., of the most efficient artistic mass media. He finds fault with the translation of literary works, the performance of cultural ensembles, and art exhibitions abroad; deplores the divorce of intellectual from moral culture; finds social services unsatisfactory, works ethics poor. And he lays the blame not only on the deficient economy, but also on individual indolence, lack of work discipline, and incompetent management.

In another article in *Rruga e Partisë* [The Party Road] (no. 4, April 1988), Çami criticizes the University of Tirana for its inefficiency in scientific research. The research institutes claim they have "studied" their respective problems. Where are the results?, Çami asks. His criticism implies that scientific research is inadequate.

4. Untightening of the Screws and First Steps of Public Criticism

Thanks to the initiative of Alia and Çami, criticism has surfaced in Tirana. It had been absent from the Albanian scenario ever since the country's rupture with China, a period which came to an end with Hoxha's death. It was during this period that the dictator, tired of trying to fill in with ideological glue the cracks in his edifice— his list includes lack of discipline, high absenteeism at work, theft and damage to socialist property, waste of raw materials, falsified statistics—sought diversion in writing. While criticizing these and other ills, Hoxha imputed them to Albania's "revisionist–capitalist encirclement," his phrase for 'isolation,' which he had assiduously engineered in order that he might be hailed, after Mao's betrayal of the ideal of world revolution, as the undisputed world leader of Marxism–Leninism.

The striking feature of the new leadership's criticism is that the flaws of system are hardly attributed to the revisionist–capitalist encirclement—a minus for Stalinist ideology. Another feature is that criticism now stresses moral decay rather than economic want—a minus for historical materialism in general. Neither of these two departures would have been possible if Hoxha still lived. Would he admit that the "purity" of Albanian Marxism–Leninism, arrived at through his continued purges, could ever be defiled? Now his very widow admits it:

> Our people has always considered theft an ugly and dangerous vice. Yet some people excuse it on the grounds that there is scarcity of some items and that the needs of the mass remain unfulfilled. This may be one of the reasons, but not the principal one.[19]

Which, then, is the principal reason? Can one infer that thievery is only a surface phenomenon, its roots being deeper?

An article in *Dielli* (July 25, 1988), reporting impressions of a recent Albanian–American visitor, speaks of "moral degeneration," resulting in mental troubles, especially depression. The article confirms that theft of public property is the most widespread 'vice.' Authorities have tried hard to inculcate respect for public property by arguing that public property belongs to the people, as made clear by the qualifier 'public.' To which the people respond: If public property belongs to us, we can take it, which is not to say we are stealing it. A further illustration, also in a humorous key, is a story—a true one— in the workers' union newspaper. Two schools in a Central Albanian town used to be surrounded by brick walls. The walls disappear one after another. The director of one of the schools complains to the Chief Executive of the district. "You're not asking me to put in writing that walls don't move, are you?" says the chief, adding: "The walls do indeed move, but they don't travel far. You can find their bricks in the new houses built in your town and mine."[20]

The examples suggest that people have begun to open their

mouths, yet their criticism is expressed cautiously, in a rather playful way, as in the following joke: "They want us to think our salaries are good. And we make them think our work is superb." Only occasionally does criticism take the form of lampoon, as in the following strophe:

> Scallion and cabbage the Shkodër people eat,
> but Muho Asllani only fish and meat.
> O Ramiz, you cleverest of bums,
> you cannot feed the people with crumbs.[21]

All considered, we can speak of an untightening of the screws. Since the new leadership came to power, it seems that no incarcerations for political reasons have been made. Yet political prisons and forced labor camps persist. The number of prisoners and internees is not known; a conservative estimate would be in four digits, though two amnesties in 1986 and 1987 must have made a difference. Internment has not been abolished, the interned being individuals and even entire families related to exiles, as well as former prisoners still considered dangerous. In its reports on the situation of political prisoners, Amnesty International has more than once called attention to the harsh treatment they receive.[22] A recent exposé by a committee of American lawyers for human rights focuses on religious persecutions.[23] Interviewed on this topic by an English journalist, Professor Aleks Buda, President of the Academy of Sciences, quoted the line of an ideologist of the Albanian Risorgimento: "The religion of the Albanian is Albanianism," adding: "I would not say that any idea has the right to exist. This would lead to the suicide of the nation."[24]

Thus speaks a retrograde conservative. The leading team is more flexible. Religious persecution has been suspended. As already mentioned, representatives of the Albanian–American clergy have been allowed to enter the country, although the leadership remains loyal to its atheistic faith and Albania's attitude towards the United States continues to be hostile. Hostility is, however, more bitter against the other superpower, and for good cause. For Albania has nothing to fear from the United States, whose only concern is not to let Albania fall back into Soviet arms. We saw that certain Common Market countries seriously consider that possibility, owing to the steady deterioration of Albania's economy. One cannot exclude the possible resurgence in the Party of a pro–Soviet faction, one which, faced with the prospect of an economic catastrophe, would appeal to Gorbachev just as Hoxha appealed to Stalin in the past. And since a Soviet intervention could topple the existing leadership, their pronounced hostility toward the 'social-imperialist' superpower should not come as a surprise.

5. The Hedgehog Comes Out of His Hedge

Hence the Party's negative reaction to Gorbachev's reforms. An editorial in the Party daily is entitled: "*Perestroika*, a program and a strategy to strengthen Soviet social–imperialism."[25] One also reads (I limit myself to subtitles): "*Perestroika* is anti–socialism"; "The Principal objective of *perestroika*: the privatization of economy"; "*Glasnost*: a trick with which to crown the ideals of the bourgeoisie." And since *glasnost's* main objective is to demolish Stalin's cult, his memory continues to be entertained by the party on a par with Lenin's, his statue occupying a place of honor in Tirana. The Army's organ, *Luftëtari* [The Combatant], has published an article (June 23, 1988) exalting Stalin for his "liquidation of the Trotskyist–Bukharinist gang and the faithless Tukhachevsky group," while also reviling "the revisionist perfidious Khrushchev–Brezhnev clique."

Nonetheless, for tactical reasons, the United States and the Soviet Union appear in tandem in the speeches of the Albanian leaders and the broadsides of the Albanian press. The speech of the Vice–Minister of Foreign Affairs before the United Nations includes the following:

> The main protagonists of th[e] unrestrained arms race . . .
> are the two superpowers, the United States of America and
> the Soviet Union, which, together, with the military blocs
> they lead, NATO and the Warsaw Treaty, account for about
> 800 billion dollars of this expenditure. . . . It is more
> than justifiable for the countries and peoples who continue
> to suffer from the consequences of colonial oppression and
> neo–colonial exploitation to feel deeply concerned with and
> indignant at seeing the very ones who have robbed and con-
> tinue to rob them of their national assets spend hundreds of
> billions on the production of all types of weapons.[26]

Associated with the Soviet Union through the common denominator of revisionism, Yugoslavia shares with the social–imperialist superstate the honor of priority in the attacks of the Albanian press.

In one of its articles *Zëri i popullit* lashes out at the unfriendly declaration of the then–President of Yugoslavia, Lazar Mojsov, concerning the Albanians of Yugoslavia.[27] The same newspaper rebukes a Serbian writer for his "slanders and attacks" aimed at proving Albanian cultural inferiority.[28] Still another editorial in the same newspaper (August 11, 1988) criticizes Yugoslavia's decision to increase the number of the special federal police in Kosovo and to intensify the activities of the courts of justice. The article points out that, since the 1981 demonstrations, 15,000 Kosovars have been jailed, and it goes on to reiterate the Albanian—and Kosovar—thesis that Serbs are abandoning Kosovo because of the province's great poverty, not because they are persecuted by the Albanians, as the Serbs pretend.

After the Belgrade Conference of the six Balkan countries (February 1988), at which the Albanian Minister of Foreign Affairs recognized that the question of national minorities is an internal one, the general impression was that Albania had dropped its quarrel with Yugoslavia concerning Kosovo. The above–mentioned articles disprove that assumption; the anti–Yugoslav attacks persist, though in a lower key. On the other hand, while tacitly supporting the Kosovar request for a republic of Kosovo, the Albanian government has continued to hand Kosovar refugees over to Yugoslav authorities—249 only from April 1981 to December 1983, according to Sinan Hasani, former President of Yugoslavia.[29] The Albanian government has never pleaded the Kosovar cause before the United Nations. Clearly, it does not want to shoulder that responsibility. Why then make poor Kosovars believe that Albania supports their claims? This unscrupulous policy only adds to Kosovars' sufferings, the advocacy of the Albanian government being interpreted as an incentive to Kosovar irredentism.

Among Balkan countries, Greece enjoys preferential treatment. The Greek socialist government abolished the 'state of war' between the two countries which had gone back to World War II, when Albania, then an Italian colony, declared war on Greece following the Italian invasion of that country. Greek personages who have visited Albania have expressed satisfaction with the way the Greek minority has been treated by the Albanian government. An Athens–Tirana air link has been established. The relations with Turkey continue to be friendly. Not so the relations with Italy, which have become stale since an entire family obtained refuge in the Italian Embassy in Tirana, where they have been living for some three years. Yet this has not prevented the Albanian government from signing a treaty for cultural cooperation with Italy (May 1988). Relations with Bulgaria have improved, whereas those with Romania remain icy. Albania entertains good relations with Switzerland; a Zürich–Tirana air link is flown twice a week. And for quite some time another Central European country, Austria, has been representing Albanian interests in countries with which Albania has no diplomatic relations. The friendly relations with France, owing much to Hoxha's French cultural background, have cooled a bit since his death. Now Albania has diplomatic relations with 110 states on five continents. No longer can one say that Albania is isolated. The former glacier has become— very much Diamatically–a torrent.

It is true that Albania has never literally been isolated, even after the break with China (with which, by the way, Albania continues to have diplomatic relations). Yet relations with Third World countries, which were of rather ideological and propagandist nature, could not modify Albania's retreat into herself. Situated in Europe and hostile to both the Atlantic alliance and the Soviet bloc, while also unassociated with the group of nonaligned countries, Hoxha's Albania, sticking to the principle of self–reliance, was isolated *de facto*. The new leadership has realized that this *lager*–like isolation risks atrophy in the economy, let alone in intellectual life. They have begun to take action—which is not easy, one must recognize. For Hoxha has mortgaged not only the Albanian economy but also Albanian thinking. Having eliminated one after the other all real or potential rivals, he has monopolized Albanian Marxism–Leninism as its only ideologist and theorist. Glorified during his life as the architect and legislator of the Albanian state, its illustrious diplomat and great army commander, the father of the reborn Albanian nation, he has been apotheosized after his death. The Albanian Stalin has become Albania's Lenin, his writings the equivalent of sacred scriptures, his ideas the mainsprings of Albanian politics and legislation.

One of those ideas is the article in the Albanian constitution prohibiting foreign investments and loans. Now Albania's economy is, as shown, in serious trouble. Its two major exports, chrome and oil, have become less profitable due to the diminished extraction quotas, and also because the price of oil has fallen considerably in the international market. The shortage translates into a lack of currency—83 million francs in 1987,[30] an amount which is badly needed to replace the out–of–service machinery. The result is never–ending repair work, on a mostly trial–and–error basis (the Greek article on defense speaks of spare parts obtained through "cannibalization" of old tanks). It goes without saying that in conditions such as these the quinquennial plans cannot be fulfilled. Hence the decline in national product, caused by jerky work–rhythms, indolence, underhanded practices in management, and fallacious optimism based on falsified statistics,[31] the discrediting of the notion of socialist property, thievery, vandalism— rumors are that in Shkodër the population has eaten bread mixed with sand (a Ministry of Interior report has called attention to the bad quality of bread).[32]

The press has become more vocal. *Zëri i popullit* stigmatizes phenomena such as "thievery, injuries, inefficiency, laziness, and red tape," interpreted as "manifestation of class struggle."[33] The same newspaper (June 17, 1988), following a Politburo decision, publishes an article on cadre rotation in some ministries more than usually susceptible to bribes and favoritism. We saw that Hoxha's widow speaks of thievery as something quite ordinary. Çami, who does not mince his words, concluded in a speech to the Academy of Sciences in March 1987 that "as long as the country's freedom and independence are protected and the social order preserved, 'other things can and must be changed when necessary.' "[34] His formula leaves the door open to a number of interpretations, one of which could well be, in the course of time, Gorbachev's formula of *perestroika/glasnost.*

6. Problems with Youth

I began this article wondering whether something is happening in Albania comparable to what is going on in the Soviet Union, considering not only that Gorbachev and Alia were elected at about the same time, but more particularly that both of them show a tendency towards decentralization, which is, however, much stronger in the former. Now Gorbachev is supported mainly by intellectuals. Can the same be said with respect to Alia and his team?

My assumption is that since Albania has been molded basically on Stalin's model of socialism, the country is bound to undergo, *mutatis mutandis*, the fate of the Soviet Union. And we shall shortly see that there are additional reasons for that assumption. Now the Soviet Union's reaction to Stalin's dictatorship was expressed mostly by young poets, two of whom, Evgeny Yevtushenko and Andrey Voznesenksy, enjoyed great popularity among Soviet youth. Albania did not have a Khrushchev, and Albanian ideology continued to be rooted in Stalin's doctrine and praxis. Yet in the late sixties, as a consequence of Hoxha's infatuation with the Chinese Cultural Revolution, Stalin was temporarily overshadowed by Mao. It was during the Albanian Cultural Revolution that Ismail Kadare and Fadil Paçrami made their debut, the former a poet and novelist, the latter a playwright. Kadare could publish his controversial novels thanks to his panegyrics to Hoxha. The victim was Paçrami, demolished by Hoxha himself, who saw him as a dangerous rival—Paçrami, chief of the Tirana Youth Organization during the war and editor–in–chief of *Zëri i popullit* after the break with Yugoslavia, later a member of the Party's Central Committee and Minister of Education, was respected by and popular with the educated youth. Other victims of the 1973 purge were the director of radio–television and the president of the Youth Organization. They were accused of "liberalism," manifested, according to Hoxha, in alien lifestyles such as wearing "long hair" and playing "jungle music."

Liberalism is implicitly linked to "anticulture" in an article in *Rruga e Partisë* [The Party Road], the Party's theoretical organ. Taking his lead from Alia's explanation of terrorism as a modern bourgeois phenomenon of moral disintegration and despair among people living in misery, the writer elaborates on the degeneration of philosophical and aesthetic thought which in turn breeds "the subcultural revolution."[35] Seemingly in reply to this article is one in *Zëri i rinisë* [The Voice of Youth], published by the Youth Organization, which comments on a clothing exhibition for young people. The writer hints that they did not care for the exhibition, finding it beneath their expectations. He distinguishes between "liberals," who find modern good taste in certain styles of clothing, and "sectarians," who call good taste "extravagant" and "alien." He criticizes the latter, the desire to dress well being seen as a legitimate aesthetic demand.[36]

Another article in the same periodical comments on a clothing exhibition in the Soviet Union. Yet here the clothing motif is merely a pretext for conveying explicit political statements. For at a certain point, the author notes that the improved relations between the United States and the Soviet Union are not limited to disarmament, then adds:

> Here success is obvious and undeniable. Successes such as this cannot possibly go unnoticed in other sectors, even in that of fashion. . . . This exhibition is a precious gift *perestroika* has given to young people on the occasion of the

new year. Next year *perestroika's* gift might be even more interesting.[37]

Whereas the Party lashes out at *perestroika*, the youth sing its praises. On the other hand, the Youth Organization organ deplores certain acts and habits of young people: violations of proletarian discipline, careless work, products of poor quality, injuries to socialist property, thievery, vulgar and coarse language (an English journalist who has had contacts with youngsters speaks of them "cursing the system").[38]

Hamit Beqja is a professor of psychology at the Tirana University. His article,[39] a good discussion of youth mentality, begins with a discussion of their lifestyle. They loathe hard work, and work *tout court*; their approach to studies is shallow; they seek to get good grades and certificates without deserving them, prefer careers in the high–ranking professions, pay lip–service to revolutionary ideals. The outcome is a sort of "parasitism." The causes are many: the heritage of a backward past, weakening of patriarchal and parental authority, imitation of foreign models, indulgence on the part of authorities. "Go for a walk in Tirana's main park. You will see trees recently hacked at—a true barbarian act." The professor grows indignant; he demands severe punitive measures, for "barbarian acts must be combatted, also, with barbarian methods." Other vices are mentioned, besides vandalism: palm–greasing, favoritism, various kinds of solicitation. Yet youthful frivolity is only part of the problem, which has its roots in an ideological stance: "To justify these alien manifestations by taking refuge behind the presence and influence of objective factors is, no doubt, to fall into vulgar mechanistic materialism." The language indirectly accuses someone or some group in the party of cultivating a Marxism–Leninism smacking of Menshevism. Beqja's silent accentuation, by contrast, of subjective and voluntaristic factors recalls Gramsci, the most–read Marxist—almost on a par with Lenin—in the Soviet Union today. The title of Beqja's article, "Intellectual culture and moral culture," paraphrases Gramsci's well–known formula of "intellectual and moral reform."

In another article, written a year later,[40] the culprits for the alienation of youth are identified as Party conservatives. For these people, everything must remain as it is, "especially the young and, in general, the relations between generations." An analysis of the generation gap follows, a theme typical of capitalist culture, usually avoided by communists. Conservatives, the professor continues, don't want to understand that the alienation phenomena among the young must be explained in context with other phenomena, such as the country's industrialization, the demographic rise, a certain degree of urbanism, the disintegration of the customary code, and the massive education of the young. One risks being branded a "liberal" by these retrogrades simply for saying that the phenomena of alienation among the young must be approached by recognizing the difficulties inherent in their intellectual and moral growth. Instead of starting dialogues with young people with a view to resolving their problems, conservatives hit them with their taboos. The holders of taboos who pose as guardians of the puritanical national heritage are in fact mouthpieces for a fanatical, patriarchal, and petit–bourgeois mentality.

Intellectuals such as Beqja are, no doubt, in the camp of Alia and his team. They don't seem to be many so far, though their number is bound to increase. What about the new generation, which makes up a third of the population? The Youth Organization's attitude toward the new leadership is lukewarm to cool. In a previous article,[41] I suggested that the end of Stalinism in Albania may depend on the alliance of the leadership and the students, i.e., the educated youth. The chances of this occurring in the near future, judging from the texts just discussed, are small. As long as the statues and busts of Stalin continue to adorn the squares of Albanian cities, the young will be loath to support a reformist movement which remains deaf to their demands. There cannot be a true cultural revolution in Albania without demolishing the Stalin–Hoxha cult.

All that can be said at this time is that the hedgehog is no longer rolling into a ball, having instead left his hedge to explore adjacent grounds. What Alia and his team have so far achieved presents a certain resemblance to what Gorbachev is doing. Western observers are unanimous in crediting the new Albanian leader with tacking slightly towards decentralization, granting some autonomy to agricultural cooperatives, and introducing incentives that diversify the salary system.[42] However, compared to such radical reforms of *perestroika* as self–financing of enterprises, creation of joint companies with participation of foreign capital, and lease of land up to fifty years—all of which amount to privatization—the Albanian reforms look like the rippling of waves in a breeze compared to the ripping off of roofs in a hurricane. The difference with respect to *glasnost* is also conspicuous. The power of the secret police has indeed been restrained; yet Hoxha cannot be openly criticized, whereas de–Stalinization in the Soviet

Union is in full swing. The bunkers dotting the Albanian landscape have been sealed, but not destroyed. The number of tourists has slightly increased (ca. 12,000 in 1988). Yet, with a few exceptions, they still have to travel in groups, and they still cannot visit mountainous North Albania. The press has become mildly critical,[43] but as yet there is no Albanian *samizdat*.

This is to say that Albania's de–Stalinization will probably take some time. But it is bound to occur if the Stalin cult in the Soviet Union is in due time (as appears likely) desecrated, and continuous international pressure is exerted on Albania to end its ideological isolation. Given the quasi–parental Stalin–Hoxha relation, the de–Stalinization process will involve the withering away of the Hoxha cult. The process, however, could come to a brusque end with a sudden ideological swerve, something which is not to be excluded considering that there have already been two such cases in the past. One more would not be a great surprise. A brief survey of Albanian communism may shed light on its queer nature.

7. Evolution–Devolution in Stages

The nature of a thing, the Italian philosopher Vico used to say, is no more than the ensemble of factors presiding over its birth. Once a seed is born a plant, its growth is the realization of the seed's entelechy. *Pace* Engels, no dialectic here. But a dialectic, though not of the Marxian type, is at work in the history of typical Stalinist communist parties, such as the Bolshevik party and its Albanian heir, where former friends turn into foes and are then duly purged. Because of the maximal centralization characteristic of such a party, the person (and there is usually only one) at the epicenter tends to act, by virtue of the party's pronounced hierarchical system, pretty much as a puppeteer manipulates his puppets. The history of such a party coagulates at his feet and becomes his pedestal, illustrated with his victories over all sorts of dissidents, whether friend or foe.

The history of the Albanian Party has gone through five stages.

Stage 1. Albanian Communism was born an orphan, with the Yugoslav Communist Party acting first as midwife and then as nurse. During the period of Yugoslav tutelage (1941–48), Albania was not really an independent state, the Albanian C.P. being practically a branch of the Yugoslav C.P. And when a government was formed, composed of incompetent and mostly half–educated people, it had to resort to Yugoslav advisors for the running of the state. Since

Yugoslav communism was at the time completely Stalinist, with Tito the darling of Stalin, Albanian communism was entirely Stalinist, too. Its main slogan: "Enver–Tito."

Stage 2. It became "Enver–Stalin" after Stalin's excommunication of the Yugoslav C.P. The Yugoslav advisors were replaced by Soviet ones, who were, however, less demanding, since the Albanian Party–State hastened to adopt almost all features of the Big Brother's system in its various sectors: Party organization, state security, army, industry, agriculture, education, language and literature, etc. Stalin was not insensitive to that kind of doglike loyalty, responding with lots of economic and technical aid, and taking Albania under his wings when the country felt threatened with partition by its neighbors. The Soviet protectorate period (1948–1961) was the golden age of Albanian communism. Things began to turn sour when Khrushchev pressured the leadership to make peace with Yugoslavia. This Hoxha would never do, for it would mean licking back all the saliva he had spit upon his former master, now his mortal enemy. So he turned against Khrushchev, denouncing him as another revisionist, while branding the Soviet Union as 'social–imperialist.'

Stage 3. The protectorate grew into an alliance during the Maoist stage (1961–1978). Soviet technicians were replaced by Chinese ones. But no advisors this time, only "Enver–Mao." Self–governance advanced, but the economy was still a long way from "self–reliance": there were five billion dollars of Chinese aid, alimentary, military, and financial. All this was written off with a stroke of the pen after the seventeen–year–old alliance degenerated into misalliance. What happened? Well, there is the story of the elephant and the rooster. The rooster sang the praises of the elephant, who fed the rooster for as long as he sang. But then Elephant befriended Vixen, who is, as everyone knows, the mortal enemy of the gallinaceous breed. The rooster stopped singing and began cackling. And that was the end of the Sino–Albanian romance.

Stage 4. A period of soul–searching ensued (1978–1985), during which Hoxha hatched the golden eggs of his disaffected mind. What came out was a series of volumes of reminiscences and other material, which constitute his title to glory as the theorist of latter–day Marxism–Lenism. He scrubbed the doctrine clean of all manner of filth attached to it by renegades and revisionists, such as Trotskyism, Titoism, social–imperialism, Maoism, Eurocommunism, and other –isms. To all of them he opposed his *Stalalbanianism* as the definitive

Koran of mankind. The Koran he liked, for it was "more complete and purer than the Bible (Torah) of the Jews, the Christian Gospel, etc.," while greatly admiring its author for being, as well as a prophet, "also 'head of state,' " and, mind you, no "autocrat," "because God was the only 'source of authority' both for the leader (Mohammed) and for the people."[44]

Stage 5. Faced with this last act of his performance, his disciples had no choice but to adore him. His cult of personality, written large on mountains and lawns, has grown, since his passing away, into a religion. The Koran contains many a purple patch. Hoxhan zealots have discovered literary jewels in the memoirs of their prophet.[45] Hoxha exalted as the Albanian Mohammed—a record achievement for Albanian scholarship. Yet Stalinist Albania can boast of many more such records, distributed along a gamut: Balkan, European, and worldwide. As they shed additional light on the nature of Albanian communism, I proceed to list them in a chapter of their own and in chronological order, beginning with some peculiar features of Albanian history of the pre–socialist period.

8. Albanian Records

Rich in generals and statesmen who served other countries[46] for want of a state of their own, Albania produced in the fifteenth century one who tried hard to create such an Albanian state. This was George Castrioti, better known as Scanderbeg, the Albanian national hero, a man celebrated in many historical and literary works in many European languages for his heroic resistance to the Turks. Now Scanderbeg was born an Eastern Orthodox, converted to Islam while a hostage to Murat II, and served in the Ottoman army, which, however, he deserted after the Turkish defeat near Niš (1443) by John Hunyadi. He then allied himself with various European Catholic princes who were fighting against the Turks. Pope Nicholas V called him '*athleta Christi.*" We don't know which were Scanderbeg's actual religious beliefs—to the popes then threatened with an invasion of Italy, fighting Turks was a good enough certificate of true Christian faith. The point is that after Scanderbeg's death, many Albanians, led by their princes, embraced Islam, and today Albania is the only European country with a Moslem majority of 72 percent (the Albanians in Yugoslavia are more than 95 percent Moslem). Moreover, Albania furnished her dominators with grand viziers,[47] big pashas,[48] kings,[49] and, in modern times, with presidents of a republic.[50] This was the main reason why Albania was the last Balkan nation to achieve independence (1912), while also losing whole regions to its neighbors. Albania was also the only Balkan country to have a Moslem king during the prewar period.

Albania was the first Balkan country to recognize the Soviet Union (1924), a step taken by the Albanian Premier, Bishop Fan Noli, later Primate of the Albanian Orthodox Church in the United States. Yet Albania was the only Balkan country not to have a socialist/communist party before World War II. It was also the only European country to have a Communist Party which was organized and tutored by a foreign Communist Party. Yet Albania was the only Communist country which dared to challenge the ideological hegemony of the Bolshevik Party in the Conference of the 81 Communist and Labor parties held in Moscow in 1960. Following which, Albania was the only country in Europe to be allied with China. It was also the country which, after Mao's death, claimed to be the only one in the world to have realized Marxism–Leninism at its purest. No wonder, considering that the quicksilver of Marxist theory stands fixed at zero degrees—another European record.

Albania is the only country in the history of mankind to have suppressed historical religions and styled itself "atheistic." It is also the European nation which has given birth to Mother Teresa, perhaps the most revered saintly figure in our times and the recipient of a Nobel Peace Prize—the only international prize Albania has ever been awarded.[51]

Albania is the only European country where the voters, having achieved a participation of 99.99 percent in several elections for their National Assembly, succeeded in rounding that figure up to 100 percent in the elections of March 1987. This is also the country where the purgers have regularly been purged in turn. From 1944, when Albania freed itself from foreign troops, to 1982, when the last big purge came to an end, of the seven Ministers of Interior and Sigurimi [Security] chiefs, all were purged, whereas four were executed.[52] With this Albania has proved to be more Stalinist than Stalin himself—Stalinism raised to the second power.

One of the first things the Albanian leadership did after taking power was to "unify" the Albanian literary language, which had for five centuries been written in two dialects, Gheg in the North and Tosk in the South. Since Albanian Communism had its roots in South Albania, where it spread rapidly, Tosk was imposed as the country's official language from the outset. According to Stalin's *Marxism and Linguistics* (1951), whenever two languages "mix," one comes out "victorious" by retaining its grammar and basic word stock while appropriating the "vanquished" language's vocabulary. This Stalin thesis was the main guideline in the reform of the Albanian "unified literary language": Tosk grammar was left almost intact, while the twice–as–rich Gheg vocabulary was Toskicized. Stalin also wrote that it takes centuries for the vanquished language to die out. It took unified literary Albanian less than two decades to suppress literary Gheg. Here the authority relied upon was another Georgian, N. J. Marr, according to whom language, a superstructural and class phenomenon, changes by reflecting revolutionary changes at the base. Since Marr's theory collided with his own, Stalin demolished it by maintaining that language does not admit of revolution, nor is it a class phenomenon. This did not prevent the Albanian linguists from revolutionizing their country's language just as they revolutionized its economy, and in about the same stretch of time (of course Marr's contribution to this concoction bearing the double stamp of Georgian genius was never acknowledged). And this is perhaps the best example of how Albanian Diamat functions, for here we have a typical case of thesis/antithesis producing a truly revolutionary synthetic—a world record in 'scientific' Marxism.[53]

Albania is the country in Europe with the highest birthrate, while being also its poorest and most backward. Yet the demographic drive is strongly encouraged by the government. Consequently, abortion is prohibited, and homosexuality punished by no less than ten years imprisonment.

Finally, Albania is the only European country to have refrained from signing the Helsinki agreement.

9. De–Europeanization

Other oddities could be added to the list. But this is enough, I think, to make one doubt the sanity of the people responsible for such deeds. The most ominous oddity in the list is the final one. It immediately excludes the country from the European community. By not signing the Helsinki agreement, Albania has in fact signed her de–Europeanization. The implication is that Albania's geographical location in Europe is a mere accident, its real connections being with Asia Minor or North Africa; in other words, with Third World countries. As a matter of fact, Albania has been treated as such.

President Bush used the phrase "from Angola to Albania" during his 1988 election campaign. And a distinguished historian of the Balkans, who certainly cannot be accused of anti–Albanianism, once wrote to me that he "became much interested in Albania from a Third World view rather than Balkan perspective."[54] The sentence suggests that Albania's 'elective affinities' are not with the Balkan countries but with those of the Third World. The idea impressed me as germane to my idea of an eastward political–cultural trend in Albania's history after World War II, a question to which I shall soon return.

Imagine now the possible reaction of a European, and indeed of any westerner, to the preceding list of records. Since Europe is overwhelmingly Christian, molded by two millenia of Christian civilization, such a reader would give the Albanians credit for their contribution to that civilization with respect to only two items on the list: Scanderbeg's defense of Europe from the Turkish invasion, and Mother Teresa's charity, following Christ's example, for the sick and the poor. The rest will cause consternation and revulsion. Will such an attitude help Albania come out of the blind alley into which Hoxha has led her? Being considered as a non–European country even while being one *de facto* must be one of those peculiar contradictions which only the Albanian Diamat can resolve. It actually did so with the famous–infamous Hoxha reply to the complaint by the Youth Organization[55] that Albania was, after all, a European country, and, therefore, "should follow . . . the course of European development." Hoxha replied,

> No, comrades, we cannot and should not follow "the European road"; on the contrary, it is Europe which should follow our road, because from the political standpoint, it is far behind us . . . far from that for which Marx, Engels, Lenin and Stalin fought.[56]

The sentence spells out Albania's de–Europeanization.

But there is something even worse. I have occasionally run into or been told of cheap detective stories and comic books in which Albanians are cast in the role of spies or bullies or other types of villains. One day, leafing through a New York periodical, I ran into a queer title, "Albanian Banalities." The article reviews a play, *Albanian Softshoe*, in which Albanians appear as alien monsters.[57] According to the reviewer, the play has little to do with Albania, which is used "rather condescendingly as a generic foreign culture." But this is exactly what struck me, namely that Albania has become in the minds of some westerners a cliché for a nation with an "alien," barbarian culture, a "subculture" to use the very term used by the writer of the article on the degeneration of bourgeois society and art published in the Party's organ. De–Europeanization has led to sub–humanization.

10. The Eastward Trend

In an article written in 1962,[58] after Albania's divorce from the Soviet Union, I noted a steady eastward trend in Albanian politics— from Yugoslavia (mainly Serbia/Macedonia) to the Soviet Union to China—and concluded, rather jokingly, that, continuing the same trend, Albania would end by joining the United States. The joke could be pursued by saying that my prediction has almost come true now that Albania, having established diplomatic relations with Canada, has at least reached the borders of the United States. What can be said in earnest, provided that the 'qualitative jump' does not add to the adventures of Albanian Diamat, is that, when it comes to establishing diplomatic relations with the two superpowers, the United States will have precedence. This can be argued on both economic and political grounds. In the United States there live today ca. 100,000 Albanian–Americans, some of them millionaires, with a good number belonging to the rising middle class. Now Albanian–Americans in general are eager to visit Albania. And if the Albanian government would open its door to them, their money would sensibly add to the foreign currency the government so badly needs to pay for imported machinery. Political considerations carry even more weight. Although the cultural level of the Albanian community lags behind other ethnic lobbies, the younger generation might catch up more quickly than expected, thus beginning to play a political role in the life of the nation. The Albanian–American intervention on behalf of the mother country when it was at risk, after World War I, of being partitioned among its neighbors, was decisive in preventing the loss of Albania's independence. The Albanian–Americans might repeat that deed with regard to Kosova, now threatened with the loss of its autonomy. What will the Albanian government do if a civil war breaks out between Albanians and Serbs? If that happens, Albania will necessarily be involved. Will Alia, born to Kosovar parents, remain neutral? Will the Kosovars of Albania fold their arms and watch as their brothers are submitted to what might degenerate into a massive massacre like the one in 1944? How apprehensive the Albanian leadership is over the possibility of such a development can be judged from its angry reaction to a publicized anti–Albania placard displayed during the recent Serbian demonstrations.[59] It serves the interests of Communist Albania to have in the stronghold of world capitalism an Albanian–American community on whose help it can rely upon under critical circumstances.

When I wrote the article on the Albanian eastward trend, I did not inquire into the factors that determined it, which were not clear to me at the time. Now I can individuate them. There is first the leadership's survival factor, which, however important, cannot possibly explain by itself Albania's weird politics. A more important factor is Albania's backward socio–political structure, the result of Albania's choice to share the fate of her Turkish rulers almost to the end. Yet this choice was in turn conditioned by a long tradition of South–Albanian Byzantine culture in its two components of medieval Bulgarian and Greek culture, these having Eastern Orthodoxy as their common denominator. When the center of Byzantine culture moved from Constantinople to Moscow and when Russia defied the Ottoman Empire, the Russian Empire became—in the eyes of Byzantine Balkan populations—their champion, exerting over them the unwritten right of a *Kultusprotektorat*. When the October Revolution occurred, the other Balkan countries were already established kingdoms, whereas the infant Albanian state was without a government and in fact occupied by foreign troops. Yet, as already said, it was Albania that was the first Balkan state to recognize the Soviet Union in 1924, when the Albanian government was headed by a South Albanian orthodox bishop. Noli's gesture, however symbolic, set a precedent. He was overthrown by Ahmet Zogu, a man without Noli's culture, but one with a whole tribe behind him, and who was also assisted by White Russian troops exiled in Yugoslavia. This man, who ruled Albania as an autocrat within the framework of a 'constitutional monarchy' (1924–1939), allied himself with Italy, had his gendarmerie organized and run by English officers, and also introduced a couple of western reforms which, however, merely scratched the surface of the nation's basically tribal–feudal structure. It was this last and most important factor which determined Albania's future. For whereas feudal remnants were still to be found in the East European countries (with the exception of Czechoslovakia) when they were forced to adopt the Soviet system, though with considerable modifications due to their more advanced and basically bourgeois system, Albania was, when Stalin-ism arose there, a society mostly tribal in the north and semifeudal in the rest of the country. During the country's occupation by Italian–German troops, the Albanian Communist Party made rapid headway by cloaking its Stalinism with the banner of the war of national libera-tion. And whereas the nationalist parties, mollified by the fascist–nazi gift of Kosova to Albania, fought the Italians (though not the Ger-mans) with a divided heart, the Communists, having grown callous to the Kosova problem so as to please their Yugoslav mentors, fought in earnest, thus earning the blessings and provisions of the Anglo–American allies. Their victory was made easier, on the one hand, by the absence of an Albanian socialist party, and, on the other, by the absence of a truly bourgeois Albanian party, the two existing na-tionalist parties having no class basis. The royalist party preserved to a great extent its tribal nature, while the National front was not even a party, but an amalgam of heterogeneous groups from left to extreme right. Had Albania possessed at that time a bourgeois class such as the ones in other Balkan countries, communism in Albania would probably not have won.

11. Tentative Conclusions

We started this article by asking ourselves whether the reforms made by Gorbachev in the Soviet Union influenced those made in Albania by Alia and his team. Based on data collected mostly from foreign periodicals, and illustrated with texts from Albanian newspa-pers and journals representative of the Party, the intelligentsia, the Youth Organization, and the working class, a first conclusion is that *the Albanian reforms present some signs of glasnost, but have only vague similarities with perestroika* (chapters 1–6).

In the second part of the article (chapters 7–10), we inquired into the deep structural causes which conditioned the evolution–devolution of Albanian socialism. To this end we glanced into the history of Albania as a nation and as a state, and commented on the trans-mogrifications through which Albanian socialism has gone. A sec-ond conclusion is that *Albanian socialism is closer to Soviet socialism than to any form of socialism in other East European countries be-cause the Albanian Revolution presents similarities with the October Revolution.* Both revolutions were basically peasant revolutions, and they were also achieved during a war—not after it, as was the case of the other European countries. But the main similarity between

the two revolutions rests in their non–Marxist, (i.e., Leninist), type
of revolution, which became characteristic of Third World countries
(beginning with China) after World War II, a revolution made by
jumping from feudalism (mixed with tribalism in Albania's case) to
socialism, without going through the intermediary stage of bourgeois
capitalism. We can thus say that the main similarity between the
two revolutions is their Eurasian character. This becomes obvious in
the case of Albania when we consider its eastward trend. Albanian
socialism began by copying Yugoslav Stalinism, went on to mimic the
Soviet model, then parodied its Chinese brand, only to fall back to
a form of Stalinism already passé in its mother country. This throw-
back, resulting in political isolation, can be explained as an atavistic
recurrence (exemplifed in Hoxha's religious relapse)[60] which is rooted
in a long tradition of Byzantine culture informing South Albania—
Albanian socialism is, let us repeat it, a South Albanian product. We
illustrated the role of the Byzantine factor through the oddity of the
Albanian language revolution, which, theorized by the Soviet linguist
N. J. Marr, was executed under Stalin's scientific patronage with typically Stalinist methods, and came to an end with the suppression of
literary Gheg. We should add that literary Gheg, and more generally
the Gheg dialect, have been molded, as have other aspects of Gheg
culture, by Roman civilization. The cultural–political relevance of the
abolition of literary Gheg by literary Tosk is made tangible when one
considers that the Albanians identify themselves with their language,
not with any form of religion or state.

A third conclusion regards the future of Stalalbanianism. Due to
its similarities with the Soviet model, as explained, the assumption
can safely be made that it will tend to follow the experience of the
model. Because of the weirdness of recent Albanian history, however,
it is risky to venture even an approximation of what is likely to happen
beyond a mere descriptive summary.

Let us begin with considerations of age. The average age in the
Politburo is sixty,[61] not a good age for daring innovations. For all
its *glasnost* departures, the leadership remains anchored in Hoxha's
legacy, although the more they turn their backs on him, the louder
they acclaim him, as if to cover the distance with the noise of his
name. A change could also occur if the party splits into factions,
the winning faction veering away from the former direction. But
the signs are that the Albanian Politburo has no factional quarrels
as yet. The differences in it are of degree, 'conservatives' led by

Hoxha's widow resisting departures favored by 'innovators' (headed by Çami), with centrist Alia and his disciples holding the balance. The fact that Hoxha's widow has not made it into the Politburo, her position being merely that of President of the Democratic Front, an umbrella organization functioning as a transmission belt, shows rumors of her hegemonic role to be groundless.

Where can the impulse for real innovation come from? Not from the unions, whose leaders have distinguished themselves as obedient servants, ready to execute the Party's orders (no case of a workers' strike in the whole history of socialist Albania). The peasants, herded into co-ops, are unlikely to protest as long as the party closes its eyes to their robbery of socialist property. The army in Stalinist countries has no power per se (as in Yugoslavia). And Hoxha imparted a lesson to ambitious generals and admirals by executing those of their number who dared to challenge his power.[62] The students, maybe? Unlike their Kosovar brothers, who in 1968, 1981, and 1988–89 spearheaded massive demonstrations against the Yugoslav regime, the Albanian students have been keeping quiet, causing no troubles to the Tirana regime. Minor disturbances have come from mostly high school students, who vent their anger by hacking off tree branches, spitting on Stalin's monument,[63] cursing the system, and wearing unbecoming clothes, the most common form of protest. But since the Party has closed its other eye to such juvenile delinquency, nothing has happened to induce the leadership to grant more leeway.

It may do so in the near future, trying to defuse a growing discontent. While fighting shy of radical reforms, the Alia group seems resolved not to give malcontents cause to rock the boat. Little by little Albania could loosen up like, say, Bulgaria, with which it has resumed contacts after a long period of silence. By participating in the Belgrade Balkan Conference, Albania accomplished a goodwill gesture which somewhat reassured her partners. A Yugoslav journal praised Albania for her "readiness to cooperate with its neighbours . . . and gradually break out of the self–imposed isolation. . . ."[64] On the other hand, and in the same year, a French journal published an illustrated article, "Immovable Albania." It showed, among other features, a parade of women soldiers carrying machine guns, and a young man in a swimsuit lying on the sand close to his bicycle, a bunker behind him. The writer has this to say about Shkodër: "Don't ask where the [Catholic] cathedral is located, one of the largest in the Balkans. The answer will be: 'You mean the Palace of Sports? It's open to the public.' " In the naves the people play basketball and volleyball. "The sacristy has been transformed into toilets."[65]

The Albanian leadership is well aware of the kind of esteem in which Albania is held abroad, a consequence of her rocambulesque Stalinism. Some of their latest overtures are attempts at having the image of Albania improved in the eyes of the western world. Hercules cleared the Augean stables by diverting Alpheus' waters into them to carry away their filth. Alia is no Gorbachev, and no one expects him to undertake such a Herculean labor. What he and his team can do, however, is to speed up the tempo of reform while at the same time trying hard to improve Albania's record on human rights, which, luckily, is not as bad as that of the Khmer Rouge. There will be a European conference on human rights in Moscow in October 1991,[66] where it is expected there will be improvement on the Helsinki agreements by supplying rules for checking on the human rights practices of the signatory states. By publicly declaring, *and without delay,* that Albania will join that conference and respect its decisions, the Albanian leadership will shake off the curse of de–Europeanization, which has turned Albania into the maverick of Europe, an object of derision and grotesque jokes. Joining the Moscow conference would be an effective and anodyne way for Albania to re–Europeanize herself. Re–Europeanization is tantamount to de–Stalinization, which means some relief may be brought into the life of the much–abused and oppressed Albanian people. *Chances are that only by de–Stalinizing itself can Albanian socialism survive* (third conclusion).

XIV. THE INTERPLAY OF SERBIAN, ALBANIAN AND KOSOVAR STALINISM IN THE KOSOVA TRAGEDY

The reader who has been following me so far must have noticed that the word 'Stalinism' does not appear in my earlier articles, where one finds 'communism' instead. The term is generic, it misses the *differentia specifica* of Albanian communism. There are many species of communism, each different from the next and some of them irreconcilable opposites. The list is long, from Plato's philosophical communism to the medieval religious communism realized by some Christian fraternities, and from there to modern communism in its two main ramifications of Anarchism and Marxism, the latter proliferating into Leninism, Stalinism, Trotskyism, Titoism, Hoxhanism, Eurocommunism, not to mention the Asian, African, and Latin American varieties.

Now communisms are ideologies, i.e., systems of theories, beliefs, and practices, particular to certain parties or groups but with pretensions to universality. They all tend to be exclusive of other ideologies, though some are more tolerant than others. For instance, Eurocommunism accepts the right to exist of other ideologies, whereas Stalinism does not; the former is pluralistic, the latter monopolistic.

As an utterly totalitarian ideology, Stalinism permeates almost all human areas of activity, such as politics, ethics, economy, philosophy, arts and sciences, and any other form of thinking and praxis. The Stalinist glossary includes compounds that stress the primacy of ideology over these other areas and forms. Two of them very much in use are 'ideo–political' and 'ideo–scientific.'

'Ideo–political' stresses the predominance in politics of Marxism–Leninism, an ideology whose goal is the conquest of world power in order to allegedly free the proletariat of all nations from capitalist exploitation, thus realizing the ideal of the classless society of the future. The conquest of power, achieved through revolutionary violence based on terror and propaganda, is then preserved through more of the same in the form of a dictatorship of the proletariat, in fact a dictatorship over the proletariat and the society as a whole by a Party oligarchy. This oligarchy, usually fated to devolve into autocracy, monopolizes power through control of the army and a formidable police apparatus. The result is a Party–State with a privileged class of functionaries known as *nomenklatura*, the rest of the society being condemned to take orders from them. The Stalinist Party–State exacts from its subjects unconditional loyalty to its ideological tenets, such as the ineluctable final victory of communism over capitalism, unrelenting class struggle between the bourgeoisie and the proletariat, the Party's monopoly of power, the dictatorship of the proletariat over enemy classes, the hegemonic role of industrial over agricultural workers, and other such shibboleths, which have to be revered whether or not they fit the physical and moral habitat of a certain society. Thus in Albania, where the overwhelming majority of the population were peasants, a working class had to be created almost *a nihilo* to satisfy the sacrosanct ideological tenet that the industrial working class is the real carrier of communism. This is of course not to say that industry in Albania should not have been developed. Yet the development should have been accomplished with consideration for the economic and cultural situation of the nation, not for the sake of doctrinal conformity.

Examples of 'ideo–scientific' phoenomena will be found in the next chapter of this essay. Here I should like to say two words on the 'ideo–emotional' variety. The reader already knows about one such case from my review of Hoxha's *The Titoites*, in which Shehu's fall was determined by his allowing his son to fall in love with a girl belonging to a declassed family. Another telling case is found in Kadare's *The Great Winter*. There a candidate Party member is subjected to a telling–off by the Party which finds him delinquent for delaying his marriage to his fiancée, the daughter of a vice–minister. Other ideo–combines I have seen are 'ideo–theoretical' and 'ideo–artistic.' And I won't be surprised someday to run into 'ideo–sportive' or even 'ideo–militaristic.' One of the first things Albania did after securing power was to establish the Lenin Party School, whose director was Shehu's wife. Later the Institute of Marxism–Leninism was founded, under the direction of Hoxha's wife, nepotism being an ingredient of Albanian Marxism–Leninism.

Albanian Stalinism appears in two varieties, as Albanian Stalinism in Albania proper and as Kosovar Stalinism in Yugoslavia's 'autonomous' province of Kosova.

1. Nature and Features of Albanian Stalinism

Writers of articles and books on the People's Socialist Republic of Albania are usually silent about her ideology, thus missing a main characteristic. In his valuable book on socialist Albania, Peter Prifti devotes a whole chapter to the [Communist] Party of Labour, including ideology as one of its characteristics, along with nationalism, revolutionary militancy, tight centralism, radicalism, and modernism. Yet these characteristics also apply, *mutatis mutandis*, to Soviet Stalinism, which is to say that Albanian Stalinism is pretty much a copy of its Soviet model. Prifti only occasionally identifies the Albanian ideology as Stalinist, giving the impression that the Albanian ideology is original to a great extent.[1] In my opinion, Stalinism so permeates the Albanian ideology as to justify the coinage of the compound 'Stalalbanianism.' For whereas other communist countries of Eastern Europe have adopted particular features of Soviet Stalinism, Albania has appropriated the latter lock, stock, and barrel, going so far as to reform her language, the very mark of Albania's ethnic distinction, by resorting to Stalin's imperialist ideas on language.

We learned from a previous chapter that Giambattista Vico stated that the 'nature' of something depends on the circumstances of its being born (*natura* from *natus*). Now the Albanian Communist Party was born with the Yugoslav Communist Party as its midwife and nurse at the time when the latter was a dyed–in–the–wool Stalinist party. The two Yugoslav emissaries who were instrumental in organizing the conference from which the Albanian CP originated were a Serb, Dušan Mugoša, and a Montenegrin, Miladin Popović. Born under Serbian–Montenegrin supervision and then tutored by the Yugoslav CP, the Albanian CP was in fact the Albanian branch of the former, which was then the strongest East European communist party. By jumping from Belgrade to Moscow, the Albanian CP changed only her orbit. And the same can be said when the gravitational locus became China, Maoism being the Chinese version of Stalinism.

After Mao's 'betrayal' of it, Enver Hoxha had dreams of making Tirana the Mecca of Marxism–Leninism. Since Albania failed to produce a Khrushchev who would make public the crimes of Hoxha and his political blunders, the dictator has ended up being extolled as the Savior of the nation, and a cult of his person has grown up, with features typical of a new fetishistic religion. The degenerative phenomenon is explained by the new leadership's fear of being swept away by the movement of protest going on in Eastern Europe. The more Gorbachev strives to bury the memory of Stalin, the more the alarmed Tirana leadership tries to keep away the *perestroika* demon by chanting spirituals to the ghost of the Albanian Messiah. They have seen how students in South Korea and China have expressed their abhorrence of military or totalitarian regimes in those countries. And Albania was too long allied with China for them to forget that students and the youth in general can cause problems to them. This explains the leadership's relative tolerance of their ideological lip-service, parasitism, western leanings, and disaffection with Stalinism.

They envy the youth of other nations who can travel abroad and make contacts with other cultures, they resent their military training (begun while children and extending to women), chafe at joining brigades for 'voluntary work,' are sick and tired of having to swallow slogans in the form of ideological pills. The adult generation, workers or peasants alike, have grown apathetic, resigned to their fate of being exploited by their own government. Deprived of much of their right to ownership and robbed of the fruits of their labors by the Party-State, the owner of both the land and the factories and plants in its double capacity as landlord and capitalist, they vent their anger by sabotaging their work and plundering the 'socialist property.' They can tell that 'socialist property' is a fiction, its belonging to the state an invented right, of the kind of rights Vico called *iura imaginaria*, presenting similarity with Marx's 'commodity fetishism.'[2] Once the state's imaginary right to own the land and the means of production is established, the bureaucrats are bound to function as its managers, thus enjoying economic privileges which make the egalitarianism of salaries sound like a joke. These privileges are a modern replica of feudal privileges, with the difference that whereas in the Middle Ages it was the king who conferred privileges upon his vassals, now the bureaucrats receive them from a Politburo headed by a Secretary General or a First Secretary whose power is at least as great as that of a king.

After forty-five years of uninterrupted dictatorship in Albania, the moral temper of the people shows symptoms of decay. Fear of falling into disgrace or being arrested for an imprudent word or a nonconformist gesture has given rise to widespread vices such as cowardice, fawning, lying, dissimulation, and spying.[3]

During the last years of his life Hoxha practically retired, devoting his full time to recording in writing his legacy to his people. His lieutenants drew a long breath of respite; they could now attend to their jobs without being checked on, while making the dictator believe they were carrying out his orders. In fact they did not, having realized that his policy of isolation, based on self-reliance as to economy and bunker strategy as to defense, was absurd. It fell upon Shehu, his longtime premier, and his heir apparent, to reshuffle the cards of the game. By the time Hoxha discovered this, which was when the Kosova riots of 1981 reproposed the question of Albania's attitude versus Yugoslavia, the differences were such as to provoke the clash resulting in Shehu's downfall. It was during this interim that a pattern of behavior took shape whose origins go back to the first half of the seventies, during which Hoxha, Stalin-like, wiped out dissenters in the cultural, defense, and economic areas. It consisted in pretending to follow the dictator's injunctions, while actually doing one's own thing. Given the pyramidal organization of the Party–State, the habit was transmitted from top to bottom. The peasant would pretend to work hard for his cooperative, while robbing it of time and energies spent in cultivating his own parcel of land. The co–op's president would tamper with percentages and pretend that the plan had been accomplished. The percentages would be manipulated in the competent agricultural office before being submitted to the minister, who would then pass the figures to the President of the Plan Committee. More or less the same would occur in industry, construction, trade, education, and other areas. In the League of Writers and Artists, Kadare, to name its most representative member, would pretend to follow the guidelines of socialist realism while doing exactly the opposite. His fellow writers would pretend not to know what he was doing, Kadare having secured Hoxha's favor. Hoxha himself would pretend not to know that Kadare, who extolled him as a rule, would occasionally pinch him. Yet he would let him do so, considering that a few negative traits would even add to his reputation as an enlightened dictator who can bear with an artist's whims. Pretension thus became a generalized feature of the Albanian frame of mind. One finds it sculpted in a popular witticism: "They want us to believe our salaries are smart. And we make them believe we're working hard."

In such a mental environment, values tend to turn into disvalues,

eroded by crudely egotistic calculations. Work is exploited worse than
in capitalist regimes, thrifty use of resources turns into waste. In
the moral domain the result is corruption; in the intellectual area,
pseudoscience and falsification of history.

I shall spare the reader a repetition of the various facets of corruption as found in chapter 13,[4] mentioning only one case, the rotation
of cadres in some ministries considered as more liable to bribery and
favoritism. A measure such as this recalls the Latin, *"Medice, cura te
ipsum!"* Which is to say that rottenness has nested in the privileged
class itself. A work on the Soviet quinquennial plans by a competent Albanian economist who lived and worked in the Soviet Union
explains why the Soviet economy could not catch up with capitalist
economies, much less outdo them. One is struck to find in this book
shortcomings and flaws of the Soviet economy which are reproduced
in miniature in the Albanian economy today: breakdowns in factories and construction for lack of spare parts and equipment, waste
of material and money, theft, inefficiency, irresponsibility, etc. The
following excerpt is particularly telling:

> I do not deny that the Soviet Union has increased enor-
> mously its industrial capacity during the last twenty years.
> Disposing of the work of more than 200 million people and of
> the seemingly inexhaustible resources of a very big country,
> the Soviet Union can achieve results, and even impressive
> ones at times. But everything they do costs them two or
> three times more than in any advanced industrial country
> of the West. They have not created the highly rational, ef-
> ficient, progressive and fair economic system promised by
> Lenin. In other words, Marxism, based on the collective
> ownership of all the means of production, the dictatorship
> of the proletariat and the permanent revolution, has not
> been an answer to the economic and social problems of our
> century. So far the industrialization of the Soviet Union has
> been obtained at a price in human suffering which no other
> nation of the West could pay. The millions of human vic-
> tims and the incalculable wastage of material wealth are the
> best proof that Soviet economy is not planned in the ratio-
> nal and scientific meaning of the word. The decisive cause of
> the failure of Soviet economic planning is the dictatorship of
> the proletariat which implies the centralized direction from
> Moscow of economic life down to the smallest detail. This

over–centralization, with the [K.G.B.] watching eagerly the slightest *faux pas*, kills all local initiative and turns men into frightened automatons. The responsible managers of the Soviet industry are always hard pressed to fulfill and overfulfill their plans, which are set beyond the normal productive capacity of their men and their machines. When a breakdown is threatening, they do not dare to stop production from fear of sanctions for sabotaging the Plan (pp. 235–36).[5]

The catastrophic economic situation that Gorbachev is desperately trying to remedy with his *perestroika* reform was anticipated by Tayar Zavalani some thirty–five years ago. Here is a book written by a competent, Russian–trained economist, familiar with the Soviet brand of Marxism.[6] Have the Albanian economists consulted his book? Did Hoxha read it? Had he read it and had he been smarter than some people think he was, he would have had second thoughts before adopting the Soviet quinquennial plan pattern with its disastrous consequences as formulated in Zavalani's excerpt.

Zavalani does not appear in the *Albanian Encyclopedic Dictionary* [AED] (1985), a collective work by the Albanian Academy of Sciences. The dictionary has duly recorded every Albanian hero and heroine killed by nazi–fascists, including one Zavalani who "fell heroically [sic!] . . . while fighting inundating waters about to drown the goat herd of his cooperative." The dictionary has duly recorded every Albanian hero and heroine killed by nazi–fascists or in defending socialist property. Yet people who have criticized, let alone opposed, Stalalbanianism, be they distinguished scholars such as Tayar Zavalani or outstanding statesmen and venerable patriots, have not been recorded. The criterion for their omission is simple: persons expunged from the dictionary are considered as nonpersons. To Stalalbanianism these persons are (paraphrasing Goethe with a slight pronominal change) "as good as if they had never been" (*"es ist so gut als wär' es nie gewesen"*). Mephistopheles' line is a pertinent comment on the treatment of history by Stalinists. Wherever an event does not suit their ideo–political or ideo–scientific viewpoint, they either ignore it altogether or distort it so as to make it unrecognizable.

Here is an example of the latter alternative. The document of the Albanian proclamation of independence bears the signatures of, among others, Midhat Frashëri, Lef Nosi, and Mustafa Kruja. The first two were members of the first Albanian government and later members of the Nationalist Front, the main rival to the Albanian

CP, while Kruja was Premier of one of the Albanian governments during the Italian occupation.[7] A photograph of the document in *The History of Albania* (vol. II, p. 499), a collective work published in 1084 by the Albanian Academy of Sciences, has the section of the document bearing Frashëri's signature covered by a picture of the house serving as the seat of the government, while the section bearing the signatures of Kruja and Nosi is covered by a picture of the delegates to the Independence Congress.* When even a document recording the proclamation of Albanian independence is falsified, one can imagine how scientific is Albanian historiography. Suffice it to mention here the AED has not only excluded statesmen and other major personalities during the Zog period, as well as leaders of rival parties during the Italian–German occupation, but has also expunged all party dissidents who were purged, including Mehmet Shehu, the Communist Premier for twenty-five consecutive years. Not a word on him even in the *History of the Party of Labour of Albania* published in 1982, i.e., immediately after his alleged suicide.[8]

Stalalbanian historiography best illustrates the pseudoscientific character of Stalalbanian scholarship. And when history is falsified in this grotesque way, one can imagine how the situation is in other humanistic sciences. Socialist realism in literature and the arts is all a *quid pro quo*, with art its own caricature.* And even music is fake, with songs that are adulterations of folk melodies ringing like military marches and sung hurriedly as if the singers were being tracked down. Dances resemble parades, the dancers' smiles stamped on their faces, their awkward movements trapped in their otherwise gorgeous costumes, the settings as weird as in science fiction. Indeed, Albanian society as represented in figurative art and moving pictures seems to belong not to the planet Earth but to another planet or star. The politics of self–isolation has bred a state–of–siege psychology permeated by xenophobia and exasperated nationalism. Albanian leaders still use 'encirclement,' a typical Stalin word, to describe their self–imposed quarantine, which has alienated the country from both Western and Eastern Europe. Albania is the only European country which does not allow her citizens to travel abroad. Isolation from the outside world has internal isolation as its counterpart. After forty–five years of rule, the regime has not yet built a railway network connecting its main cities, thus discouraging even internal communication.

---

*See pp. 218–22 in this volume.

The communications shortage is reflected in transportation capacity, this in foreign trade and the economy in general. The economic situation is so desperate that the Albanian government has knocked at Germany's door for help. And this Germany with which Albania has signed a treaty of mutual economic and technical aid is not Stalinist East Germany, but West Germany, a capitalist country part of the Atlantic Alliance and ruled by a Christian Democratic government. In other words, atheist communist Albania has come to terms with Christian capitalist Germany, its chief ideological enemy. In so doing, Albania has replayed a Soviet precedent occurring more than half a century ago, the difference being one that emphasizes Albania's ideological backslide. For whereas the Stalin–Hitler pact was one of nonaggression, Albania's treaty with West Germany implies financial assistance, forbidden by the Albanian constitution. According to German sources, West Germany has granted Albania industrial equipment costing 16 million Deutschmarks and 10 million in capital aid.[9] In my 1962 article on the eastward trend of Albanian politics I predicted the reversion of that trend once the alliance with China was over. The reversion has now begun, and once begun it is bound to proceed, thus joining the de–Stalinization process going on in the Soviet bloc.

2. The Kosovar Variant

While Albanian Stalinism is emphatically ideological, Kosovar Stalinism is characterized by pragmatism, ideology there being a layer of veneer. Scratch it, and you will find a thick crust of Albanian nationalism, which is thicker and harder than nationalism in Albania proper because of the Kosovars' exposure to Serbian, Montenegrin, and, more recently, Macedonian nationalist pressure.

Kosovar Stalinism is weak because Kosovar nationalism is strong, the former being limited to the leadership and some groups, but the latter extending to the entire Albanian population of the province. It is weak also because not autochthonous.[10] It was imported by Kosovar youth studying in Albania at the Shkodër State Gymnasium and at the Elbasan Normal School during the second half of the thirties, when a communist movement made its appearance in Albania with its two main centers in Shkodër and Korçë.[11] Since almost all of them were boarding school students living on a miserable state stipend, communism was quick to stick to them. Having completed their secondary studies, they returned to their homes where they established contacts with Yugoslav communists belonging to a Party with a certain tradition, thus falling under their influence. It was these people who constituted the older Kosovar Stalinist core, their communism being an amalgam of Gheg communism and South Slav (mostly Serbian) communism, i.e., an ideology which is neither autochthonous nor representative of the Kosovar ethnic nation. These Kosovar communists could not possibly forget that the ideology they professed was basically the same as the ideology of those who had oppressed them for almost a generation during Yugoslavia's royalist period and for two more decades during the rule of Communist Yugoslavia. Consequently, their loyalty to the Yugoslav kind of Stalinism could not but be ambiguous. The phenomenon is a case of the Hegelian 'unhappy consciousness' in which consciousness is split into two conflicting parts. Such a state of mind explains the older leadership's paradoxical behavior of adopting the Tirana flag and the official Tirana language at a time when Stalinist Albania was the number one enemy of Titoist Yugoslavia.

After the bloody repression by Yugoslav Partisans of the 1945 Kosovar insurrection, the Kosovars experienced the reincorporation of their homeland into Communist Yugoslavia as a foreign occupation. Kosovar leaders collaborating with Serbs and Montenegrins were looked down on. In order to establish some legitimacy, they had to prove they were nationalists. In 1968, the year when a revolutionary euphoria swept the student bodies of many a European country (including Yugoslavia), it was students who, according to witnesses, pressed on their professors to adopt the Tirana language. The leadership, now Kosovar in greater part, was quick to agree in order to win the students over. They even allowed them to fly the Albanian flag, an unequivocal showpiece of Albanian nationalism.

The nationalist movement gained momentum after the Constitution of 1974 promoted Kosovar to an autonomous unit of Federal Yugoslavia. Kosovars began acting as masters, making Serbs and Montenegrins feel like subjects. They complained but were not listened to. The cultural exchange with Tirana grew in volume, which is to say that more textbooks and literary works were reprinted in Prishtina and more visiting professors were lecturing there. The liberal Serbian leadership then in power did not intervene. It did so only after the riots of 1981, when in the student–led demonstrations, together with nationalist slogans, others appeared hailing the Tirana regime.

As the Albanian mass media inveighed against the ensuing re-presssion, defending the Kosovars' right to have their own republic, the Kosovar leadership, led by Fadil Hoxha and Mahmud Bakalli, were accused of promoting Kosovar irredentism. They therefore had to go, making room for another leadership, amenable to meeting Serbian demands. The new team, led by Azem Vllasi, a former president of the Kosovar Youth and a *persona grata* to Serbs, unleashed a campaign of arrests and jailings which was such as to elicit protest even from some liberal Serbian academicians.

I have often asked myself how a leadership could act so cruelly against its own people. The older leadership had tried to prove their nationalism by coming to terms with Kosovar demands, thus angering Serb nationalism. The younger leadership sought to prove their loyalty to Yugoslavia by cracking down on Albanian nationalism. There was a reversion of roles. The cultural exchange with Albania was suspended, Kosova became a police state. In an interview on the International Conference on Kosova held in New York in November 1988,[12] I expressed the view that for Kosovars to gain their republic they should "differentiate" themselves from Albania in the cultural field,[13] beginning with the correction of the blunders made by the older leadership when they adopted the Tirana language and the Tirana flag. The younger leadership continued their use, thus continuing to identify themselves with Stalinist Albania. The identification was of course symbolic. But even so, it could not fail to arouse suspicion among Serbs.

In 1986, more than 200 leading Belgrade intellectuals signed a letter of protest addressed to the Serbian and Federal Assemblies, accusing the Yugoslav government of 'national treason' for allowing Albanians to 'expel' from Kosova Serbs and Montenegrins. The document describes the Kosovar leadership as a Tirana agency exercising 'Stalinized chauvinism.'[14]

3. Serbian Stalinism and the Kosovar Revolt

The petition of the Belgrade intellectuals marked a turning point. The anti-Albanian Serbian nationalist wave swelled when the radical nationalist faction, headed by Slobodan Milošević, defeated in Fall 1987 the liberal Stambolić–Pavlović leadership. On January 4, 1988, a hearing on the crisis in Yugoslavia took place in the European Parliament in Strasbourg.[15] Hardly anyone at the time could imagine that the crisis would end with the province's loss of her autonomy.

Milošević managed to bring Kosova back under Serbian control by launching a state-backed campaign of chauvinism through massive rallies aired over the broadcast media and favorably commented on by major Belgrade newspapers. Mounted under inflammatory slogans calling for the liberation of Kosova from Albanians, the rallies included intimidation tactics. Milošević forced the Voivodina leadership to resign by sending to Novi Sad a cabal of his zealots who threatened to storm the headquarters of the autonomous province. Soon after, he tried to bring down the leadership of Montenegro by having his devotees there foment a huge rally of protest in Titograd. Here he failed.[16] He even tried to hold a rally in Ljubljana, in order to hush Slovenes who had been lashing out at him for his totalitarian methods, reminiscent of the fascist *squadristi* and the nazi brownshirts.

Milošević's raids against Voivodina and Montenegro were rehearsals for his attack on the Kosovars. He knew this was not to be an easy deed. He first tried to persuade the leadership to give up the province's autonomy willingly. Having met with a strong resistance he resorted to a roundabout approach. Since Kosova's autonomy was guaranteed by the 1974 constitution, he set out to amend it, including a set of clauses which empty autonomy of much of its content.

Milošević's proposal for constitutional amendments galvanized the Kosovar resistance. On November 17, 1988, some 3,000 miners from the Trepča mine near Titova Mitrovica began a 70-mile march to Prishtina to protest a meeting of the Provincial Committee of the League of Communists (LC) of Kosova taking place the same day. The meeting was expected to sanction the planned resignation under duress of Kaqusha Jashari, President of the Provincial Committee, and of Vllasi, then a member of the Executive Bureau of the League of Communists of Yugoslavia (LCY). The miners' march set in motion demonstrations of protest in Prishtina and other cities of Kosova. People from all parts of the province rushed to Prishtina for five consecutive days.[17]

The miners' march was intended to be a shot in the arm for the wavering body of the LC Provincial Committee, submitted as they were to Serbia's heavy pressure. They succumbed to it. This Kosovar leadership had never been a friend to Kosovar resistance. A reading of *Rilindja* [Renascence], Kosova's official Albanian daily, shows that the

Provincial leadership had long accepted the Serbian charges against the popular nationalist movement, even adopting their labels condemning it as 'counterrevolutionary,' 'irredentist,' and 'separatist.' Following the November demonstrations, the LCY Executive approved Milošević's proposal for the amendments. A date was set for the approval of the Kosova Assembly. The storm was approaching. The signal did not come from the sky or the sea, it came from the bowels of the earth. On February 21, 1989, 1,300 miners stopped working in the shafts of the Stari Trg mine, declaring a hunger strike. These were the same miners who in November 1988 had marched to Prishtina. They protested the change of the constitution with a petition to the United Nations, and threatened not to come out of the shafts if the pro–Serbian replacements of Vllasi, Jashari, and another member of the LCY Executive did not in turn resign. They also let it be known that they had with them a sufficient quantity of dynamite.[18]

The hunger strike of the Trepča miners, the first of its kind in the history of Yugoslavia, if not also in the history of Europe, had a tremendous political impact. The President of the LCY, Stipe Šuvar, visited the mine, trying in vain to dissuade the miners from their resolve. English and Danish trade–unions sent telegrams and petitions,[19] and a German delegation of workers tried to contact strikers. Donations arrived from Croatia and Slovenia in the form of money as well as food and clothes for the strikers' families. The European press eagerly followed the course of events. After days of deliberations in the Provincial Committee, the replacements resigned. That was a great victory for the Trepča miners, won over the Provincial leadership condemning the strike. The historic event drew a sharp line between the leadership on the side of the Serbs and the Kosovar people on the side of the miners, thus doing away with ambiguities and double dealings, "distinguishing," as the Albanian proverb goes, "the alum from the sugar."

The miners' hunger strike prompted an avalanche of protest and counterprotest never experienced before in Yugoslavia. Workers in other mines and other work places joined the strike; students in Prishtina and other cities boycotted classes, shopkeepers closed their shops. On February 22, 1989, the day after the miners barricaded themselves underground, an appeal signed by 215 intellectuals and addressed to the Serbian Assembly expressed disapproval of the Serbian move to change Kosova's constitution. On February 24, Albanian writers in the Kosova Writers' Association made public a statement endorsing the strikers' demands. They called the so-called 'counter-revolution,' the outcome of an eight-year political and clerical anti-Albanian campaign, 'a big lie.' A couple of days later, the same group of writers addressed a petition to the Yugoslav President and to the Presidency of the LCY Central Committee, condemning "the anti-Albanian hysteria." And hysteria there was. The day after the Trepča miners went on strike, seven miles away, 800 Serbian and Montenegrin workers in the Kopaonik mine went on a counterstrike, with demands diametrically opposed to those of their Albanian fellow miners. Massive counterprotest rallies in Belgrade and other Serbian cities followed.

On February 26, the Federal Assembly approved the changes to the constitution of Serbia together with the decision to introduce the "special measures."

Of all the republics of Yugoslavia, only Slovenia protested the state-of-siege. On February 27, a meeting of protest took place in Ljubljana. Jože Skole, President of the Slovene Youth Federation, opened the discussion by pointing to a badge on his coat with the inscription, "Kosova my homeland," printed by the Youth Federation of Slovenia. He warned that what happened to Kosova might happen also to other ethnic groups if intolerance were to prevail. Milan Kučan, President of the Central Committee of the LC of Slovenia, compared the hunger strike of the Trepča miners to Gandhi's methods of nonviolent resistance. As a small nation, he said, Slovenes are bound to be in solidarity with Kosovars, who are a minority in Serbia.[20] An article in the German press[21] observed that, notwithstanding Ljubljana's strong protest against the introduction of the 'special measures,' the Slovene delegates in the Yugoslav Assembly voted for it a few days later. Their excuse that the Slovenian leadership failed to instruct them is refuted by a more convincing explanation. According to it, even before the Voivodina *putsch*, the LCY had agreed to accept Serbia's demands for constitutional changes to make possible an anodyne solution to the Kosova crisis.[22] Yet Milošević wanted the crisis solved by a show of force, which would then reflect on his person as Yugoslavia's strong man. In Serbia there exists a radical ideology, apparently shared by Milošević, according to which a national crisis entailing a state of emergency is a necessary condition for that ideology to achieve victory. And if the condition does not exist, it must be created.[23] The fact that the question of constitutional changes was coordinated with that of the state-of-siege supports the thesis that the Kosova crisis was, to Milošević, his stalking horse. The Trepča hunger strike was continued by partial strikes in the Goleš mine during the next month. In the meantime, Vllasi and other Kosova leaders had been arrested under the state of emergency provision. Now tanks rolled in city streets, and airplanes and helicopters circled. On March 23, the Kosova Assembly sat in session to decide on the amendments to the province's constitution. Of the 187 delegates present, only 10 voted against them, with two abstaining (*Tages Anzeiger*, March 29). *Der Spiegel* (April 3) noted that intimidation was used. Yet Radio Ljubljana commented that all the Kosovar forums competed with each other to ease the Serbian demands.[24] The President of the Provincial Assembly, Vukašin Jovanović, had the nerve to say that the amendments left the citizens' rights intact. Five days later, in the session for ratification in the Serbian Assembly, the Albanian delegates there behaved no differently from their fellow ethnics in Kosova's Assembly. The third act of Kosova's tragedy was over, the first two acts having been played at the end of World War I, when the Kosova *vilayet's* greater part was incorporated into royalist Yugoslavia, and at the end of World War II, when the Yugoslav part of the province was reincorporated into Communist Yugoslavia.

Tragedies are supposed to end with bloodshed—with bloodbath, when the protagonist is a collectivity. According to official data, there were only twenty–four deaths. The revolt began the very day the Provincial Assembly was meeting, and it lasted six days. It was general, and it took place in, besides the capital, almost all Kosova's cities: Uroševac (Ferizaj), Podujevo, Gnjilane (Gilan), Ljipljan, Suva Reka, Peć (Pejë), Orahovac (Rahovec), Djakovica (Gjakovë), Dečan, Dušanovo, and also in a village in the Zhur district. One characteristic of the revolt was the participation en masse of teenagers, some of them in their early teens, who pelted with stones the security forces—another characteristic. There were also some shootings; two policemen, one of them Albanian, were killed. The security forces responded with tear gas, water cannons, and firearms.[25] The number of demonstrators varied from tens to hundreds and sometimes thousands, mostly young people, including girls. Many workers joined them. Four mines in Stari Trg, Kišnica, Goleš, and Novo Brdo went on strike. Slogans included "No to Constitutional Changes!," "We have pledged to die for Kosova," and "Better the grave than a slave."

4. Press Review of the Repression

The brutal repression of the Kosova revolt was condemned by the press and radio stations of European and other countries—an exception being the Soviet Union, for obvious reasons concerning its own national problem.[26] *Corriere della sera* (March 29) spoke of the new Serbian constitution "born in blood." A correspondent of the London *Times* who visited the hospital in Titova Mitrovica learned from the chief doctor that most of the fifty wounded people would probably die.[27] A correspondent of the *New York Times* asked a man in Peć (Pejë) what he thought of the state of emergency. The answer was : "Occupation." The Greek *Ethnos* (March 31) stigmatized the Serbian leadership for its brutality. An article in *The Economist* (April 1) was entitled "The Intifada in the Balkans." An article in *Die Welt* (February 28) ended with the word "Lebanon."[28]

The Economist (October 8, 1988) called Milošević 'Mussović,' with clear allusion to Mussolini. According to the Madrid *El Pais* (March 7), many non–Serbian Yugoslavs referred to the Serbian leader as 'Benito Milošević.' An article in *Le Monde* (January 29–30) noted Croatians' fear of Milošević's "neo–Stalinist" drive to reconstitute Greater Serbia. *Der Spiegel* (April 3) reported Stipe Šuvars' allusion to Milošević as a "neo–Stalinist." Milan Kučan was more diplomatic when he spoke of Milošević's "mild *coup d'état*" (*Tribune de Genève*, January 31, 1988). *L'Hebdo* (October 6, 1988) described his ideology as a "kind of national Stalinism."[29]

Albanian ethnics in various cities of Europe (Brussels, Stuttgart, Bern, Zürich, Geneva), United States (New York, Washington), and Australia (Sydney) staged demonstrations of protest.[30]

The insurrection subsided after six consecutive days. The March 30 issue of *Corriere della sera* described Prishtina adorned with flags "to celebrate its defeat." Yet three days later bombs were thrown at a troop truck (*The Independent*, April 3). *Der Spiegel* (April 3) noted that the sheiks of the Persian Gulf had expressed willingness to help their Kosovar Moslem brothers. That same day, an article in the Zagreb *Vjesnik*, "The Absurd Country," pointed out that the bloody repression underscored Yugoslavia's alienation from Europe, causing her to lose much of the little credit she still has in the civilized world. What she has earned is "a millstone hung at her neck."

On May 30, Prishtina University was again in an uproar. It started with a small group, led by girls, which grew into a demonstration of about 1,000 students shouting against the new Kosovar chief, Rahman Morina, and hailing the old chief Fadil Hoxha. That same day in Podujevo, a group of youngsters wearing masks appeared. They were met with tear gas and bullets. One of them was killed and several wounded.[31]

Having quelled in blood the Kosovar uprising, the special security forces proceeded with their campaign of arrests and detentions, layoffs and purges. The first voice of protest came from the Ljubljana Committee for the Protection of Human Rights in Kosova. The document rejects the charge of counterrevolution through reference to Kaqusha Jashari's contention that the demonstrations were joined by a majority of Kosova's Albanian population. The collusion of night watchmen and militiamen in some Serbian villages was seen as a typical "apartheid policy," the emergency measures being applied only to Albanians.[32] The appeal of the Yugoslav Helsinki Committee to the SFRY Presidency charged that the Yugoslav state had violated the civil and constitutional rights of the Albanians, explaining the political crisis in Kosova as a consequence of those violations.[33] The Slovenian PEN Center described the persecution of the 215 intellectual signatories of the Appeal to the Assembly of Serbia as a purge "in the classic form of Stalinist purges."

The Slovenian campaign in defense of the Kosovars (a Slovenian Youth petition carried 300,000 signatures) was instrumental in eliciting the strong action taken by the European Parliament.[34] Its resolution, signed by representatives of all political parties, calls attention to "the explosive situation in Kosova, which finds herself on the verge of civil war," and expresses "indignation" at the numerous victims and arrests. Considering that the approval by the Kosova Assembly of the changes to the constitution of 1974 was, according to the Committee for Human Rights in Kosova, "reached through manipulations and threats," the European Parliament warns that further inciting of nationalist feelings endangers peace "with possible consequences for Europe as a whole"; reminds the Yugoslav government of its obligations, taken on by signing the Helsinki Accords, to guarantee respect for minorities' human rights and equality before the law; and demands the liberation of political prisoners and the setting up of an investigation committee for establishing the responsibility of civic and military agencies for having produced so many victims. An appeal is made to the Yugoslav authorities to have comprehension and compassion for the Albanian population in Yugoslavia while also calling for Kosova's

Albanian majority to respect the rights of the Serbian minority. The resolution welcomes the invitation of the Yugoslav Assembly to the European Parliament to send to Kosova a visiting delegation. At the end of May, a five-person delegation of the European Parliament visited Prishtina. According to preliminary agreement, the delegation was to meet not only with Yugoslav officials, but also with people not sharing their views. Since officials did not live up to their words (they even discouraged the delegation from meeting Kosovar intellectuals), the delegates had to arrange the meetings themselves. They were dissatisfied with the officials' answers to their questions concerning arrests, detentions, and the ruthlessness of the repression—the University of Prishtina demonstration and the Podujevo demonstration in which a young man was killed occurred while the delegation was in Prishtina. Not having received the full information they wanted, the delegation left, after expressing their "disappointment" to the Yugoslav premier, Ante Marković. They also told him that a grant of economic aid by the European Community would be made easier if democracy obtained in Kosova.[35] According to the Parisian AFP (June 1, 1989), the delegates departed without shaking hands with their escorts. A joint communiqué underscored that the visit had accomplished nothing.[36]

The condemnation of the Yugoslav repression could not be more forceful. Another condemnation, this one couched in neutral statistical terms, is the report on Kosova of Amnesty International.[37]

According to official figures, during the period 1981–88, over 1,750 Kosovars were sentenced to up to fifteen years of imprisonment, and about 7,000 more to sixty days for minor political offences.

On March 19, it was officially announced that 44 people had been arrested, including 13 officials from the Trepča zinc mine, 3 from the Goleš magnesite mine, and 2 from the Kišnica pit. From the introduction of "special measures" (March 26), some 300 Trepča miners and some 800 shopkeepers who had closed their shops in solidarity with the strikers were sentenced to up to sixty days of imprisonment, or suspended from their jobs, or fined.

Deaths were probably more numerous than the official toll of 24. The figure of the International Press Agency Reuters (March 31) is about 100, that of Ljubljana radio, 140. The official 24 includes a sixteen-year old girl and two boys, one aged thirteen and the other fourteen. According to the London *Times* (April 1), Dečan people stated that police opened fire without warning. Reuters (April 2) reported that in Zhur, where one man was killed and many injured, demonstrators did not attack the police station, as the official version maintains. The Slovenian *Mladina* (April 7) announced that those who came to collect the bodies of their relatives at Prishtina's mortuary on March 29 "were only allowed to take their dead after they had countersigned a death certificate which stated that the person had died a natural death."

An unknown number of people are being held in 'isolation' (the Yugoslav term for administrative detention), detainees having no right of access to lawyers or even to their families, who need not be informed of their whereabouts. Among them were, according to unconfirmed reports in the press, 65 intellectuals who signed the petition opposing constitutional changes. Amnesty International warned Yugoslav authorities (May 10, 1989) that 'isolation' as practiced violates Articles 177 and 178 of the Yugoslav Constitution.[38]

5. Kosova's Tragedy Albania's Shame

Lawlessness is a characteristic of totalitarian regimes, and no such regime can compare with the Stalinist apparatus as to its craftiness in making simple people believe in its lies and forgeries. The heirs of Ranković have learned the lesson. The anti–Albanian campaign since Milošević's coming to power has depicted Kosovars as barbarians, predators, rapists, whose goal is the expulsion of Serbs and Montenegrins from Kosova, and has vilified their leaders.[39] Serbian propaganda, fanned by Belgrade newspapers such as *Politika* and NIN, degraded into Milošević mouthpieces, was able to convince Serbs that the high birthrate of the Kosovars was cultivated as a political strategem to cleanse Kosova of Slavs. By 1987, laws were being passed to profit Serbs at the expense of the Albanians.[40] By that time Milošević had managed to discredit the Tito–Kardelj constitution of 1974 by posturing as the one who would defeat their sinister plan of mutilating Serbia.[41] Hitler seized power by proclaiming himself as the one destined to save the German nation from the Jewish conspiracy. And Stalin became a demigod after purging the Soviet Union of all kinds of traitors in the service of Western imperialism. Stalinism and nazism are ideologies in which the cult of personality thrives on the myth of a conspiracy threat. Milošević became a Serbian champion by slyly hinting that the Croat Tito and the Slovenian Kardelj conspired to dismember Serbia, which he is first to 'unify' and then raise to hegemonic status.

The previous chapter has sufficiently shown that the backward drive of Serbian Stalinism, haunted by nostalgic dreams of reviving Stefan Dušan's Empire in the Balkans, has already suffered a defeat on three superposed levels: on the national one, by Slovenia, the most civilized Yugoslav republic; on the coninental level by the European Parliament; and on a global level, by a humanitarian institution, Amnesty International, respected all over the world.

Belgrade radio recently reported that in the Niš garrison three Albanian soldiers have been charged with planning terroristic acts. Yugoslav authorities have been reticent to make public courtmartial verdicts gainst Albanians in the Yugoslav army. Rumors of horrible episodes of torture and murder have circulaated, suggesting that manifestations of Albanian nationalism in the army are met with terror. In September 1987, in the Paračin barracks, a former university student killed five fellow oldiers and then committed suicide. The counterterrorist act, called "an attack against the Yugoslav army," raised a hue and cry in the anti–Albanian campaign. With the reinstated state of emergency in Kosova, life in the army for ethnic Albanians is bound to get harsher.

An article in *Borba* (April 15–16, 1988) by Miloš Antić comments on a pamphlet by the People's Movement for the Republic of Kosova, addressed "to the Albanian people, workers and peasants, university students and schoolchildren," stating that the movement seems to hold the reins of the 'counterrevolution' in its hands. Official sources used to speak of a fragmentary movement of nine large organizations and ninety–five groups from 1981 to 1988. Now the talk is of a more centralized movement. Who are those who direct it? In a press conference following the March uprising, Rahman Morina, now President of the LC Provincial Committee, answered questions.[42] He denied that the population has been abused during the uprising, and rejected the opinion that a clash had occurred between the Party and the intelligentsia. A journalist retorted by calling 'an illusion' the Party's pretension that the population is behind the Party. Is it, he asked, because a 'parallel' leadership has emerged, the so–called Djakovica group,[43] whose influence on the masses is stronger than that of the legal leadership? Morina brushed aside the geographic element, placing the fault with the leadership. He made a distinction between political mistakes and criminal counterrevolutionary actions, implying that the latter cannot possibly apply to him, who, as Kosova's former Secretary of the Interior and Police Chief, was responsible for the almost half a million police proceedings against nationalists and separatists during the period 1981–88.[44] I don't know for how long Morina was chief of police. But even if he acted in that capacity for only one year, the figures he presented qualify him as a worthy disciple of Ranković, setting him soundly in the Stalinist lineage, from Yagoda to Beria, and from Koçi Xoxe to Mehmet Shehu.

My question of how the younger Kosovar leadership could be so cruel to their own people can now be answered. The answer is Serbian Stalinism of the Ranković brand, the worst kind of Yugoslav Stalinism. That Stalinism in Yugoslavia did not disappear after Tito's break with Stalin should be clear to anyone who considers such features of Titoism still existing today as the single–Party system, the Security apparatus patterned after the KGB, the fraud of 'self–management' (the label suggesting that the workers manage factories and plants which are instead managed by Party functionaries), as well as, not last and not least, the possibility for a person such as Milošević to emerge, Mussolini–like, as a national superhero. Borislav Mihailović, Vice President of the Serbian Association of Writers, a declared anti–Tito person turned a Milošević fan, had this to say to a French correspondent: "After the war, Josip Broz first drove his Stalinian apparatus into our asses, and then, after the break with Stalin, took out half of it."[45]

Quisling rulers are usually despised by their people. But the amount of contempt varies with the degree of their servility. The old Hoxha team can still command some respect for their attempt to wrestle from Serbs as much freedom as possible. Telling in this regard is an exchange between Draža Marković and Fadil Hoxha in 1971. Replying to Hoxha's insistence on promoting Kosova to the status of a republic, Marković replied that Kosova could not become a republic because the Serbs would be put in a position of inferiority. Hoxha then "threatened" that Kosovars might take to the streets. To which Marković retorted that "it was less dangerous to take to the streets in Prishtina than in Belgrade."[46] What he meant is that Serbs would not tolerate a Kosova made into a republic. History has proved Marković right. Hoxha and his team had to go, after they had allowed, as seems likely, for the demonstrations of 1981 to occur. Vllasi's role in the demonstrations of 1988–89 has not yet been ascertained. But if he did encourage them, this was perhaps out of remorse for having long persecuted his people. Converted persecutors can occasionally become saints. But this probably won't happen to Morina, whose team will have to be an almost one hundred percent quisling team, with no chances for redemption. They may last as long as the state of Yugoslavia does, but they won't be remembered. Servants leave no memory of themselves.

In fighting for independence, Kosovars lost their autonomy. Shall we blame them for their hubris? We should praise them for their courage to fight for a just cause. This time they lost, next time they may well succeed. Defeats can be lessons, for they temper the spirit and they add wisdom to courage. And if Kosovars lost their autonomy, the loss was not without gains. What they gained was an intelligentsia they did not have, one that came of age in an emergency situation marking a historic date. What they gained is a revolutionary working class which proved itself in battle. Workers and intellectuals joined in protest in the best tradition of revolutionary socialism. They marched in front, they put their bodies to the Party–State machine to stop it. The Kosovar youth rushed after them, followed them, surpassed them. They challenged the enemy, who responded with fire. Some of them fell. But the rest will remember the outcry that makes a nation out of an amorphous human mass: "Better the grave than a slave."

But courage is not only a military virtue. There is also something called civic courage, and still another courage which informs intellectual and moral life. A literary historian, Ibrahim Rugova, defined the intellectual as one who dares express what he thinks. And he did express unequivocally what he thought, something Kosovar intellectuals could not do in the past. They accuse me as a nationalist, Rugova said, because I have criticized "Stalinist methods" used by State agencies to hush the Albanian demands for freedom and democracy, economic independence and equal political rights.[47] Another gain in the defeat is that it cleared the ground for further resistance action, identifying those who sold out from those who hold on. Obtaining or preserving power by serving the occupier is a form of national treason. France condemned Pétain, a national hero. In times of oppression, freedom may choose to dwell in jails. And siding with the oppressed is the mark of true nobility. In a novel, *The King's Hour*, Boris Hazanof, a Russian writer, has a Scandinavian king who is also a university surgeon frustrate the nazi plan to make him into a collaborator. And when his resistance is no longer tolerated, he sews onto his coat the Star of David which the Jews of his kingdom are obliged to wear, and walks with it in the streets, thus walking to his death. I was reminded of the Scandinavian king in Hazanof's novel when I learned of the Slovenian youth wearing the badge with the inscription, "Kosova my homeland."

But perhaps the biggest gain in the Kosovar defeat is the lesson Kosovars have imparted to their brothers in Albania, who for almost half a century now have been accepting an undignified existence under an anachronistic and ossified regime that has made Albania the butt of cruel jokes. Kosovars have given luster to the name of Albania, which the Stalalbanian leadership has sullied and debased, by joining the movement of protest against Stalinism in Eastern Europe. Whereas Slovenia, a Slav nation located hundreds of miles from Kosova and with which Albanians had no relations in the past, took the case of Kosova to its heart, all that the motherland has done for Kosovars is to blow some hot wind with their broadcasts and pay lip-service to the Kosova cause with a couple of articles in their press. The Albanian workers did not lift a finger for the Trepča strikers, and the Tirana university students did not even send a telegram to their brothers at the Prishtina university. Likewise, the League of Albanian Writers and Artists remained mute before the vigorous protest of the Kosovar writers. A statement of the Albanian Telegraphic Agency contains the following:

> The defense of the national and democratic rights of the peoples and nations of Yugoslavia, including the Albanians, must be made also by those whose desire is to see the much-suffering Balkan [peoples] live in peace and security.[48]

When this text was broadcast, the Kosovar miners had already begun their hunger strike in the Stari Trg pit. Not a word about them. The tone of the statement is subdued and evasive, that of a spectator who comments on events unrelated to him. The moral obligation of the Albanian government to defend Kosovars about to lose their autonomy is diverted to an impersonal "those" who care about "peace and security" in the Balkans. The concern is for "the peoples and nations of Yugoslavia," not for Kosovars who figure only parenthetically.

An editorial in *Zëri i popullit* commenting on the repression has a striking title, "Kosova's Tragedy, Yugoslavia's Shame,"[49] in which "shame" appears as equiponderant to "tragedy." How deeply the writer feels about Kosova's tragedy surfaces when he concludes that "the bullets that hit the Kosova masses who defended their rights have also hit the whole of Yugoslavia." Have they? From the same article we learn that Belgrade celebrated the bloody victory.

An article by Professor Luan Omari, editor of the scholarly *Studia Albanica*,[50] mentions the Trepča strike and notes the sympathetic echo it has aroused in Europe and Yugoslavia. Yet Slovenia is not mentioned, and for good reason: Slovenia's defense of Kosova is Albania's shame.

In another article, by Professor Sofokli Lazri,[51] an official representative of the Albanian intelligentsia, the tone has changed, becoming accusatory and vituperative. Nationalism is said to have "clouded the reason" of Milošević and his "clan," and the Kosovar leaders are called, one a "spineless character," another a "lackey," and a third a "fossil." Yet the shift of the stress from Kosova's tragedy to "the danger of Yugoslavia's Balkanization" persists. The professor forgets that the danger in question is also a consequence of the quixotic attempt of the Albanian leadership to Stalinize Kosova. He forgets that the roots of the Kosova tragedy go back to the national treason of the Albanian CP who delivered Kosova to Serbian Communists. He forgets that the actual Kosovar leadership he excoriates is only following a vassalage pattern set out by the Albanian CP, and that the insulting epithets of "spineless character," "lackey," and "fossil" fit Enver Hoxha better than anyone else.

The editorial in the Party newspaper and the articles by the two Albanian professors do not coincide in all points with the official position of the Albanian government towards Yugoslavia, which is one of great caution caused by fear of aggression. The official position was reasserted by the Deputy Foreign Minister, Sokrat Plaka, who made it clear that Albania will continue to hand over to Yugoslav authorities Kosovar fugitives seeking shelter in Albania: "They are Yugoslav citizens, they have to live there."[52] Reading this cynical sentence, one thinks of the Hungarians who have opened their borders to Transylvanian fugitives, and also of Turkey, which has been ready to shelter the Turkish minority in Bulgaria who refuse to be Bulgarized. Hungary has formally protested Romania's treatment of Transylvania Hungarians with a petition to the United Nations. And the irony is that whereas the Albanian government has failed to bring forth for discussion in the U. N. the tragedy of two million Albanians living in Yugoslavia, the Yugoslav government has already raised the question of a few thousand South Slavs in Albania before the U. N. Social Committee of the Socio–Economic Council.[53]

The truth is that the Albanian government is not interfering directly in Kosova's politics while continuing to pour fuel on the ongoing conflict.[54] The recent tactic has been not to advocate openly, as in the past when Hoxha was alive, Kosova's right to have its republic, while supporting Kosova's claim for equality of rights. The Albanian leadership fears a rival Republic of Kosova. They know that some Kosovars entertain thoughts of a Piedmont Kosova destined to unite all Albanian lands into Greater Albania.

What happened in Kosova cannot be explained without bringing into the picture the role of Albanian Stalinism. The responsibility for the Kosovar tragedy lies with all three parties involved, the Serbian, Albanian, and Kosovar leaderships, Stalinist all three, though in varying degrees. Albanian–born Kosovar Stalinism, political and pragmatic rather than ideological during the long rule of the older Kosovar leadership, absorbed during the rule of the younger leadership a strong dose of Serbian Stalinism. This Stalinism, dominant during the Ranković era but later contained by the liberal wing in the Serbian LC, resurged after Tito's death more virulent than before, taking advantage of the blunders made by the 'Djakovica leadership' in flirting with the Tirana leadership. The responsibility of the latter consists in trying—and to some extent succeeding—to divert Kosovar nationalism into its own ideological channel. Considering that Albania and Yugoslavia became sworn enemies after Yugoslavia's split from the Soviet bloc, Albanian ideological penetration turned Kosovars into ideological scapegoats in the ideo–political feud between the two states. My opinion is that the tragedy of Kosova could have been avoided if the Hoxha–Alia leadership had refrained from pouring fuel into the Serbo–Kosovar conflict.

Document of the
Proclamation of Albania's Independence
November 28, 1912
from *Dielli*, December 1, 1984

The signatures circled are those of Midhat Frashëri,
Lef Nosi and Mustafa Asim Kruja

Document of the
Proclamation of Albanian Independence
November 28, 1912
from *Historia e Shqipërisë*, Vol. 2, Tirana, 1984

The signatures of Midhat Frashëri, Lef Nosi and
Mustafa Kruja have been covered

Albanian Socialist Realism

(by Abdurrahim Buza)

Albanian Socialist Realism

(by Abdurrahim Buza)

Albanian Socialist Realism

(by Abdurrrahim Buza)

XV. PROSPECT OF ALBANIA'S FUTURE

The spectacular changes modifying the 'ideo–political'[1] map of Eastern Europe repropose the question of whether the *perestroika* hurricane will reach the dormant shores of the Adriatic Sea, where, in the fifties, a diminutive country worried the NATO allies because it harbored a USSR submarine base. So far the hurricane has struck Poland, Hungary, East Germany, and Czechoslovakia, all North and Central East European countries, without causing serious trouble to the Communist Balkan countries. Judging from a first shake–up of her leadership, Bulgaria will wind up by joining the other four Warsaw Pact countries. Another Warsaw Pact country, Rumania, is bound sooner or later to follow suit. Yugoslavia has long had its own *perestroika*, which does not at all exclude a rearrangement of her whole system, considering the aggressive tendencies of Serbian neo–Stalinism. Albania may very well be the last to be affected because it has characteristics strikingly different from those of other East European countries.

1. Peculiar Albanian Differences

1. The Albanian [Communist] Party of Labor remains the most Stalinist party in Europe because Albania has all but copied the Stalinist Soviet system in almost all its aspects: agriculture and industry, the security apparatus and the military, education and welfare, literature and the arts, whereas the other East European countries have adopted only some characteristic features of the Stalinist system. The bible of Albanian Communism, the *History of the Party of Labor of Albania* is almost the facsimile of the Stalinian *Short Story of the Communist [Bolshevik] Party*. Stalinist ideology is so permeating and overwhelming as to justify calling the Albanian variety of Stalinism 'Stalalbanianism.'

2. This is so because Albania, just as the Soviet Union, achieved socialism by short–cutting the road to it. According to Marx,

socialism will obtain as a necessary solution of the otherwise insoluble contradictions of the bourgeois capitalist system. Yet czarist Russia had an embryonic bourgeoisie when the Bolsheviks launched the October Revolution. Likewise, the Albanian bourgeoisie was embryonic when the Albanian Communist Party was founded in Italian–occupied Albania in November 1941. On the other hand, while all other East European countries were Stalinized after going through bourgeois governments, Albania jumped to dictatorial socialism from a tribal and semi–feudal social system.

3. Now it is the existence of varieties of this backward social system that characterizes Stalinist–Maoist revolutions in Asia, Africa, and Latin America. Stalalbanianism has thus been a model for varieties of Third World socialism. While being geographically a European country, Albania has acted as a non–European country. After breaking with Yugoslavia, her alliances have been first with the Soviet Union, a Eurasian country, and then with China, a far–East Asian country. Consequently, Albania has moved farther and farther from Europe, thus de–Europeanizing herself. Albania has not even signed the Helsinki Accords, in this too unlike other Communist East European countries and European countries *tout court*.

4. The main reason for this oddity and others as well is that whereas all other East European countries have a socialist tradition, with established Communist parties long before World War II, Albania has no such tradition. Moreover, the Albanian Communist Party came into existence during World War II thanks to the organizational efforts of the Yugoslav Communist Party through its delegates who were instrumental in the founding of the Albanian Communist Party, from which Enver Hoxha emerged as Acting Secretary General. Until Albania broke loose from Yugoslavia's tutelage in 1948, the Albanian Communist Party was practically a branch of the Yugoslav Communist Party. When the Cominform was founded in 1947, Albania was not represented, Yugoslavia functioning as her advocate.

5. Another major difference with the other Communist East European countries, with the exception of Yugoslavia, is that Albania is not a member of the Warsaw Pact, which she joined in 1955 and then denounced in 1968, in protest of the Soviet Union's invasion of Czechoslovakia (when the Soviet Union invaded Hun-

gary in 1956, Albania hailed that invasion).

6. Unlike Yugoslavia, a non-aligned country entertaining normal relations with the two superpowers, Albania, also a non-aligned country, remains the sworn enemy to both, despite repeated attempts by the two superpowers to reestablish diplomatic relations. And whereas some Communist countries such as China, Cuba and Yugoslavia have joined the loose alliance of non-aligned Third World countries unrelated either to NATO or the Warsaw Pact, Albania—while acting practically as a Third World country—has avoided joining that loose alliance, thus achieving total political and cultural isolation.

7. Unlike all other Communist East European countries, Albania has outlawed the practice of religion, celebrating herself as the first atheist state in the history of humankind.

8. Matching that strange world record is another one, even more self-congratulatory. Of all the existing Communist countries, Albania is the only one who claims to have kept Marxism-Leninism pure of 'revisionism.' This makes Tirana the epicenter of orthodox Communism, much as Mecca is the epicenter of Islam, and Rome of Catholicism.

9. While theoretically a political ideology, Albanian atheism is practically a religion, different as such from those two theistic religions in that Stalalbanianism is a godless religion. It has, however, a prophet: Enver Hoxha, its founder. One must add that Albania shares the honor of this particular world record with North Korea, the Hoxha cult being comparable to that of Kim Il Sung.

2. Image of Albania as Seen by Foreigners

Such idiosyncratic features make Albania a political *unicum*. Foreigners who have visited the country refer to the visit as "a journey back to the 1950s";[2] describe the country as a "dam against time,"[3] a "twentieth century anachronism" and a "utopia . . . of all utopias . . . surely the most grandiose";[4] associate it with African countries: "from Angola to Albania,"[5] ". . . people in Albania or Burkina Faso";[6] or call the Albanians "aliens" and "monsters."[7] The attraction Albania exerts on foreigners is that of an exotic rare animal in a zoo.

Forty-five years of the Stalalbanian regime have not cured endemic Albanian poverty. Collectivized agriculture has not been a success, wheat continues to be imported. Most of the work in the fields and groves is done by women. Lines outside state food stores, usually "bare of goods,"[8] are a customary sight. Even water and electricity are rationed, because of consecutive dry years (a divine punishment?). People cannot move from one place to another without written permission. Travel abroad is granted to very few, usually trusted people. No automobiles are to be found in Albania, except those of Party leaders and high functionaries. Transportation of people is done by decrepit buses;[9] the fragmentary single-track railroad network serves people also, but it was intended to carry minerals and agricultural products. In the streets bicycles and a few motorcycles alternate with horse- and ox-carts.

The older generation who lived during the revolutionary period are about to become extinct. Those who were born after the Party seized power have adjusted to the situation, resigned to their fate. The younger generation who can watch on television how Europeans live vent their anger by ripping apart plants in public parks and by spitting on Stalin's monuments.[10] The happy ones are the children, who are well taken care of in kindergartens and elementary schools. They are instructed to spy on their parents, for which they get good grades.[11]

The privileged segment of the population, the *nomenklatura*, i.e., the new ruling class, can shop in special state stores, have access to various perquisites, and can cure themselves abroad. Workers, theoretically the backbone of the regime, are made to work hard while being paid poorly, exploited much more so than in capitalist countries. They react with absenteeism, laggardness and slapdash work. Peasants in cooperatives are better off because they can sell the surplus of products priced by themselves (a typically capitalist device introduced recently). They can also steal socialist property. Theft is, for that matter, a generalized feature of the system, as also are bribery, palm-greasing, and favoritism of all sorts.[12]

The intellectuals—doctors, teachers and technicians—are slightly better off. The best rewarded are writers and artists. "The courts are governed by the class struggle principle."[13] Students with suspect political records (bourgeois kinship, lack of enthusiasm) are denied access to university studies. Thousands of people languish in prisons and forced labor camps. Yet dissidence expressed even in its mildest form is punishable. No private cultural clubs or sportive associations are tolerated, no journals or books are published that are not state-owned and state-censored. And of course no *samizdat* either. Strikes are forbidden. Not even one strike has occurred in the history of Stalinist Albania, except one in a forced labor camp, ruthlessly repressed. A modicum of criticism regarding most visible flaws in the economy and the administration was introduced after Hoxha's death. On the other hand, it has become obligatory to attribute every possible and imaginable achievement to Hoxha's omniscient genius. The organ of the Party Youth published recently an editorial about three new oil drillings. The merit for the discovery goes to Hoxha's "recommendations" to search assiduously for oil fields.[14]

3. Two Possible Scenarios

What can one infer from such historical premises with respect to the future of the country? Given that the regime has features so different from those of other East European countries and considering the apathetic attitude of the people in the absence of even a minimum of liberal institutions, one can hardly expect Albania to follow in the wake of the emancipatory movement of East European countries. Eastern Europeans were able to resist and also defy the dictatorship of their Communist parties thanks to the existence of anti-bolshevik institutions such as Christian churches, the survival of democratic parties however emasculated, the memories of a social-democratic tradition and, last but not least, a higher level of civilization. None of these factors is to be found in Albania today. The Catholic Church, the only well-organized and highly cultured Albanian church, was demolished from the very beginning. Albania had no democratic parties, except for the short 1920-24 period. Trade unionism was unknown in an overwhelmingly agricultural country with almost no industry and with a weak social-democratic group trying in vain to contain the influence of the Communist Party. And the level of civilization of the country was low.

It has grown considerably in the meantime, but it still lags behind as compared to that of other East European countries, while also being polluted with Stalalbanianism. In these circumstances, I am afraid that even after Ceaşescu's disappearance from Romania's stage, Albania will continue to be Stalinist for some time—if, for no other reason, then because the European community will not be displeased to house a natural live museum preserving the race of the Stalinist anthropoid.

Chances are, however, that this prison–like museum will not last a long time, but will be destroyed by the inmates themselves. Albania's economic situation has worsened to the point of her knocking at Germany's door. Not at the door of East Germany, mind you, but at that of West Germany, the leading European capitalist country, which is, moreover, ruled by a Christian Democratic–Liberal government. I am willing to bet that Hoxha's ghost, upon hearing the news, will rise from his grave to strangle the authors of that most unprincipled 'revisionist' deed. For it is Hoxha who used to say that the Albanians will feed on grass rather than beg for capitalist aid. But I doubt the Albanians will obey his order, obeying which will irrevocably qualify them to deserve living in a zoo behind bars.

I foresee two scenarios. One is that the Alia team will continue to distance themselves from Hoxha's legacy through cautious moves of liberalization and decentralization and, in foreign policy, by opening more to the West. By so doing, they will in fact imitate Gorbachev's tactics, while at the same time decrying them—in typical Stalalbanian style. A way to speed up reform could be to have students demonstrate for more democracy, thus weakening the influence of the conservative Hoxhan wing in the Party. But will Alia risk this maneuver after what happened in China? That may, however, be his only chance.

A more probable scenario is that the de–Stalinization process in East Europe will have repercussions on Stalalbanianism, the repercussions reflecting on the person of Hoxha and, as a consequence, discrediting his cult. Western pressure for improvement of human rights as a condition for economic aid will do the rest. Stalinist Albania shows signs of acute need for improving its bad image no less than its poor economy. A new party person, one who has not identified with Hoxha, should be able to challenge his ghost, joning the *perestroika* chorus. If even Romania, the other hard–line Stalinist Balkan country, joins it, then a shake–up in the Albanian leadership is bound to occur. This is not to say that Albania will return to the Eastern family of nations. If something has been learned from Albania's eastward drift, it is that Albania's destiny is to be an Adriatic country.

APPENDIX: 1. IN THE CANAL*

An episode of forced labor in the Maliq Marsh, Summer 1948

That day at the end of July was exceedingly hot. The sun began to scorch down more than usual, flooding the swamp with a bright light that caused the black mud, dug from under the water, to shine like anthracite.

Nicolas felt thirsty, but there was no water left in his flask. The worst was knowing that he would probably not get it refilled that day: no one had been seen carrying drinking water along the canal. It was not the first time that, on the hottest days, water service had been neglected. If he had been in the part of the canal where people were working in dry soil, he would have dug a hole in the earth and drunk from the water which would have seeped into the little pit. The water, of course, would have been repulsive, somewhat salty, and flowed into his stomach like molten lead; but, nevertheless, such a liquid would have helped to quench his torturing thirst.

Nicolas stopped shoveling for a moment. He wiped the sweat from his brow and asked Muko, the fellow toiling closest to him, whether he had a drop left in his flask. The other showed surprise:

"Why should I have? Do you think the sun is kinder to me than to you?"

He continued jokingly:

"You are happy enough to be up to your waist bathing in the quagmire. Think of buffaloes in your village! Why don't you do as they do? Your thirst, I guarantee, would be quenched at once."

Nicolas heard Muko's malignant laughter. He was sure that Muko had water in his flask; he had seen him, not long ago, steal

* Published in *Zâni i Katholikvet Shqiptarë në Mërgim—La Voce dei Cattolici Albanesi*, No. 5, September–October–November 1959.

from Liman's flask, when Liman had been ordered away by a guard. He knew Muko was not the kind of person ready to help his fellow man. He repented having asked a favor of such a person.

Muko had scarcely made his joke when Nicolas heard another voice behind him:

"It seems you have a liking for what buffaloes do!"

Nicolas turned his head in the direction of the speaker. He had recognized him at once: it was Corporal Zia, one of the most brutal camp guards.

The corporal was standing a few steps from him, on the edge of the canal. He had approached the workers from behind the embankment. The prisoners had not heard him because of the humming noise made by the wheelbarrows which removed the muddy heaps beyond the embankment. He carried a short, knotted stick, taken possibly from the kitchen woodpile.

Now he shouted:

"You, son of a bitch, why do you lag behind, instead of doing your job? Did we put you here for jesting and joking? Come on here, quick!"

Muko hastened towards him through the marsh and stopped in front of him. He had grown pale. In a standing position, holding the shovel with both hands as if it were a gun, he lowered his head, not daring to meet the guard's cruel gaze.

The voice now grew sharper.

"I see, you want to corrupt people here and keep them from doing their duty. Your jokes! I'll show you how to make fun."

The knock of something hard hitting something else hard was now heard. It was followed by another and still another succession of sounds, varying according to the part of the body beaten, as the prisoner twisted his head and shoulders, his back and arms. There was a cracking sound, and Nicolas saw the guard staring at the half-broken stick in his hand. He threw it away, and began kicking the contorted body with his boot. He kicked so many times that the body ceased to make any resistance whatever.

"Throw him in the water!" shrieked the corporal.

Two of the prisoners who were nearby started for the body. Nicholas did not move, although he was the closest. The corporal looked at him angrily.

"It seems that you are not in a hurry to help your friend."

The next moment he was yelling to the two prisoners who managed to lift the body onto its legs:

"Throw him in! you ruffians! Fling him down!"

Muko had only fainted. The violent impact with the water brought back his senses. He emerged from the water, clumsily brandishing his hands, trying to grasp something. Then he collapsed, rose up again, now squatted on his knees, then began to grope his way toward the shore, painfully, awkwardly.

"Don't let him get out!" rose the infuriated voice. "Keep him down!"

A third person was meanwhile drawing near the unfortunate Muko. Nicolas knew him well. He was a young man, named Vojo, formerly a thief and now a spy, who more than once had helped the guards carry out the manifold tortures inflicted upon 'the enemies of the people.' He was not one of Nicolas' working team, but apparently had been accompanying the corporal on a trip along the canal. Attracted by what was going on, he volunteered to carry out the guard's orders.

He snatched a shovel from someone's hands and rushed into the marsh to prevent Muko from leaving it. He fell on him at once, threatening him by shaking the shovel close to his face. Then he thrust it out and sent the half-conscious man splashing into the water, to the corporal's great excitement and loud laughter. Muko managed to get up again, but his time Vojo kept shoveling mud and water against the victim with such a swift motion that the latter was nearly stifling.

The corporal screamed and roared with laughter.

"The buffaloes! Ho! Here you have it!"

He shouted to the two fellows who had remained spectators:

"Give a hand, you rascals! Do you pity him?"

Just at that moment Nicolas spoke to the corporal:

"You'll kill him."

The guard looked at him, at first astonished. Then, after a pause, he said:

"So, you pity him."

No answer came.

"Come on!" said the corporal, in a voice which was the more frightening for being cold and low.

Nicolas walked out slowly and stood in front of the corporal, at some distance from him, looking him straight in the eyes.

The corporal stepped forward. For a while he scanned the prisoner from head to foot and suddenly knocked Nicolas in the face with all his strength.

Nicolas staggered, but did not fall. He recovered, and kept looking at the corporal, while slowly wiping with his palm the blood that flowed from his nose.

The other blurted out, grinding his teeth:

"Get into the canal!"

Nicolas walked in slowly.

"Stop! Get down into the water!"

Nicolas sat down in the water, leaving only his bloody head exposed.

"Down with your head!" the enraged voice yelled.

This time the prisoner plunged into the morass and emerged with a black-stained face oozing streams of slime.

"Again! . . . Again! . . . Again!"

Each time the corporal yelled, Nicolas repeated the same motion, like a robot, or like an escavator which dives into the water at regular intervals.

This finally bored the corporal. It looked like, instead of a torture, the parody of it.

"Give him a shovel!" he ordered with a lowered tone that was no longer angry. "And let all sluggards and saboteurs remember! That's what they'll all get."

Then he stepped away, whistling a song.

APPENDIX: 2. *VENERIADA*

Nepërmjet lutjevet të Nênë Terezës, Arbëria (A), një **grua afèr** gjashtëdhjetavet, është lejuar të vizitojë Skëterrën e Dante-s. Duke përshkuar qarkullin e fundëm të sajin, Arbëria ndeshet me Hoxhën (H), i cili, duke ndërprerë grindjen e tij ideologjike me Stalinin (S), i hakërrohet Arbërisë. Kjo e mallkon.

H. Shqipëri, tri her' të shita,
    edhe borxhet t'i resita!
    Si shpërblim ti çfar' më dhè?
    As edhe një mauzolè!

A. Mauzolè unë s' të bêra
    që të mos i dukej vêra.
    Nuk e pe ç' pësoi yt mjeshtër?
    Kêmbëshkurtër kjo gënjeshtër.

S. Ç'nunuris kjo palo femër?
    Nuk e di kê shklet me thembër?
    Kur musteqet un'i vrênja
    Eurazis'i dridhej rrênja!

A. Sot jo mê. Lëpin sot plagët
    nga Katynët, nga gulagët.
    Të përmjerrin sot mbi rrasë
    proletar'e të paklasë.

H. Po û ç'faj i kam atdheut?
    Pse ja dola Skënderbeut?
    Shqipëri, unë të bêra,
    unë, me vithet e gjêra!

S. O bandill, të lumtë bitha!
    Ajo i shpjegon të gjitha.

Ç' duhen dituri e mênd
kur njeriu ka fatin tênd?*

Bukurosh, të lumtë llapa!
Kush të pa që s't'erdhi prapa!
Por harrove, o tungjatjeta:
të shpëtoi Dyzeteteta!

A. Ti Kosovën tregëtove,
    ti me Jugon më martove.
    Shite mua dhe Kosovën,
    shite Jugon për Moskovën.

S. Po 'dhe mua m'tradhëtove,
    Çinmaçinit i lakmove.
    Tej e flake pasi e vole.
    Socializmin mir'e mole!

H. Shok, nga ti e kam ungjillin:
    Pas Hitlerit, me Çurçillin!
    Û ta ngrejta lart doktrinën
    kur Krushçevi i solli shpinën.

S. E ç'doktrin', o budallà!
    Çorba jote pordhallà!
    Atheizmi shpallur fè,
    me Tiranën për Qabè!

A. Vrave, preve, vare, ndoqe,
    miq, armiq, shok'edhe shoqe,
    cilindo që t'bênte hije,
    gati t'a zhdukje, t'a fshije.

    Dhe tani pa turp kërkon
    një kolltuk në pantheon
    me klasikët e marksizmit,
    ti, xhambaz i komunizmit?

    Vendi yt në mauzolè,
    tok me mjeshtrin, në halè!

    _____

    * It. *'aver culo,'* 'të keshë fat.'

Krushçevi ju foli hakun:
atij vêrën, ty kapakun!

Stalinuc i Shqipërisë,
paç haram qumësht e sisë!
Paç mallkimin e një nême:
pizeveng, doç i satême!

2. VENERIAD

Through the prayers of Mother Teresa, Albania (A), now in her late fifties, has been granted her request to visit Dante's Inferno. In crossing over its bottom circle, she is recognized by Hoxha (H), who is engrossed in an ideological quarrel with Stalin (S). The following thrust-and-reply occurs.

H.   Thrice, Albania, you I sold,
     wrote your debts off, new and old.
     Didn't I deserve at least
     a mausoleum, once deceased?

A.   Setting no such glorious crypt up
     spared us seeing marble ripped up.
     You recall your master's shame?
     Lying words are always lame.

S.   What's this dirty woman mumbled?
     Can't she see on whom she's stumbled?
     My mustachios' slightest shaking
     set Eurasia's roots a-quaking!

A.   Once; but now she licks the wounds
     left by Katyns, gulags, goons.
     Proletarians, declassés
     both piss on your grave these days.

H.   Yet in what did I fail you?
     Daring Scanderbeg to outdo?
     I, Albania, made you, yes,
     I, the one with this big ass!

S.   Romeo, blest be your ass!
     That explains it all, I guess.

Who needs science, wit, or pluck,
when he's got what you've got—luck?*

Bless your tongue, too, Ganymede!
Who but followed where you'd lead?
Don't forget, though, dearest soul,
Forty–eight's what kept you whole.

A.   Poor Kosova first you traded,
    me to Yugo gave and mated.
    Sold us both, but to the wrong man,
    then sold him to Moscow's strong man.

S.   I in turn saw you defect
    to the Mau Mau Dragon sect.
    Dropped it, too, when once you'd bilked it.
    Socialism, how you milked it!

H.   Your example was my text:
    Hitler first and Churchill next!
    I upheld your doctrine boldly
    when Khrushchev had spurned it coldly.

S.   Fool! My doctrine? What baloney!
    Your bouillabaisse–minestrone!
    Mullah atheism chanted,
    Mecca in Tirana planted!

A.   You who shot, hanged, persecuted
    foe or comrade, any suited
    to eclipse you in your station,
    marking all for liquidation,

    now you dare, from this abysm,
    you horsetrader of communism,
    bid the pantheon admit you
    and with Marxist classics sit you?

    Your seat there is in the restroom,
    with your master, as his groom.

---

* 'To have luck' translates Ital. *'aver culo.*

There Khrushchev gave each his due:
him the hole, the lid to you.

Petty Stalin of Albania,
woe that my breast nursed your mania!
Have your mother's curse and scorn,
you, her pander, bastard–born!

Albanian text (quem vide) by Arshi Pipa.
English version by Arshi Pipa and Jeffrey Fruen.

NOTES

Notes to Chapter I

[1] Because quisling Albania, following Italy's example, declared war on Greece.

[2] Haxhi Qamil was the leader of an anti-national peasant movement intended to restore Turkish domination.

Notes to Chapter IV

[1] *Bajraktar* [flagbearer] is the Turkish name for an Albanian tribal chief who, in the event of war, leads his men to battle.

[2] Albania's relation to fascist Italy fits the concept of dependency describing the relations of the Latin American countries with the United States.

[3] After World War II, Albania assisted and sheltered insurgent Greek communists, thus angering the Greek government, which, according to reports, seriously considered an invasion of South Albania. On October 22, 1946, two British destroyers were struck by mines in the Corfu Canal. The Hague's Court of Justice found the Albanian government guilty of having placed them and sentenced it to pay damages to Great Britain.

[4] Nicola Pašić, Premier of Yugoslavia at the time.

[5] China was admitted to the United Nations in 1971 on Albania's request.

Notes to Chapter VI

[1] Enver Hoxha, *Kur lindi Partia* [When the Party Was Born], Institute of Marxist–Leninist Studies at the Central Committee of the PLA [INLSCC], Tirana, 1981, p. 220.

[2] *History of the Party of Labour of Albania* (no author(s)) (IMLSCC, Tirana, 1981), p. 65.

3 E. Hoxha, *Kur lindi Partia*, p. 430.

4 E. Hoxha, *Selected Works*, vol. 1 (IMLSCC, Tirana, 1974), p. 140.

5 This is how Ismail Kadare portrays his execution in his novel *Dimri i madh* [The Great Winter], Tirana, 1981, 3rd ed., pp. 105–06: "Anastas Lulo, you have betrayed the International." He stood before them pale, looking with empty eyes on now one now another. Partisan courtmartial. "Don't hurry, my boys, wait a moment, you don't know what the International is. You are young. Don't rush, summon here a competent comrade. I want to discuss with him questions of principle. A comrade from the center, one who is conversant with theory." They listened to him for a while. His imploring voice kept increasingly repeating resonant foreign words, which sounded more and more absurd in that scorched plain. "This comrade here is conversant with theory," the company commander finally interrupted him, pointing to a young man with blondish hair and a stubbed nose, a partisan from the village of Brataj. The partisan lowered his eyes. "Çoçol, explain to him the question from a theoretical viewpoint," the company commander said. "And you, Muqerem, assist him." The man charged with treason opened wide his eyes, his mouth writhed. And instead of uttering resonant foreign words, he only said, "no," "no." They took him to a place some fifty steps away. And there they gunned him down.

6 He was allegedly killed by Liri Gega. See Stavro Skendi, (ed.), *Albania* (Praeger, New York, 1956, 2nd ed.), p. 85.

7 E. Hoxha, *The Titoites* (IMLSCC, Tirana, 1982), p. 135.

8 *Ibid.*, p. 415.

9 *Ibid.*, p. 256.

10 See Arshi Pipa, "Komunizmi dhe shkrimtarët shqiptarë" [Communism and Albanian Writers], *Shqiptari i lirë* [The Free Albanian] (New York, February 18, 1959, and March 31, 1959).

11 The conspiracy of engineers, allegedly masterminded by H. T. Fultz, a member of the U. S. Military Mission and former director of the American Vocational School in Tirana, is the subject of a prize–winning novel, *Këneta* [The Marsh] by Fatmir Gjata. See A. Pipa, *Albanian Literature: Social Perspectives* (Trofenik, Munich, 1978), pp. 175–78.

12 E. Hoxha, *The Titoites*, p. 159.

13 *Ibid.*, p. 160.

14 *Ibid.*, p. 449.

15 *Ibid.*, p. 380.

16 *Ibid.*

17 *Ibid.*, pp. 430–31.

18 *Ibid.*, pp. 435–36.

19 *Ibid.*, p. 449.

20 *Ibid.*, p. 450.

21 *Ibid.*, p. 466.

22 E. Hoxha's *With Stalin* (IMLSCC, Tirana, 1979) includes after p. 208 a picture bearing the following caption: "Comrade Enver Hoxha signing the oath of the Albanian people on the occasion of the death of Joseph Stalin, March 10, 1953."

23 E. Hoxha, *With Stalin*, p. 216.

24 E. Hoxha, *The Titoites*, p. 482.

25 *Ibid.*, p. 556.

26 *History of the Party*, p. 263.

27 See S. Skendi, *Albania*, p. 86.

28 See Nicholas C. Pano, *The People's Republic of Albania* (John Hopkins Press, Baltimore, 1968), p. 92.

29 Among the twenty–eight victims executed with due procees were a writer, Manush Peshkëpia, and a woman professor, Sabiha Kasimati.

30 *History of the Party*, p. 270.

31 *Dokumenta kryesore të PPSH* [Main Documents of the PLA, vol. 3] (Tirana, 1970), p.449.

32 Khrushchev mentioned her case in his speech at the 22nd CPSU Congress (October 1961). See William Griffith, *Albania and the Sino–Soviet Rift* (MIT Press, Cambridge, Mass., 1963), p. 235.

33 In his *Conversations with Stalin* (Harcourt, Brace & World, New York, 1962), Milovan Djilas reports: Stalin responding to his explanation as follows:: "We have no special interest in Albania. We agree to Yugoslavia's swallowing Albania! . . . ." At this he gathered together the fingers of his right hand and, bringing them to his mouth, he made a motion as if to swallow them (p. 143).

Later, he repeated the offer to Djilas. Yet, since the conversation took place in January 1948, i.e., not long before Stalin denounced Yugoslavia's leadership, it is possible that Stalin's offer was a provocation.

34 Robert Lee Wolff, *The Balkans in Our Time* (Harvard University Press, Cambridge, Mass., 1974), p. 606.

35 The expression is part of the title of Chapter 7 in the *History of the Party*, which is divided into five subchapters. "Revolution," "revolutionization," "revolutionizing," and "revolutionary" appear twelve times in the titles of the subchapters.

36 The first two volumes of Hoxha's *Works* (in Albanian) were published in 1968. By 1971, eight volumes had appeared. Volume 37 came out in 1983.

37 E. Hoxha, *Selected Works*, vol. 4 (IMLSCC, Tirana, 1982), p. 819.

38 *History of the Party*, p. 504.

39 *Ibid.*, p. 467.

40 Peter Prifti, *Socialist Albania since 1944: Domestic and Foreign Developments* (MIT Press, Cambridge, Mass., 1978), p. 215.

41 *History of the Party*, p. 506.

42 Pirro Dodbiba, Minister of Agriculture and Politburo candidate member, was fired in April 1976.

43 *History of the Party*, p. 506.

44 Part of the title of subchapter 5 in Chapter 8 of the *History of the Party*.

45 P. Prifti, *Socialist Albania*, p. 82, and note 65, p. 273.

46 R. L. Wolff, *The Balkans*, p. 607.

47 *Ibid.*

48 Mehmet Shehu, *Report on the Fifth 5-Year Plan* (Tirana, 1971), p. 147.

49 Between 1978 and 1982, the following books authored by Hoxha appeared, all published by IMLSCC: *Yugoslav Self-Administration-A Capitalist Theory and Practice* (1978); *Imperialism and the Revolution* (1978); *With Stalin, Memoirs* (1979); *Reflections on China*, 2 vols. (1979); *Eurocommunism is Anti-Communism* (1980); *The Khrushchevites, Memoirs* (1980); *Kur lindi Partia* [When the Party Was Born, Memoirs] (1981); *The Anglo-American Threat, Memoirs* (1982); *The Titoites, Historical Notes* (1982).

50 *History of the Party*, pp. 570-71.

51 *Ibid.*, p. 570.

52 E. Hoxha, *Report Submitted to the 8th Congress of the Party of Labour of Albania*, November 1, 1981 (Tirana, 1981), p. 102.

53 "Address to the Second All-Russia Congress of Communist Organizations of the Peoples of the East," in Lenin, *Selected Works*

in One Volume (International Publishers, New York, 1971), p. 508.

54 "The Immediate Task of the Soviet Government," *Pravda*, April 28, 1918, in Lenin, *Selected Works*, pp. 407–08.

55 " 'Left–Wing' Childishness and Petty–Bourgeois Mentality," *Pravda*, May 9, 10, 11, 1918, in Lenin, *Selected Works*, p. 438.

56 *History of the Party*, p. 468.

57 *Ibid.*

58 E. Hoxha, *Report to the 8th Congress*, p. 102.

59 T. Campanella, *The City of the Sun: A Poetic Dialogue*, trans. D. J. Donno (University of California Press, Berkeley, 1981), p. 69.

60 I have combined and slightly paraphrased Shehu's intervention in the Hoxha–Krushchev confrontation. According to E. Hoxha, *Albania Challenges Khrushchev Revisionism* (Gamma Publishing Co., New York, 1976, p. 177), both Mehmet Shehu and Hysni Kapo replied to the Soviet leader when he used the name of MacMillan: "Comrade Enver is not MacMillan, so take that back." The following, "Put it in your pocket," was pronounced by Mehmet Shehu alone.

61 E. Hoxha, *Reflections on China*, vol. 1 (IMLSCC, Tirana, 1979), p. 369.

62 *Ibid.*, vol. 1, p. 23.

63 *Ibid.*, vol. 1, p. 97.

64 *Ibid.*, vol. 1, p. 690.

65 "The Echo of Our Article 'The Theory and Practice of Revolution,' " in *Reflections on China*, vol. 2, p. 564.

66 "Why Were Police, Violence and Tanks Used Against the Albanians of Kosova," April 8, 1981; "Who Incites Hostility Amongst the Peoples of Yugoslavia," April 23, 1981; "The Status of a Republic for Kosova Is a Just Demand," May 17, 1981.

67 E. Hoxha, *The Titoites*, p. 625.

68 R. L. Wolff, *The Balkans*, p. 467.

69 *Ibid.*, p. 471.

70 *Ibid.*

71 *Ibid.*, pp. 480–81.

72 *Ibid.*, pp. 409 and 365–66.

73 "Notes on the Cultural Revolution in China. The Party is not Purged from Outside but from Within," *Reflections on China*, vol. 1, p. 366.

[74] E. Hoxha, *The Titoites*, p. 35.
[75] *History of the Party*, p. 64.
[76] *Ibid.*, p. 166.
[77] *Ibid.*, p. 319.
[78] *Ibid.*
[79] E. Hoxha, *The Titoites*, p. 187.
[80] *Ibid.*
[81] *History of the Party*, p. 530.
[82] E. Hoxha, *Imperialism and the Revolution* (IMLSCC), Tirana 1978), pp. 262-63.
[83] *Ibid.*, p. 25.
[84] E. Hoxha, *Eurocommunism is Anti-Communism* (IMLSSC, Tirana, 1980), p. 249.
[85] *Ibid.*, p. 227.
[86] E. Hoxha, *Imperialism and the Revolution*, pp. 134-35.
[87] *Ibid.*, p. 142.
[88] Quoted by R. L. Wolff, *The Balkans*, p. 277.
[89] M. Djilas, *Conversations with Stalin*, p. 146. Stalin asked Djilas about Hoxha during their January 1948 conversation.
[90] Lenin, *Selected Works,*, p. 432.
[91] *Marx-Engels. Collected Works* (International Publishers, New York, 1975), vol. 4, p. 110.
[92] *Early Writings [of] Marx*. Trans. R. Livingstone and G. Benton (Penguin Books, 1977 repr.), p. 357.

Notes to Chapter VII

[1] According to the 1981 census, the population of Macedonia was 1,760,000, that of Montenegro, 565,000.
[2] About 600 people had been expelled from the Party at the end of 1981. Michele Lee, "Yugoslavia's Albanian Crisis: Wrong Turn in Kosova," *Labour Focus on Eastern Europe* 5(1982)1-2:51.
[3] A total of more than 1,800 years in jail (until March 1982), distributed among people of various categories, mostly intellectuals and students, including workers.
[4] Groups ideologically related to Tirana have been engaged in subversive activities. One of them, The Movement of the Albanian Socialist Republic in Yugoslavia, publishes a periodical in Switzerland: *Zëri i Kosovës* [The Voice of Kosova].
[5] *History of Yugoslavia* by V. Dedijer, I. Božić, S. Ćirković, M. Ekmečić, (McGraw Hill, New York, 1974), p. 60.

⁶ Alain Ducellier, "Les Albanians et le Kosovo," *Le Monde*, June 2, 1982. See also Ducellier's "Conclusion générale" in his *La Façade maritime de l'Albanie au moyen âge* (Institute for Balkan Studies, Salonika, 1981).

⁷ *Srbi i Arbanasi (njihova simbioza u srednjem vijeku)* (Belgrade, 1925).

⁸ First partially published by S. Ljubić. "Skadarski Zemljišnik od god. 1416," in *Starine* 14(1882):30–57. Fulvio Cordignano published the Cadaster together with the concessionary acts in the codex, *Catasto veneto di Scutari e Registrum Concessionum* 1, 2 (Tolmezzo–Roma, 1944, 1942) as well as a study of the names and toponyms in the former, *Onomastico del Catasto di Scutari e Registrum Concessionum* (Tolmezzo, 1945). Giuseppe Valentini made a new edition of the codex, which constitutes vol. VIII of *Acta Albaniae veneta saeculorum XIV et XV* (Trofenik, Munich, 1970). Vol. IX of the series (Trofenik, Munich, 1970) is an index of the cadaster, provided with statistics. An Albanian translation and edition of the codex was made by Injac Zamputi: *Rregjistri i Kadastrës dhe i koncesioneve për rrethin e Shkodrës 1416–1417* (Institute of History, Albanian Academy of Sciences, Tirana, 1977).

⁹ H. Hadžibeć, A. Handžić, E. Kovačević, *Oblast Brankovica*, I, II (Sarajevo, 1972).

¹⁰ Selami Pulaha, *Le Cadastre de l'an 1485 du Sandjak de Shkodër* I, II. Presentation, introduction, translitteration, traduction et commentaire (Institute of History, Tirana, 1974).

¹¹ Edith Durham quotes Strabo describing the Dardanians as "an entirely savage people, so much so that they dig caves beneath dung–heaps, in which they dwell." Durham adds that most probably the dwellings of the Dardanians had been reduced to ashes by the Romans when Strabo visited the province. *Some Tribal Original Laws and Customs of the Balkans* (Allen & Unwin, London, 1928), p. 13.

¹² See especially Norbert Jokl, 'Rumänisches aus Albanien," in *Studia albanica* (1964)2:75–79.

¹³ See Peter Bartl's article "Kosova and Macedonia as Reflected in Ecclesiatical Reports," *Studies on Kosova* (1984), pp. 32–39.

¹⁴ 238,106 in 1910, according to Turkish statistics. Antonio Baldacci, *L'Albania* (Istituto per l'Europa Orientale, Rome 1930), p. 199.

[15] 742,509 in 1910, according to Turkish statistics. *Ibid.*, p. 200.

[16] 599,582 in 1910, according to Turkish statistics. *Ibid.*, p. 201.

[17] 340,477 in 1910, according to Turkish statistics. *Ibid.*, p. 200. About 400,000 in 1912, according to Antonio San Giuliano, *Briefe über Albanien* (Leipzig, 1913), p. 143.

[18] In his book, *Serbs and Albanians* (in Serbocroatian), Dimitrije Tucović protested against the cruel repression of the Albanians: "The bourgeoise press called for merciless annihilation and the army acted upon this. Albanian villages, from which the men had fled on time, were reduced to ashes. At the same time, there were barbarian crematoria in which hundreds of women and children were burned alive. . . . It once again confirmed that the popular revolt of the most primitive tribes is always more humane than the practices of standing armies used by modern states against such revolts." Quoted in *History of Yugoslavia* (see note 5), p. 436.

[19] By peripheral Albanian regions are meant the Albanian regions in Montenegro and Macedonia.

[20] See note 11.

[21] Michel Roux, "Le Kosovo; développement régional et integration nationale en Yugoslavia," *Hérodote* (1982) 26 (2nd quarter), p. 13.

[22] Albanian is an indoeuropean language with two main dialects, Gheg, spoken in the North, and Tosk, spoken in the South. The differences are mostly in phonology and, to some extent, in morphology.

[23] *Rilindja* (17 November 1980, p. 13), published an article by Academician Idris Ajeti, President of the Society of Teachers of Albanian Language and Literature in the Autonomous Socialist Province of Kosova, on the situation of the teaching of the official Albanian language in the elementary and secondary schools, which was described as "not at all good" and "disturbing." The main causes for this situation were "the lack of an organized social activity for the appropriation of the Albanian literary language on a vast social level," and "the low level of knowledge of the literary language by the teachers" themselves. The document is proof of the general lack of interest in a language which is not germane to spoken Kosovar and results in artificial writing— Kosovar literature has lost its impetus and flavor.

24 See Ibrahim Rugova, *Vepra e Bogdanit 1675-1685* (Rilindja, Prishtina, 1982).

25 The Kosovars have been strangely silent about this important sector of their oral poetry. Two Harvard Professors, Milman Perry and Albert B. Lord, collected epic songs from Albanians. A first volume, *Serbocroatian Heroic Songs*, was published in 1954. To my knowledge, the first Kosovar article on this volume is dated April 2, 1983, published in the newspaper *Rilindja* [Renascence].

26 Peter Bartl, *Die albanische Muslime zur Zeit der nationalen Unabhängigkeitsbewegung (1878-1912)* (Harrassowitz, Wiesbaden, 1968), p. 153.

27 Stavro Skendi, *The Albanian National Awakening* (Princeton University Press, Princeton, 1967), p. 335.

28 Hima was sympathetic to the idea of a Balkan Federation. See Hasan Kaleshi, *Biographisches Lexikon zur Geschichte Südosteuropas*, vol. II (Oldenbourg, Munich, 1976), p. 163. Hima and a Vlach (Aromunian), Dimitri Papazoglou, founded what seemed to have been a joint Albanian-Vlach Committee in Paris in 1902 (Skendi, *The Albanian National Awakening*, p. 325.).

29 *Ibid.*, pp. 342–43.

30 *Ibid.*, p. 427.

31 Bartl (1968), p. 182.

32 The Acting Chief of the European Division at the Library of Congress told me (Spring 1981) that purchases of Kosovar publications have been conducted through dealers, direct contact having failed. The situation is even worse at the British Museum, where Kosovar publications are not even listed in the catalogues. The person in charge of Albanian in the Slavonic and East European Branch there explained to me that they are now receiving the more important publications (not yet catalogued in Spring 1983).

33 In this respect one case is particularly telling. The Modern Language Association of America publishes a yearly, *MLA International Bibliography*, in many volumes, covering books and articles on the language, literature, and folklore of practically all the countries in the world. The compiler of the bibliography of Albanian literature and folklore in that periodical has more than once written to the University of Prishtina asking for their contribution to a venture which is in the interest of Kosovar and Albanian culture in general. His letters have not been answered

and no attempt has been made to correct the unfortunate situation.

[34] M. Roux (1982), p. 38.

[35] *Ibid.*, p. 35.

[36] *Politika*, May 18, 1982.

[37] M. Roux (1928), p. 30.

[38] *Ibid.*, p. 30.

[39] Catherine Verla, "Après les émeutes du Kosova. Une question nationale explosive," *Inprecor*, June 1981, p. 10.

[40] See for this L. S. Stavrianos, *Balkan Federation. A History of the Movement toward Balkan Unity in Modern Times* (Archon Books, Hamden, Conn., 1964).

[41] Academician Vasa Čubrilović wrote a memorandum to the Royal government in Belgrade in March 1937, "The Expulsion of the Arnauts"—Arnaut is the Turkish name for the Albanians.

[42] Dimitrije Tucović was the founder of the Serbian Social Democratic Party. See note 18.

Notes to Chapter VIII

[1] This must be the son whom Hoxha accuses of having installed a radio broadcasting mechanism at Shehu's home. A third son who happened to be in Europe when his father committed suicide now lives in Sweden.

[2] Tuk Jakova, Organizational Secretary of the Party during the period 1948–1951, was removed from his position for maintaining, among other things, that "it was they [the Yugoslavs] who had created the Communist Party of Albania" (*History of the Party of Labour of Albania*. IMLSCC, Albanian 2nd ed., 1982, p. 287).

[3] Harry Fultz was Director of the American Vocational School when Shehu graduated from it. Fultz was a member of the American Delegation after Albania's liberation. The delegation, accused of espionage against the Albanian government, left in 1946. See Joan Fultz Kontos, *Red Cross, Black Eagle, A Biography of Albania's American School*, East European Monographs LXV (Boulder, 1981).

[4] Disease as an attribute of revisionism (the *genus* of liberalism) is spelled out in the following sentence: "What is the explanation for this custom of revisionists? Do they all copy each other, or does their disease drive them to find the same cause?" (489).

[5] *Dimri i madh* [The Great Winter] (Tirana, 1981, 3rd ed.). Citations are from this edition.

6 The following are some excerpts, in chronological order, from letters that Hoxha sent to Shehu (and his wife), as well as from various speeches. Letter of April 14, 1944 to Mehmet Shehu: "You should not . . . endanger your life at any moment, like an ordinary partisan. You are not permitted, except at extremely critical moments . . . to expose yourself to danger" (*Enver Hoxha. Selected Works [EHSW]*. The Institute of Marxist–Leninist Studies of the CC of the PLA, Tirana, 1974, vol. I, p. 269). Letter of April 22, 1933 to Fiqret Sanxhaktari (Shehu): "Following your work, help, and guidance there has been an obvious improvement in the situation of the brigade [the First Brigade, commanded by Shehu, with Sanxhaktari as Commissar] from every point of view, especially as regards the level of the cadres" (*EHSW* I, p. 271). Report to the Tirana Party activitists on the 11th Plenum of the CC of the CPA, October 4, 1948: "Comrade Mehmet Shehu deserved neither the accusations brought against him nor the condemnation he received [from Xoxe and his faction] . . . . Comrade Mehmet Shehu is a comrade who has fought well. We say this, for in the analysis of the 9th Pelnum efforts were made to obscure this very positive aspect of his. Mehmet has military ability, and has made a valuable contribution to the struggle, and to the organization and modernizing of our army. Comrade Mehmet Shehu has defended both the general line of the Party and our correct line in the army with determination worthy of a member of the Central Committee" (*EHSW* I, p. 802). Speech at the 17th Plenum of the CC of the PLA, July 11, 1960: " . . . Mikoyan wanted to see me the next morning to discuss some important questions. 'Agreed,' I told him, 'but I shall take Comrade Mehmet [Shehu] with me, too.' He replied, 'They told me only you,' but I said that Mehmet had to come too." " . . . Fifteen days before the counterrevolution took place in Hungary, Mehmet and I, at a meeting with Suslov in Moscow . . ." (Enver Hoxha, *Albania Challenges Khrushchev Revisionism [ACKR]*. Gamma Publishing Company, New York, 1976, p. 32 and p. 38). Closing speech at the 17th Plenum, July 12, 1960: "As all of you have stated, and as Comrade Mehmet [Shehu] correctly expressed the view of the whole Party, in a Marxist–Leninist way . . ." (*ACKR*, p. 46). Radiogram to Shehu in New York, September 28, 1960: "We liked your speech very much" (*ACKR*, p. 117). Speech at the

Albanian Stalinisn

Chinese Embassy, September 30, 1960: "As is known, the regular
session of the United Nations Organization has opened in New
York and its proceedings are continuing. There, the Chairman
of the Government of the People's Republic of Albania, Comrade Mehmet Shehu, expressed the will of the Albanian people,
of our party and our Government for the preservation of peace in
the world. He condemned colonialism. Comrade Mehmet Shehu
defended China and insistently demanded that it be admitted
to the United Nations Organization and the Chiang Kai-Shek
puppet regime be ousted . . ." (*ACKR*, p. 126). Radiogram
to Shehu in New York: "Fiqret and the children are well. I embrace you and we are eagerly awaiting your return" (*ACKR*, p.
143). In *Kur lindi Partia* [When the Party Was Born] (IMLSCC,
Tirana, 1981, p. 426), Hoxha writes that he cried when he heard
that Shehu's mother had died.

7 That a split and liberal Marxist–Leninist party ceases to exist
as such is made clear by Hoxha himself: "The Marxist–Leninist
party . . . is not a party of words, but a party of revolutionary
action. If its members are not engaged in concrete actions and
struggle it will not be a genuine Marxist–Leninist party, but a
Marxist–Leninist party only in name. At given moments such
a party will certainly be split into different factions, will have
many lines which will coexist, and it will be turned into a liberal
opportunist and revisionist party" (E. Hoxha, *Eurocommunism
is Anti-Communism.* IMLSCC, Tirana, 1980, p. 258).

8 *Histoire du Parti du Travail de l'Albanie* (Institut des Etudes
Marxistes–Lenistes près le Comité Central du Parti du Travail
d'Albanie, Tirana, 1982).

9 Chapter 2 of Kadare's *The Great Winter* contains an episode
that illustrates Hoxha's role as a publicity figure. The editor-
in-chief of the journal for which the journalist works, dissatisfied
with a series of pictures depicting Hoxha among women workers,
has the head of the photography laboratory look for another
picture to be printed in the journal. The head wonder why, the
development of the film having been faultless. The journalist
provides the answer: "Perhaps we should look for a shot where
Comrade Hoxha is seen somewhat smiling" (32).

10 This sentence, expunged from the English edition, is found in
the Albanian edition of the volume: "*u fut në dhe si qen . . .*"
(*Titistët* INLSCC, Tirana, 1982, p. 578).

[11] *Origin of Family, Private Property and State*, chapter on "The Family" (2nd para.).

Notes to Chapter IX

[1] See Arshi Pipa, "The Political Culture of Hoxha's Albania," in Tariq Ali (ed.), *The Stalinist Legacy—Its Impact on 20th Century World Politics* (Penguin Books, London, 1984).

[2] Paul Lendavi, *Das einsame Albanien* (Zurich, 1985), p. 70.

[3] So far there is little indication of this: in March 1986 Enver Hoxha's widow was elected president of the Democratic Front of Albania, a post previously held by Hoxha himself. This is the only function of the departed leader not taken over by his successor Ramiz Alia.

Notes to Chapter XI

[1] "The Heirs of Stalin," in Tariq Ali, *The Stalinist Legacy* (Penguin Books, 1984), p. 549.

[2] *With Stalin* (IMLSCC, Tirana, 1979), pp. 14–15.

[3] *Perestroika. New Thinking for Our Country and the World* (Harper and Row, New York, 1987), excerpts in *U. S. News and World Report*, November 9, 1987, p. 71.

[4] *Ibid.*

[5] A photo after p. 208 in *With Stalin* shows "Comrade Enver Hoxha signing the Oath of the Albanian People on the occasion of the death of Joseph Stalin, March 10, 1953."

[6] " 'We shall certainly carry out your instructions, Comrade Stalin,' I said . . ." (*ibid.*, p. 216).

[7] See "Party Ideology and Purges in Albania" in this volume.

[8] See the three previous essays in this volume.

[9] The Yugoslavs needed my article to have it as a 'certificate of good behaviour' for Yugoslavia and Tito," E. Hoxha, *The Titoites* (IMLSCC, Tirana, 1982), p. 449.

[10] "Figure universelle," in Ramiz Alia, "Drapeau de la lutte pour la liberté et le socialisme," *Studia albanica* 23(1986)1, p. 7; "oeuvre immortelle" in Foto Çami, "Le camarade Enver Hoxha, fondateur, organisateur et dirigeant de notre glorieux Parti," *ibid.*, 22(1985)1, p. 8; "gloire eternelle à l'oeuvre monumentale" in Ramiz Alia, *op. cit.*, p. 9.

[11] IMLSCC, Tirana, 1984.

[12] Reuters Agency, Bonn, October 23, 1987.

Notes to Chapter XII

[1] The gravity of the economic situation in Yugoslavia was under- lined by the President of the European Commission, Mr. Jacques Delors, and the West German Foreign Minister, Hans–Dietrich Genscher, both of whom used the phrase "possible economic collapse" in considering what may result from the hypertrophying debts and balance of payments crisis. *The Guardian*, March 7, 1988.

[2] Branko Horvat, "The Kosovo Question," *Labour Focus on Eastern Europe*, July–October 1987, p. 33. The article is a selection of extracts by Michele Lee from the article published in *Književne Novine*, the organ of the Serbian Writers' Association. According to Horvat, "against 210,000 employed in the social sector, 114,000 had no jobs" (*ibid.*).

[3] On this see the July–October issue of *Labour Focus*, containing a letter to the journal's Editorial Collective by the former editors of *Praxis International*: Zagorka Golubović, Mihailo Marković, and Ljubomir Tadić, in protest against a previous article by Michele Lee in which, according to them, Lee implicitly accuses them of "betrayal of their former socialist views and alignment with nationalism." The same issue includes a reply by Lee and her translation of the "Petition by 200 Leading Belgrade Intellectuals."

[4] *Labour Focus*, July–October 1987, pp. 31–32.

[5] On this topic see two articles by Victor Meier in *Frankfurter Allgemeine Zeitung*, dated February 19, 1988, and March 29, 1988.

[6] Branko Horvat, "The Kosovo Question," p. 33.

[7] Peter Bartl, "Die *Këlmendi*. Zur Geschichte einer nordalbanischen Bergstames." *Shêjzat* [Le Pleiadi]. Festschrift for Professor Ernest Koliqi, 1978, p. 135.

[8] Carlo Tagliavini (*La stratificazione del lessico albanese*, Riccardo Patron, Bologna, 1965, p. 13) gives the names of two villages: Hrtkovcki and Nikincki.

[9] *Labour Focus*, July–October 1987, p. 31.

[10] A. Pipa, "The Other Albania: A Balkan Perspective," in this volume, p. 138.

[11] Koçi Xoxe, the main Yugoslav agent in Albania's Communist Party, was, in his capacity as Organizational Secretary of the

Party and Minister of the Interior, Albania's strongman during
the period of Albania's dependency on Yugoslavia (1944–48). He
was executed after Albania became a Soviet protectorate.
[12] *Narodni Odbor Autonomne Kosovsko-Metohiske Oblasti, 1943–
1953* (Prishtina, 1955), p. 10.
[13] Here is a telling joke. A Kosovar is swimming in a pool in a
Serbian city. Suddenly he suffers a cramp and is in danger of
drowning. He cries for help. No one budges. He then shouts:
"Kosova Republic!" Immediately one of the bystanders jumps
into the water and saves him. The Kosovar thanks his rescuer,
who coolly produces a pair of handcuffs, saying, "Sorry, I'm a
policeman."
[14] An Albanian soldier, a former university student, ran amok in the
Paračin barracks, killing five Slav soldiers and then committing
suicide.
[15] Pedro Ramet speaks of more than one thousand casualties in
"Problems of Albanian Nationalism in Yugoslavia," *Orbis* 25
(1981) 21:369–88.
[16] *Rilindja* (Prishtina), July 1, 1987.
[17] In June 1986, Representative Joseph J. Dioguardi and Senator
Robert Dole presented two concurrent resolutions lamenting violations of Kosovars' human rights. On July 17, 1987, a second concurrent resolution was introduced, Dioguardi's text this
time being signed by fifty–six congressmen, and Dole's version
cosponsored by Senator Paul Simon, both Dole and Simon being
candidates for the presidency of the United States.
[18] Translation distributed by Committee to Aid Democratic Dissidents in Yugoslavia, New York, July 1986.
[19] Branko Horvat, "The Kosova Question," *Labour Focus*, July–
October 1987, p. 33.
[20] Amnesty International Report, 1985, "Yugoslavia."
[21] Daniel Alberte, *Journal de Genève*, Sept. 29, 1987.
[22] Vehbi Ibrahimi was murdered in Brussels on October 10, 1981.
On January 17, 1982, the brothers Gërvalla and a freind were
ambushed and killed in the neighborhood of Stuttgart. Amnesty
International reports the comment of the president of a West
German court: "It cannot be tolerated that hired assassinations
are carried out in our territory, instigated by foreign states trying to solve their internal problems." (Amnesty International
Report 1985, "Yugoslavia.") Kosovars retaliated by attacking

the club 'Yugoslavia' in Brussels, killing one person on March 3, 1982. On June 14 of the same year, the Yugoslav Embassy in Brussels underwent an armed attack which ended with the death of an officer and the wounding of two people. Terror has also been exercised against Albanians serving in the army. According to oral reports, some have been tortured, others shot. Reported also is the case of a soldier returned to his family in a metal box containing ashes. The Paraćin barracks murder of five Yugoslav soldiers and the wounding of many others by a Kosovar recruit has an explanation—not a justification—when set in this terroristic context.

23 Darko Hudelist, "The Kosovo Autumn of 1987," *Start*, October 31, 1987.

24 According to these statistics, from March 1981 to October 1987 two Serbs/Montenegrins were murdered by Albanians, both murders occurring in 1981. During the same period, three Albanians were murdered by Serbs/Montenegrins. Between 1982 and 1986, 16 Serbian/Montenegrin women were raped by Albanians, and there were also 19 attempted rapes. During the same period, Albanian women suffered 138 rapes and 152 attempted rapes at the hands of Albanians, Serbs, and Montenegrins, the largest number of rapes involving attackers of the same nationality as their victims. The alleged rape at a primary school was in fact not even an attempted rape. And the case involving a bomb planted in a primary school was pure invention.

25 Paul Shoup, *Communism and the Yugoslav National Question*, Columbia University Press, 1968, p. 104.

26 Paul Shoup, "The Government and Constitutional Status of Kosova: Some Brief Remarks," *Studies on Kosova.*, *op. cit.*, 1984, p. 233.

27 *Ibid.*, p. 237.

28 *Ibid.*, p. 235.

29 *New Statesman*, October 23, 1987, p. 18.

30 The foundations of 'unified literary Albanian' [ULA] rest with Stalin's thesis—in *Marxism and Linguistics*—that when two languages mix, one comes out victorious while the other dies out. The victorious language preserves its grammatical structure and its basic word stock, while enriching itself with the vocabulary of the defeated language. Now the victorious 'language' in Albania is the Tosk dialect, Albanian communism being a predominantly

Tosk phenomenon. Inspired by Stalin's thesis, and under the injunction of Enver Hoxha, himself a Tosk, Albanian linguists have invented a Tosk variant which, phono–morphologically, is almost completely Tosk, while borrowing abundantly from the richer Gheg vocabulary and phraseology, duly given a Tosk varnish.

[31] Characteristic of this phenomenon is the attitude of Adem Demaçi, a writer considered by many as the spiritual leader of the Kosovar resistance. *Borba*, the newspaper of the League of Communists of Yugoslavia, has recently published an interview with Demaçi, still in prison after almost thirty years of captivity for his pro–Tirana stance. Asked whether he continued to entertain the idea of union with Albania, Demaçi answered as follows (I quote from the translated text of the interview in the Italian communist newspaper *Il Manifesto*, April 9–10, 1989): "The idea of union with my mother country is no longer convincing if the process of equalization between Albanians and other peoples of Yugoslavia will obtain. . . . I am ready to give my life for Yugoslavia, if my stepmother is attacked. But I love my people, without, however, being a nationalist, for a nationalist hates other peoples. . . . I would prefer to see my own son killed rather than a Serb. . . . While in Kosova, I shall always side with Serbs and Montenegrins who are minorities there. But while in Yugoslavia, I shall always side with my Albanian people." Asked whether his attitude toward Hoxha had changed, Demaçi replied: "No, I remain a great admirer of Enver. A large portrait of him in my home I never hid, and often had myself photographed close to him."

[32] The brothers Gërvalla, who were murdered by the Yugoslav State Security, are reported to have maintained that their objective was the unconditional union with their mother country, regardless of the form of regime there, be that a monarchy, a bourgeois democratic republic, or the dictatorship of the communist party.

[33] "Certainly, the stand towards minorities and their treatment is an internal question of each country, a field of its complete sovereignty, which is treated in compliance with the state system and the laws of each country. [Missing is any reference to international law—Albania has not signed the Helsinki agreement.] The People's Socialist Republic of Albania has never raised the question that the issue of the minorities should be solved by changing borders and interfering in the internal affairs of one another. But we think this does not rule out the legitimate interest of neigh-

bours in their minorities, especially in those cases when this interest is based on the will and the sincere desire to contribute
to the strengthening of the good neighbourliness and friendship
among peoples, to the general security in the Balkans." *Review
of International Affairs* (Belgrade), No. 910, March 5, 1988, p.
19.

[34] While Tito's name was mentioned in the speech of the Yugoslav
Secretary for Foreign Affairs, Hoxha's name was not in Malile's
speech.

[35] In a reception for the Albanian delegation headed by Hoxha in
Belgrade in December 1946, Tito sat not Hoxha but Xoxe at
the head of the table. A. Pipa, "Party Ideology and Purges in
Albania," in this volume, p. 59.

[36] On this see Victor Meier's article, "Discrimination Makes One
Self–Conscious" (*Frankfurter Allgemeine Zeitung*, November
1985). After stating that the Kosovar intellectuals perceived the
Yugoslav suspension of the cultural exchange as a discriminatory
policy against them, he writes: "What is new is that at the same
time they are beginning to look at their Kosova as an independent cultural land." And in another article, "Cultural Awakening
in Kosova" (*Frankfurter Allgemeine*, December 5, 1985), Meier
adds: "Already in the seventies and perhaps due to an earlier
tradition [the allusion is to the League of Prizren (1879–1891),
marking the birth of the Albanian National Awakening move-
ment] among the Kosovars an opinion took shape, according to
which they are destined to play an 'awakening role' also with
respect to Albania proper. Tirana's fear of the Kosovars as well
as its strivings to establish good relations with Belgrade rather
than Prishtina is rooted, apart from economic considerations, in
that opinion."

[37] In the 1987 catalogue of Rilindja, the Prishtina–located official
Kosovar publishing house, among 407 titles (including translations and children's books) I spot only 15 titles of books printed
in Tirana (ca. 3.3 percent), mostly linguistic and children's
books, with a few novels translated from contemporary authors.
Their names, as well as those of their characters, and geographical names, continue to be spelled according to the Cyrillic phono-
logical system used in Serbia and Macedonia (thus John Keats
becomes Xhon Kits), which was adopted by Albania when it was
practically a Serbian protectorate, in spite of the fact that Alba-

nians use a Roman script, just as do Croats and Slovenes, who write those names as they are written in the original languages.

38 What Kosovars write today is not 'unified literary Albanian,' but a language which is neither Tosk nor Gheg, but a mishmash of Kosovar patterns of speech mixed up with clichés borrowed from official Albanian and also from Serbocroatian. Reading Kosovar newspapers, one runs into sentences whose spurious wording does not make sense; their scholarly writing suffers from verbosity and awkwardness, and the poems they write are simply not poems. A recent example from the April 17, 1988 issue of the official *Rilindja*, published in Prishtina, may suffice. The director of the Kosova Archives, Dr. Hakif Bajrami, is quoted as admitting illegal acts perpetrated by Kosovars against Serbs and Montenegrins: " . . . It is a fact that there have been misuses with respect to those families that were colonized (*u kolonizuen*) in Kosova during the two [world] wars." The verb in the sentence should not be in the passive, as it stands, but in the active: ". . . the families that colonized [settled as colons in] Kosova . . . ." The candor of the speaker who does not pass over in silence the improper deeds of his fellow nationals is the more to be lauded as he confesses his own misuse of the Albanian language: "To tell the truth, and in spite of my strivings, I am not satisfied with the level of my knowledge of my mother language."

Notes to Chapter XIII

1 Two American missionaries, Dr. and Mrs. Edwin E. Jacques, precede their unpublished report on their visit (November 17–27, 1986) with a note: "This report was deliberately kept low key so as to be shared with six Tirana dignitaries with whom we had contact." The statement of the Very Reverend Arthur E. Liolin, Chancellor of the Albanian Archdiosese in America, who toured Albania in July–August 1988, has "lyrical" praises for the Albanian government, but not a word of criticism for its politics of religious persecution (*Dielli-The Sun*, Oct. 25, 1988). Imam Vehbi Ismaili, primate of Albanian–American Moslems, had no comments.

2 Elez Biberaj, "Albania's Economic Reform Dilemma," *The World Today.*, October 1987, pp. 180–81.

3 Edith Lhomel, "Albania 1986–1990: vers plusdu réalisme?," *Le Courrier des Pays de l'Est*, no. 316, March 1987, p. 75.

4 Patrick Artisien, "Albania at Crossroads," *The Journal of Communist Studies*, Sept. 1987, p. 237.

5 E. Lhomel, "Stagnation persistante de l' économie albanaise en 1987," *Le Courrier des Pays de l'Est*, no. 330, June 1988, p. 67.

6 Statistical shortcomings, especially concerning agriculture, where the annual growth rate has been no more than 4 percent at best, are stressed by E. Lhomel, "L' économie albanaise en 1987," *Le Courrier des Pays de l'Est*, no. 320, July–August 1987, p. 58.

6bis In *JPRS-EER-87-162*, December 22, 1987.

7 Interview with Gérard Valet, *Le Soir* (Brussels), June 18–19, 1987.

8 Quoted by P. Artisien, *op. cit,*, p. 235.

9 *Zëri i popullit*, April 23, 1987.

10 Giorgios Angeles, "Albania into the 'Light' after 40 years . . .," *Mesimvrini*, Oct. 27, 1987, pp. 18–19, in *JPRS-EER-87-162*, Dec. 18, 1987, pp. 16–18.

11 "Decree on the organization of the Albanian courts of justice" includes the following sentence: "In their actions, the courts are governed by the class struggle principle" (*Gazeta zyrtare* (Official Journal), November 5, 1987.)

12 Kleanth Zoto, "The personality of the school grows in the struggle against alien manifestations," *Mësuesi*, organ of the Ministry of Education, January 13, 1987.

13 Ramiz Alia, "Socialist culture, great active force for the fatherland's progress," *Nëntori* (November) 1988, no. 3, p. 17.

14 *Ibid.*, p. 13.

15 *Ibid.*, p. 8.

16 Foto Çami, "For the multilateral progress of socialist culture and its growing role in the whole life of the nation," *Ibid.*, pp. 21–54.

17 *Ibid.*, p. 26.

18 See also Alia: "Our film studios produce an average of more than one movie per month, which is good. But we would like to see one or two good and even very good movies among them" (*ibid.*, pp. 13–14).

19 Nexhmie Hoxha, "Our cultivated person is inconceivable without mastering Marxism–Leninism," *Zëri i popullit*, March 9, 1988.

20 Ndoc Logu, "Legends of Walls," *Puna* [Work], March 1, 1988.

21 S. Rushani, (Untitled), *Dielli*, Sept. 15, 1988. –Muho Asllani, a native of Shkodër and a Politburo member, is presently the

President of the Executive Committee for the Shkodër district. Ramiz Alia was also born in Shkodër.

22 See especially the booklet, Amnesty International, *Albania, Political Imprisonment and the Law,* 1984.

23 *Albania: Violations of the Right to Freedom of Thought, Conscience and Religion,* Minnesota Lawyers International Human Rights Committee, Minneapolis, August 1988.

24 Edward Stein, "Albania Sticks to Atheistic Line," *The Independent* (London), May 13, 1988.

25 *Zëri i popullit,* June 24, 1988.

26 *Albania Report* (New York), Bulletin no. 66, June 1988.

27 Gjok Sokoli, "Revival of the old crusade of the Belgrade anti-Albanian propaganda," *Zëri i popullit,* May 21, 1988.

28 Javer Malo, "On the article published in *Borba* by a specialist in things Albanian," *Zëri i popullit,* June 3, 1988.

29 *Rilindja* (Prishtinë), March 21, 1986.

30 E. Lhomel, *op. cit., Le Courrier des Pays de l'Est,* no. 330, June 1988, p. 70.

31 Someone had written that in 1986 "363,433 conversations to disseminate medical information had occurred" (*Zëri i popullit,* April 8, 1987). A journalist decided to verify the figure by interviewing personnel in the Ministry of Public Health. They dismissed the figure as exaggerated. Yet the journalist found that in that same year the number of infant diseases and mortalities was considerably higher than the previsions of the ministry itself. Musa Ulgini, "The Directory Comrades at the Ministry [of Public Health] say: 'We too don't believe these statistics," *Zëri i popullit,* April 8, 1987.

32 "Albania during and since Hoxha," Wilson Center, Smithsonian Institution, Washington, D.C., March 1988.

33 *Zëri i popullit,* June 12, 1988.

34 Quoted by E. Biberaj, *op. cit.,* p. 181.

35 Qemal Xhaçka, "The subcultural revolution. Reflection on the crisis pervading modern bourgeois–revisionist art and society," *Rruga e Partisë,* March 1987.

36 Preç Zogaj, "Attractive clothes of young people," *Zëri i rinisë,* April 18, 1987.

37 Sokol Muho, "Variations on the theme of peace: A clothing exhibition," *Zëri i rinisë,* January 6, 1988.

38 Neal Ascherson, "Albania's dam against time," *The Observer*, November 22, 1987.

39 Hamit Beqja, "Intellectual culture and moral culture," *Zëri i popullit*, April 23, 1987.

40 Hamit Beqja, "Against taboos that block the revolutionary education and formation of the youth," *Zëri i popullit*, June 17, 1988.

41 Arshi Pipa, "Stalin and Hoxha: the Master and the Apprentice," in this volume, p. 143.

42 E. Lhomel, *op. cit.*, *Le Courrier des Pays de l'Est*, no. 330, June 1988, p. 70.

43 *Puna*, the workers' newspaper, has denounced favoritism in retail sales (H. Reka, "Goods for friends," *Puna*, March 3, 1987), or in public services, when these are self-serving (Namik Dokle, "Daily viewpoints: The seed of indifferentism," *Puna*, March 18, 1988).

44 Enver Hoxha, *Reflections on the Middle East* (8 Nëntori, Tirana, 1984), pp. 464, 483, and 484.

45 I remember Giuseppe de Robertis, my professor of Italian at the University of Florence (this was in 1941), shuddering with horror and growling a "What?!" that stuck in this throat when a fellow student asked permission to write a paper on the style of Mussolini in his speeches.

46 Two generals of European reputation listed in Bayle's *Dictionnaire historique et critique* are Nicola Basta and Giorgio Basta, Italo–Albanians. Francesco Crispi, twice an Italian premier (1887–1891 and 1883–1896) was also an Italo–Albanian. Many of the leaders in the Greek War of Independence—Botsaris, Bubulina, Kunduriotis—were Arvanites (Greco–Albanians) speaking Albanian. — See also notes 47, 48, 49, below.

47 The Köprülü family governed the Ottoman Empire through a series of grant viziers and viziers from the second half of the seventeenth century through the first three decades of the next.

48 Ali Pasha Tepelena carved out a big pashalik comprising South Albania and most of Greece at the beginning of the nineteenth century. Pashko Vasa (Vasa Pasha) was a governor of Lebanon (1883–1892) until his death.

49 Mohammed Ali, appointed Viceroy of Egypt by the Sultan (1805), founded the royal dynasty which ruled Egypt until Nasser's *coup d'état* in 1952.

50 Mustafa Kemal, called Atatürk, the builder of modern Turkey,

was an Albanian on his father's side. And the present president
of Turkey, Kenan Evren, is also of Albanian origin.
[51] Mother Teresa was born in 1910 to a Catholic family in Skople
(Shkup in Albanian) at a time when the city was part of the
Ottoman empire and was (as it still is) inhabited by a great
number of Albanians. — Mother Teresa's application for a visa
to enter Albania was rejected by the Albanian government.
[52] Here are their names: Haxhi Lleshi (1944–46); Koçi Xoxe (1946–
48); Nesti Kerenxhi (1949); Mehmet Shehu (1949–1950); Tuk
Jakova (1950–51); Mehmet Shehu (1951–54); Kadri Hazbiu (1954–
1978); Fiçor Shehu (1978–1982). Of these, Xoxe, Mehmet Shehu,
Hazbiu, and Fiçor Shehu were put to death. — For a comprehensive article on the purges, see Arshi Pipa, "Party Ideology
and Purges in Albania," in this volume.
[53] My book, *The Politics of Language in Socialist Albania* (1989)
centers on this question.
[54] "The reason is that Albania seems to be one of the very few Third
World states to be having success with it social innovations. So
I wrote repeatedly for clearance to visit Albania, but no person
or institution bothered to reply—to my deep regret" (From a
letter dated August 23, 1982). — The January–February–March
1989 calendar of the Textile Museum in Washington, D.C., includes a textile exhibition "Albanian Wedding Attire" (March
19, 1989). Other textile exhibitions during the three–month period are "Textiles from Northern Ivory Coast," "Palestinian National Costumes," "Moroccan Embroidery," "Chichicastenango
Textiles," "Weaving and Costume in Central Ecuador," "Baluch
Rugs," and "Oriental Carpets." Albania is in good company
with Third World countries.
[55] This happened in 1973, shortly before Hoxha began the purge
against liberalism.
[56] Enver Hoxha, "Everything in our country is done and built for
the youth," *Speeches, 1971–73*, p. 240. Quoted by Peter R.
Prifti, "The Labor Party of Albania," in Stephen Fischer–Galati
(ed.), *The Communist Parties of Eastern Europe*, Boulder. Distributed by Columbia University Press, 1979, p. 29.
[57] "In act II, the scene shifts to Albania and environs, where two
American women are enjoined by a local leader, Achmet Bey, to
search the ice moons of Saturn for some stolen cheese and a man
named Pancake. An odyssey ensues involving alien monsters

(Albanians!)." Jonathan Kalb, "Albanian Banalties," *Village Voice*, February 1988. – The play was presented at the New York City William Field Redfield Theatre sometime in January–February 1988.

58 "Zhvillimi politik i shtetit shqiptar" (The Political development of the Albanian State), *Shqiptari i lirë* [The Free Albanian], November–December 1962.

59 The placard bore the inscription: "Go ahead Slobodan, if necessary as far as Tirana!" *Zëri i popullit* (October 14, 1988) replied with an editorial, "Do not play with fire!," in which one reads: "In the demonstrations organized by Belgrade's chauvinistic political staff, which have been likened by world press to prewar fascist–nazi manifestations in Italy and Germany, slogans and streamers appeared such as 'We want weapons,' 'Let's wipe out the Albanians!' As far as we are concerned, our answer to those appeals is that those who can frighten the Albanians are not yet born. As history has proved repeatedly, those who have marched on Tirana, have there left their bones."

60 'Hoxha' is the Albanian spelling of 'hodja,' but is pronounced pretty much like the English word. The name is frequent as a last name among Moslem Albanians whose forefathers were Moslem priests. Enver Hoxha belonged to a Bektashi family, Bektashism being a Shia sect considered heretical by Sunni Moslems—his father and uncle used to be addressed by relatives with the honorific title 'mullah.' Hoxha hailed the Iranian revolution as an "anti–Imperialist revolution of the Iranian people [which] had a class character, was in essence a social revolution and not a revolution of a religious character" (E. Hoxha, *Reflections on the Middle East, op. cit.*, p. 245).

61 Only one Politburo member is under 50; four are in their 50s, seven in their 60s, the eldest one 70.

62 Rear Admiral Teme Sejko was executed in 1961, accused of heading a "revisionist–imperialist" plot. Generals Beqir Balluku, Petrit Dume, and Hito Çako suffered the same fate sometime in 1974–75 for apparently having scoffed at Hoxha's defense map, punctuated by bunkers.

63 *Dielli*, September 15, 1988.

64 Milorad Komatina, "Albania and the Balkan Meeting," *Review of International Affairs* (Belgrade), March 20, 1988, p. 13.

65 Edouard Bailby, "Immobile Albania," *Géodécouverte*, 1988, p.

244.
[66] *The Economist*, January 7, 1989. — Speaking about the Vienna
Conference on Security and Cooperation in Europe, which termi-
nated its work on January 19, 1989, the journal points out that it
was attended by "all the European countries minus Albania" (p.
40). All the communist countries of the Soviet bloc, as well as Yugoslavia, signed the concluding document, in which "the rules for
checking other countries' human–rights records have been made
more intrusive" (*ibid.*). Albania did not participate in this conference because she has not yet decided to improve her human
rights record, which would thus be confirmed to be worse than all
other European countries—another European record for Stalinist
Albania.

Notes to Chapter XIV

[1] Peter R. Prifti, *Socialist Albania since 1944* (The MIT Press,
Cambridge, Mass., 1978).
[2] See the chapter *'Iura imaginaria* and commodity fetishism' in my
"Marx's Relation to Vico: A Philological Approach," in *Marx
and Vico. Affinities and Contrasts*, G. Tagliabue (ed.) (Humanities Press, Atlantic Highlands, 1982).
[3] Literature offers many examples. In Koço Kosta's "The Two of
Them and Others, Too" (*Nëntori* 1986, No. 4), a novel whose
first part somehow eluded censorship, a carpetswagger type who
has managed to get a fish at a Tirana food store explains to his
friend, who compliments him on this feat, that the fish is for his
boss. In a short story in *Nëntori* by the same writer, a poacher
who kills a fox to sell its fur is asked by a friend whether he
is not afraid of being fined. He answers that, if caught, he will
pretend that he killed the fox while it was attacking his chicken.
Dhimitër Xhuvani's *Back on His Feet* (Tirana, 1970), a novel
honored with a Republic's prize, tells of a young man who had
his legs cut off by a train. He makes himself prosthetic wooden
legs, obtains a job in a junk yard which he turns into a spare
parts shop, and invents a hydraulic piston for trucks. Feted by
his fellow workers as a hero of socialist labor, he walks out of the
banquet without his cane, a born–again man, accompanied by
what seems to be his girlfriend. The novel, hailed by Albanian
critics as a representative work of Albanian socialist realism, is
realistic the way a joke is serious. In fact the novel is a bitter

satire—the author wrote it after his more realistic novel featuring a disaster of socialist construction was vilified as antisocialist.

4 See pp. 171-77 in this volume.

5 The author, Tayar Zavalani, lived and worked five years in the USSR, then returned to Albania where he was one of the leaders of the Moscow-oriented trend. He translated into Albanian Gorky's revolutionary novel *The Mother* and wrote many articles in liberal and leftist journals of the time. The Italian occupation found him abroad. He opposed both the fascist aggression and the nazi invasion. In London, where he settled, he wrote a scholarly book, *How Strong Is Russia?* (Hollis and Carter,1951), a detailed analysis of the Soviet quinquennial plans.

6 Besides being an economist, Zavalani wrote a *History of Albania* in two volumes. He also edited an anthology of Albanian literature for *Arena* (March 1964 issue), a journal published by the London Center for Writers in Exile. He was a polyglot, speaking, besides Albanian, Italian, French, German, Russian, Greek, and Turkish.

7 *History of Albania*, vol. 3, Albanian Academy of Sciences, 1984. Nosi was put to death after the Communists seized power, while the other two died in exile. Nosi and Kruja do not appear in AED. Frashëri does, insulted as a traitor. He was a longtime editor of a learned journal, *Diturija* [Knowledge], President of the Congress of the Albanian Alphabet, and also author of a volume of short stories which is, chronologically, the first of that genre in the language.

8 *History of Albania* (vol. 3), published in 1984, mentions him six times—invariably as an American and Yugoslav spy.

9 Georg Paul Hefty, "Albania in Search of a Way Out of the Poorhouse," *Frankfurt Allgemeine Zeitung,* April 25, 1989, p. 5.

10 Asim Kelmendi, the major figure of Kosovar communism, was born in Djakovica (Gjakovë), but lived first in Albania and then in the Soviet Union, ending his brief career (1900-1939) as probably Komintern's chief man on Albania.

11 In the Shkodër Gymnasium studied Asim Vokshi, Mehmet Hoxha, Sadik Bekteshi, Xheladin Hâna, Hajdar Dushi, Emin Duraku, Murat Pâci (the last four killed during World War II). Another student there was Haki Taha, a nationalist who killed Miladin Popović. Students of the Normal School were Fadil Hoxha, the Number 1 of Kosovar communism, Xhavit Nimani, Ismet Shaqiri,

and quite a few others. In his book, *Sukobi na Kosovu* [Conflicts in Kosova] (Narodna Kniga, Belgrade,1984, 2nd ed., pp. 73 and 85), the author, Spasoje Djaković, mentions other Kosovars educated in Albania: Xhevdet Hamza, Xhevdet Doda, Mazllum Kpuska, Veli Deva, Ymer Pula, Hysni Zajmi.

[12] "Kosovo between Yugoslavia and Albania," interview with Arshi Pipa by Michele Lee, *Labour Focus on Eastern Europe*, No. 5, Summer 1982; reprinted in this volume, pp. 42–53.

[13] "Differentiation" is the leitmotif of my article, "The Other Albania: A Balkan Perspective" (see pp. 92–103, above), first published in *Studies on Kosova*, East European Monographs 155 (Boulder, distributed by Columbia University Press, 1984), containing the Acts of the International Conference.

[14] "Petition of 200 Leading Belgrade Intellectuals," *Labour Focus on Eastern Europe*, July–October 1987.

[15] It was presided over by Otto von Habsburg, spokesman for the Central and Eastern European Parliamentarian Group, with the participation of Dr. Franc Buçar, Professor Emeritus, Ljubljana University, Professor Mate Mestrović, Fairleigh Dickinson University, and Professor Arshi Pipa, University of Minnesota. The text of my address, worked out in collaboration with Dr. Sami Repishti, was published under the title "For a Solution of the Kosova Crisis" in *Dielli*, July 25, 1988, and was reprinted as "Reflections on the Kosova Crisis" in *Across Frontiers*, Winter–Spring 1989).

[16] A couple of months later he succeeded by deftly manipulating popular discontent at the republic's disastrous economic situation.

[17] An estimated 150,000, according to *Journal de Genève* (November 24, 1988).

[18] Albanian oral tradition includes an epic song in praise of Oso Kuka, a Shkodër Moslem, commander of an Albanian border guard on the Montenegrin frontier. Besieged in his bastion by Montenegrin troops and invited to surrender, Oso ignited what ammunition he had, which exploded, killing himself, his men, and many Montenegrin assailants.

[19] According to Albanian sources.

[20] Tanjug, February 27, 1989, in *FBIS-EEU-89-039*, March 1, 1989.

[21] *Frankfurter Allgemeine Zeitung*, March 20, 1989.

22 Michele Lee, "Will the Center Hold?" *Labour Focus on Eastern Europe,* vol. 10, no. 1, 1989, p. 40.

23 This ideology smacks of Stalinism in that it reduces all human relations to the ally/enemy paradigm. *Ibid.*

24 Ljubljana Domestic Service, Vito Augustin talk, March 24, 1989, in *FBIS-EEU-89-057*, March 27, 1989.

25 Swedish Radio Program, April 20, 1989, Ann–Mari Boström reporting.

26 The following press review is based on a selection of newspapers and magazines mostly provided by a friend living in Geneva, which explains why the review is limited to Switzerland and its limitrophe countries.

27 *The Times,* March 31, Richard Bassett reporting.

28 *Der Spiegel* (April 3) pointed out that "annexation" is not the solution to Yugoslavia's two million unemployed and 1000 percent inflation. The Zagreb *Vjesnik* (April 3) called the Yugoslav victory a "Pyrrhus–like" one. *La Suisse* (April 9) compared the situation created in Kosova to that in Northern Ireland and the Basque Provinces. The Parisian *L'Hebdo* (April 6) described Kosova as "a cancer of Europe," reporting, among other things, what a girl with a ponytail said to the magazine's reporter in English: "They may punish me for talking to you. Don't pay any attention to their accusations of nationalism and separatism. Say that the Albanian people is united." *Le Monde* (April 14) reported Slovenes comparing Albanians in Yugoslavia to Jews in nazi Germany. *Tribune de Genève* (March 20) featured a group of miners, all of them young, displaying the part of the flag showing the Albanian eagle while hiding the Yugoslav star. *Daily News* (March 27) carried the picture of a militiaman hitting a young man in the head with his truncheon, two other militiamen holding him fast. *Das Bund* published a picture in which a man is seen protecting his head with hands from a truncheon blow. In *Neue Zürcher Zeitung* another such picture shows four children walking defiantly in front of armored vehicles.

29 *Tages Anzeiger* (March 25, 1989) underlined his "neo–Stalinist methods." *Corriere della sera* (March 30), commenting on an article in Ljubljana's *Delo*, condemned the illegal Stalinist–like arrests made in Kosova. And the *New York Times* (April 10, 1989) began an editorial, "Bullying in the Balkans," with the sentence, "Only a cynical demagogue would recklessly inflame

ancient ethnic hatreds for the sake of his own political ambition."
30 On March 2, 1989, 200 Kosovar workers gathered before the Palace of Nations in Geneva. A three–thousand–strong demonstration of Kosovars took place in Bern on March 25; they petitioned for a United Nations delegation to Kosova and the lifting of the state emergency. On February 26, 1989, the Pan–Albanian Federation of America VATRA celebrated in New York the eightieth anniversary of its organ, *Dielli* [The Sun]. On that occasion, telegrams were sent calling on the President of the U. S. and the premiers of European countries to step in on behalf of respect for Kosovar human rights. That same day a group of Kosovars staged a hunger strike before the United Nations in New York in solidarity with the Trepča miners; the *New York Times* published their appeal to the U. N. Secretary General. The Voice of America broadcast messages of protest by U. S. Albanian intellectuals. On March 10, more than 500 demonstrators representing the Albanian political parties in the U. S. protested Serbia's pressure on Kosova. On March 13, some 800 Kosovars in New York repeated the protest. A rally of more than 1,000 Albanian–Americans took place on March 22 on the lawn before the White House, with the participation of three congressmen, the President of VATRA, and other notables of the Albanian ethnic group. An academic round table discussed the Kosova crisis on March 31 at the CUNY Graduate Center. And on April 2, some 1,000 Kosovar workers in Zürich protested Yugoslavia's brutal repression of Kosovar resistance.
31 Another such protest occurred the next day in Ljipljan. According to *La Reppublica* (March 29), during the March uprising demonstrators used firearms, including machine guns, and even heavier weapons, with which they damaged two helicopters. *Le Monde* (March 30) wrote that the protest was organized, the moves synchronized.
32 Public Release No. 5 of the Committee for the Protection of Human Rights in Kosova," Ljubljana, March 3, 1989, in *FBIS–EEU–89–070*, April 13, 1989.
33 Ljubljana *Delo*, April 8, *FBIS–EEU–89–070*, April 13, 1989.
34 Europäisches Parlament, Gemeinsame Entschliessungsantrag,, April 12, 1989.
35 Tanjug, June 1, 1989, in *FBIS–EEU–89–105*, June 2, 1989.
36 Tanjug, June 1, 1989, in *FBIS–EEU–89–105*, June 1, 1989.

[37] Amnesty International. Yugoslavia. Recent Events in the Autonomous Province of Kosova. May 1989.

[38] The letter further states that, according to Article 9 of the International Covenant on Civil and Political Rights ratified by Yugoslavia in 1971, authorities must immediately inform anyone who is arrested of the reasons for the arrest, arrested persons being entitled to address a court so that it may decide without delay whether or not detention is lawful.

[39] Branka Magaš, "The Spectre of Balkanization," *The New Left Review,* 174, March–April 1989, p. 14.

[40] "Factories started to be built in Kosova for Serbs only, Albanian families were evicted from Serb villages, sale of Serb–owned land to Albanians was prohibited, rape declared a political crime." *Ibid.*

[41] Magaš reports an event which paved the way for Milošević's ascendancy. In April 1987, the Belgrade University journal *Student* named Milošević's acolytes as part of a Stalinist group at the university Party *aktiv*. The *aktiv* denounced the journal as anti–Tito. When Dragiša Pavlović, then head of the Belgrade Party, defended *Student,* the *aktiv,* supported by *Politika,* extended the anti–Tito label to Pavlović himself. Instead, the label fits Milošević well, his centralization trend being opposed to Tito's decentralization policy, advocated by Stambolić, Pavlović, and the liberal wing of the Serbian Party. "The liberals were defeated in the end not by force of argument, but by a party machinery based on Stalinist conceptions of unity and democratic centralism." "The Spectre of Balkanization," *op. cit.,* p. 22.

[42] Miloš Antić, "The Special Measures Defended Yugoslavia," *Borba,* May 26, 19889, in *FBIS–EEU–89–105,* June 2, 1989.

[43] The Djakova group, led by Fadil Hoxha, includes Mahmud Bakalli, the brothers Nimani, the brothers Agani, as well as two dead leaders, Emin Duraku and Hajdar Dushi.

[44] *Zëri i popullit* (March 5, 1989) has an article by the historian Luan Omari, who mentions the following official figures given by Morina: 75,000 condemnations for penal acts, 95,000 for minor political offenses, and 314,000 for interrogation, a total of 484,000.

[45] Alain Campiotti, "Et si la Yougoslavie explosait . . .," *L'Hebdo,* October 6, 1988, p. 27.

[46] Branko Horvat, *Kosovsko Pitanje* (Globus, Zagreb, 1988), note

pp. 94–95.

47 Interview with Ibrahim Rugova, President of the Albanian Association of Writers, by Jolyon Naegele, correspondent of the Voice of America, April 27, 1989. — Rugova rejected the charge that the Albanians of Yugoslavia want to join the state of Albania. He called "demagogic" the official propaganda that the amendments to the 1974 constitution did not affect Kosova's autonomy. And he cited three other dates, 1945, 1956, and 1981, as proof that Kosovars have been treated as enemies and subjected to repression.

48 *Zëri i rinisë*, February 25, 1989.

49 *Zëri i popullit*, March 29, 1989.

50 Luan Omari, "The Road of Violence Does Not Solve the Kosova Problem," *Zëri i popullit*, March 5, 1989.

51 "Serbian Nationalism and the Danger of Yugoslavia's Balkanization," *Zëri i popullit*, April 18, 1989, in *FBIS–EEU–89–079*, April 26, 1989.

52 Georg Paul Hefty, "Albania in Search of a Way out of the Poorhouse," *op. cit.*

53 *Borba*, May 20–21,1989, in *FBIS–EEU–89–099*, May 24, 1989.

54 In the Kosovar demonstrations of March 13 in New York, Tirana flags were displayed.

Notes to Chapter XV

1 'Ideo–political' is a term of the Stalinist jargon which emphasizes the predominance of the Marxist–Leninist ideology in politics.

2 Marvin Howe, "No Hint of Change Where Liberalization Has Long Been Suspect," *New York Times*, 13 Nov. 1989.

3 Neal Ascherson, "Albania's Dam Against Time," *The Observer*, 22 Nov. 1987.

4 Christian Tyler, "The Mouse That Roars," *Financial Times*, 15 Oct. 1988.

5 President Bush in his electoral campaign.

6 Francis Fukuyama, *The New York Times Magazine*, 19 Nov. 1989, p. 14.

7 "An Odyssey ensues, complete with adventure–packed episodes, involving alien monsters (Albanians!)." Jonathan Kalb, "Albanian Banalities." Review of *Albanian Softshoe*, a play by Mac Wellman, presented at the New York City William Redfield Theatre. *Village Voice*, Feb. 1988.

[8] C. Tyler, "The Mouse That Roars," *op. cit.*

[9] *Zëri i rinisë* [The Voice of Youth], 1 Nov. 1989.

[10] See A.Pipa, "Glasnost in Albania?" *Telos*, 79, Spring 1989, p. 191.

[11] C. Tyler, *op. cit.*

[12] A. Pipa, *op. cit.*

[13] *Gazeta zyrtare* [Official Gazette], 5 Nov. 1987.

[14] *Zëri i rinisë*, Nov. 1989.

INDEX

Italics indicate key page reference.

Basque Provinces, 266 n. 28
Basta, Giorgio, 260 n. 46
Basta, Nicola, 260 n. 46
Bauer, Bruno, 91
Bekteshi, Sadik, 265 n. 11
Belgium, 254 n. 22. *See also* Brussels
Belgrade, 59, 114, 159, 248 n. 41, 256 n. 35; Balkan Conference in
   (1988), 161, 175, 191; petition of 206 intellectuals, 145, 146, 148,
   150, 160, 164, 203
Belishova, Liri, 64, 77, 78, 82, 127–28
Beqja, Hamit, 179–80
Berat, 32
Berat Plenum, 59
Beria, Lavrenti Pavlovich, 80, 213
Berkeley Free Speech Movement, iii, 86
Berlin, Congress of, 95, 96
Bible, 183. *See also* Gospel; Torah
Blushi, Xhoxhi, 61
Boccaccio, Giovanni, 38
Bogdani, Pjetër, 98, 158
Bolshevik party, 181, 184. See also *History of the Communist Party
   (Short Course)*
Bonati, Jul, Fr., 12–13
Bosnia, 39
Botsaris, Markos, 260 n. 46
Brezhnev, Leonid, 137, 174
British Museum, 247 n. 32
Brussels, 129, 254 n. 22
Bubulina, 260 n. 46
Bučar, Franc, Dr., 265 n. 15
Buda, Aleks, Prof., 173, 199
Bujan resolution, 150
Bukharin, Nikolai Ivanovich, 139, 140, 174
Bulgaria, Bulgarians, 29, 79, 80, 95, 147, 155, 158, 176, 188, 191, 216
Bulgaro–Macedonians, 99
Bush, George, 186, 269 n. 5
Buza, Abdurrahim, 220, 221, 222
Byelorussia, 5
Byzantine Empire, 103, 120, 188

Prifti, Peter, 195
Prishtina (Priština), 76, 99,, 101, 102, 144, 149, 204; 1968 demon-
    strations in, 93, 147; 1981 demonstrations in, 92, 147, 148, 152;
    University of, 92, 99, 100, 162, 164, 208, 209–10, 215, 247 n. 33
Prishtina, Hasan, 99
Prizren, League of, 1, 95, 99, 256 n. 36
Progressive Party (Albanian), 31
Provisional Central Committee, 56
Provisional National Liberation Government (Albanian), 32
Pula, Ymer, 265 n. 11

Qamil, Haxhi, 5, 239 n. 2

Rajk, Laszlo, 80
Ranković, Aleksandar, 80, 93, 145, 147, 155, 156, 161, 203, 211, 212,
    217
Red Army (Soviet), 70
Red Guards (Chinese Cultural Revolution), 86
Regional National Liberation Council of Kosova and the Dukagjin
    Plain, 62
Repishti, Sami, Dr., 265 n. 15
Roman Empire and civilization, 14, 190, 244 n. 11
Romania, Romanians, 72, 79, 103, 176, 216, 223, 227, 228
Rome (Catholicism), 225
Royalist Party (Albanian), 32
Rugova, Ibrahim, 214, 269 n. 46
Russia, 95, 224. *See also* Soviet Union
Russian Empire, 188

Sanxhaktari, Fiqret. *See* Shehu, Fiqret
Sarajevo, University of, 159
Scanderbeg (George Castrioti), 1, 2, 5, 39, 183, 186. *See also* Ap-
    pendix 2
Sejko, Teme, Rear Admiral, 64, 78, 262 n. 62
Serbia, Serbs, 29, 38, 54, 55, 92–103 (*100, 102, 103*), 106, 175, 187–
    88, 201, 202, 203, 206, 211, 248 n. 42; constitution of, 206, 207;
    Kosova cherished by, 152; and Kosova problem, 144–65, 193–
    217; radical ideology in, 206, 266 n. 23; Stalinism in, 193–216
    (*212–13*), 223, 266 n. 23. *See also* Kosova (Kosovo)
Serbian Academy of Sciences, 153
Serbian Communist League, 162, 163

122, 123, 137, 148, 149, 151, 165, 167, 168, 173, 174, 177, 178, 179, 180–81, 182, 184, 187, 188, 189, 190, 195, 198–99, 201, 207, 214, 223, 224–25, 253 n. 11, 264 n. 10. *See also* Stalin, Joseph Vissarionovich

Spahiu, Bedri, 63–63, 77, 78, 82

Spain, 25, 72, 107, 115, 129, 166

Special Court for the Trial of War Criminals, 59

Spiru, Nako, 57, 58–59, 59–61, *60*, 64, 65, 78, 82, 107, 115, 116, 130–31, 139; his widow's murder, 128

Stafa, Qemal, 56, 80, 82

'Stalalbanianism,' 141, 142, 182–83, 190, 195, 199–200, 215–17, 223–25, 227, 228. *See also* Albania, Stalinism in

Stalin, Joseph Vissarionovich, 4, 15, 23, 35, 36, 55, 57, 62, 63, 68, 74, *75–77*, 79, 86, 87, 90, 91, 106, 108, 115, 116, 118, 119, 122, 127, 131, 132, 136, 142, 155, 160, 174, 176, 177–78, 180, 181, 182, 184, 186, 191, 195, 196, 197, 201, 211, 213, 241 n. 22; *glasnost*, his myth vs., 137; Hoxha as heir to, 137–40; Hoxha's oath to, 249 nn. 5, 6; Hoxha's worship of explained, 61; Hoxha, Stalin's view of, 89, 130, 244 n. 89; *Marxism and Linguistics*, 185, 254–55 n. 30; *Short Course*, 58, 83; and unified literary Albanian, 158; on projected Yugoslav annexation of Albania, 241 n. 33. *See also* Appendix 2

Stalinism, 58, 193–94, 199–200, 269 n. 1. *See also* under Albania, Kosova; Serbia; Yugoslavia

Stambolić, Petar, 203, 268 n. 41

'Stara Serbia,' 94, 97, 164, 208

Stil, André, 88

Stojnić, Colonel, 59

Strabo, 94, 245 n. 11

Strasbourg, 144

Sudan, 90

Šufflay, Milan, 94

Šuvar, Stipe, 205, 208

Sweden, 88

Switzerland, 38–39, 176, 266 n. 26

Tadić, Ljubomir, 252 n. 3

Tadjik people, 4

Taha, Haki, 264 n. 11

Tashko, Koço, 64, 77, 78, 80, 82